POEMS
BY
ROBERT
BROWNING

RAFAEL·MADE·A·
CENTVRY·OF·SONNET

ONE WORD MORE

BYAM·SHAW

POEMS
BY
ROBERT
BROWNING

WITH INTRODVCTION

BY

RICHARD GARNETT LLD

AND ILLVSTRATIONS

BY

BYAM SHAW

BELL & HYMAN
LONDON

Published by
BELL & HYMAN LIMITED
Denmark House
37–39 Queen Elizabeth Street
London SE1 2QB

First published in 1897 by
G. Bell & Sons Ltd
Reprinted four times
Reissued in 1979

This edition
© Bell & Hyman Limited 1979

ISBN 0 7135 1177 X

Printed and bound in Great Britain at
The Camelot Press Ltd, Southampton

INTRODUCTION

No modern English poet comes so near as Robert Browning to presenting a panorama of life. He was a man of very wide reading and a corresponding compass of knowledge; he had overflowing human sympathies and the keenest eye for the picturesque in man and nature; he had lived much in foreign countries; above all, he was objective to a fault. Goethe, the great prophet and example of healthy objectivity, was subjective too, both in his lyrical gift and his conscious self-portraiture. But Browning was probably less endowed with the faculty of pure spontaneous song than any other poet of his calibre, and he never sat to himself for his own portrait, although poems like *Two in the Campagna* may be autobiographic as far as they go. Whatever he would say is usually conveyed in the character of some other person, occasionally, as in the Paracelsus and Aprile of his early poems, typifying some element in his own nature; but in his later work more commonly studied entirely from the outside, and frequently expressive of characteristics most alien to his own. The one thing needful is that the person, circumstance, or feeling depicted should be interesting, especially if in connection with some moral or psychological problem. This is as much as to say that he was before all things a dramatist. But his *personæ* were not, as is so frequently the case, the per-

NOT
HIMSELF

INTRODUCTION

sonified moods of his own microcosm, but represented a goodly portion of mankind.

If Browning had been a dramatist upon the accepted pattern, he would have yielded most unfit material for a book of selections. Nothing, as a rule, should appear in an anthology that is not complete in itself: and, the more perfect the drama, the closer the coherency of its parts, and the greater the injury of detachment alike to the part and the whole. Had Browning lived in the age of Shakespeare he would have been the second English dramatist, and his works would not have afforded material for a selection. To his detriment as a poet, but his great gain as a moral and intellectual influence, he lived in an age in which the poetical drama of Shakespeare's period had become well-nigh impossible. Play-goers could not receive it unless when hallowed by the conventional consecration of tradition; nor, if they had been capable of this, could the poets have given it. The ancient crater was choked, and the subterranean fire must make new vents for itself. There seem some indications that these may eventually be found in a powerful prose drama on a lower level than the poetical play in a literary point of view, yet not less capable of fulfilling the serious ends for which the drama exists. That Browning could have performed this work well, he has shown in the second act of his *Soul's Tragedy*, dramatically the most perfect of his plays. But he would not have attempted it, except as an occasional condescension. He was a poet no less than a dramatist, and would not have consented to forego the beauty and dignity acquired by submission to the restraints of metrical form. He therefore fell back upon a species of composition which did not exist till long

vi

INTRODUCTION

after Shakespeare's time, and which may be described as a miniature drama, the dramatic romance, idyll, or monologue. In Browning's case this seems to have been gradually developed out of the ballad, for which he at first showed a special inclination, and to have progressed by slow degrees until it found its ultimate perfection in those marvellous monologues, such as *Cleon, Andrea del Sarto, Bishop Blougram's Apology,* in which, with such charitable sympathy, such scrupulous impartiality, but at the same time such poignant irony, he contrives to exhibit simultaneously the man as he appears to himself and the man as he appears to his Maker. This interpretation of an isolated figure, although requiring wonderful gifts, is still an easier matter than the attainment of the same result by depicting the personage in collision with others. This Browning never achieved; in Shakespeare's age he would have accomplished it with ease, but the contagious enthusiasm which in that day made even playwrights into poets was wanting in ours. Had Shakespeare wished to depict Caliban's apprehension of divine things he would have made the delineation grow naturally out of the plot, and despatched it in a few sufficient words: he would there as elsewhere have been Caliban's Demiurgus, not his Velasquez. But, superior as his method of presentation might have been, he could not within the compass of a drama have rivalled Browning's minute elaboration, nor could he have seen more piercingly into the core of the matter itself.

The main point for us, however, is that, by making the most striking dramatic creations complete in themselves, whether in the form of brief impassioned lyric, dramatic romance, or elaborate monologue, Browning has rendered it possible to offer the best of his work in the form of a volume of selected poems. This would not have been feasible if his realism had consisted in painting everything that came in his way. On the contrary, he is a great eclectic. He searches long and chooses curiously before he will exclaim—

> Now Robert Browning, you writer of plays,
> Here's a subject made to your hand!

Like Shakespeare, who never introduces an English contemporary except into some trivial comic part, he generally finds these subjects either in the remote picturesque past, or amid modern environments unfamiliar to the mass of his readers. No modern poet has done more to expand the intellectual horizon of the average Englishman. Such poems as *Protus* and *The Bishop orders his Tomb in St Praxed's Church*, for example, seem to condense into a few lines the essence of massy volumes on Byzantine and Renaissance eras. Whatever of the Dryasdust element may have clung to these ancient volumes has disappeared in the process; the descriptions could not be more fresh, vivid, and real, if they related to things of yesterday. The feelings of the modern Florentine gentleman bemoaning the dulness of the country are nearer to us in time, but no nearer in sympathy and comprehension than those of Cleon, ranging the gifts of the Greek despot in the days of Nero.

The Ring and the Book and *Paracelsus* can, of course, only be published separately, or as portions of a complete edition of Browning's works; and considerations of space also exclude *Pippa Passes* and *A Soul's Tragedy*. With these exceptions, the present volume may be said to include the most vitally important portion of such of

INTRODUCTION

Browning's work as is animated by a dramatic spirit. The dramas composed with a view to representation fall short of the mark, the requirements of the stage excluding the minute psychological analysis of which Browning was a special master, and the defect not being compensated by more strictly dramatic qualities. With an occasional almost startling exception, like *Halbert and Hob*, and *Tray*, the poetry subsequent to *Dramatis Personæ* and *The Ring and the Book*, though still most remarkable, is not such as a lover of Browning would care to admit into a selection designed to display him at his best. The cause seems to have been not so much a decline of power as a lapse into merely mechanical habits of composition. "He always," Mrs Sutherland Orr tells us, "counted a day lost in which he had not written something." Very different from the method of former years, when Mrs Browning attests that "Robert waits for an inclination, works by fits and starts; he can't do otherwise, he says." The new habit was one very likely to be engendered by habitual application to long blank verse poems like the *Ring and the Book*, designedly kept for hundreds of lines together little above the level of prose, and thus admitting of regular daily increment. According to Mrs Orr, Browning also suffered from a delusion very pleasant but very perilous to a veteran author, "the constant conviction that the latest must be the best, because the outcome of the fullest mental experience and the longest practice in his art." As if mental experience and poetic practice might not be wasted upon an unsuitable subject, or could avail anything in the absence of true inspiration. A poet, nevertheless, who is sure that he is writing his best is not likely to take sufficient pains to make it so. Browning warmly resented the imputation of negligence; and the probability is that he did take sufficient pains to please himself, but did not consider that his reader could not stand on the same plane as the author. He is not so much enigmatic as cryptic: he has a meaning evident to himself, but leaves it half-expressed or merely hinted at. The result is detrimental to style as well as matter, for ideas half-formulated cannot be translated into perfect speech. Compare the ineffective presentation of *The Pope's Net*, with the clear cameo-cutting of such poems as *A Light Woman* and *Memorabilia*. In so far, however, as Browning's obscurity is due to the opulence and fecundity of his thought, he suffers from a cause which has produced the like effect in Shakespeare.

Although, then, the later poems of Browning, had he written nothing else, would have entitled him to the highest praise he can receive, that of being the only absolutely independent and original English poet of his age, they contain, with one or two striking exceptions, little to excite any serious regret for their inevitable exclusion (due to the exigencies of copyright) from this volume, which is even advantageous in so far as it demonstrates what otherwise might not have been so clear, the utter inapplicability of the charge of obscurity to the most important part of his writings. Few sides of Browning's mind are left without illustration here; if such there be, they will be found in the long poems for which room could not have been made under any circumstances. A mind in which poetry and intellect were equally balanced, which, conceiving as its mission the interpretation of man to man through the medium of drama, and disabled from obtaining a footing on the stage by its own peculiarities and the unfavourable

INTRODUCTION

circumstances of the time, created in lieu of acted plays a series of dramatic studies, unsurpassed for truth of representation when they concern historical or other actual personages, and for ideal truth when these figures are the emanation of the poet's brain. So numerous are these creations, comprehending as they do by far the larger part of Browning's poetical works, that they may almost be said to form a literature of themselves, and it is impossible to compute how greatly the intellectual life of England has been stimulated and enriched by familiarity with them. Nor has he been less a benefactor to the land of his predilection and frequent residence. No one imbued in any measure with the spirit of Browning can be other than a lover of Italy.

The accompanying illustrations, it is believed, will commend themselves to all as the production of an artist who has imbibed the spirit of Browning, and proved himself competent to reproduce imaginative thought as visible form, with no loss of vigour or abatement of the sense of reality. R. GARNETT.

CONTENTS

xiii

CONTENTS

MEN AND WOMEN

CONTENTS

CONTENTS

NOTE.—The poems in this volume are reprinted from the
first collected edition of Browning's Poems (2 vols., 1849)
and from the first edition of "Men and Women" (2 vols.,
1855). A few irregularities of spelling and punctuation
have been corrected.

LIST OF ILLUSTRATIONS

xvii

LIST OF ILLUSTRATIONS

LIST OF ILLUSTRATIONS

JOHN BYAM SHAW

Browning's poetry, with its flamboyant characters and dramatic situations, lends itself to illustration by a sympathetic artist, and this volume is the product of just such a commission. Originally issued as one of the first titles in the Endymion series of illustrated poets in 1897, it was the work of a 25-year-old artist, Byam Shaw. Byam Shaw's combination of fanciful detail with strong portraiture was ideally suited to the subject, and the result is undoubtedly an 'illustrated' rather than 'decorated' book. There are 67 drawings in all, many of them full page.

John Byam Shaw was born in Madras in 1872, where his father held a legal appointment. He went to the St John's Wood School of Art, and later to the Royal Academy schools. His first painting, 'Rose Mary', was exhibited at the Academy in 1893. The present edition of Browning was his first major commission in the realm of book illustration and a number of other books followed, including a series of Shakespeare illustrations and others for subjects as diverse as Boccaccio, Edgar Allan Poe and *The Pilgrim's Progress*. In 1911 he founded the Byam Shaw School of Drawing and Painting in Kensington, which still continues. His paintings were frequently hung in Royal Academy exhibitions; perhaps the best-known was 'Love the Conqueror' (1899). He died in 1919.

"Hist!"—said Kate the Queen;

BYAM·SHAW.

POEMS·BY ROBERT BROWNING

SONG FROM PARACELSVS

Heap cassia, sandal-buds, and stripes
    Of labdanum, and aloe-balls
Smeared with dull nard an Indian wipes
    From out her hair : (such balsam falls
    Down sea-side mountain pedestals,
From summits where tired winds are fain,
Spent with the vast and howling main,
To treasure half their island-gain).

And strew faint sweetness from some old
    Egyptian's fine worm-eaten shroud,
Which breaks to dust when once unrolled ;
    And shred dim perfume, like a cloud
    From chamber long to quiet vowed,
With mothed and drooping arras hung,
Mouldering the lute and books among
Of queen, long dead, who lived there young.

3

SONGS FROM "PIPPA PASSES"

I

ALL service ranks the same with God ·
If now, as formerly He trod
Paradise, His presence fills
Our earth, each only as God wills
Can work—God's puppets, best and worst.
Are we ; there is no last nor first.

Say not "a small event !" Why "small"?
Costs it more pain this thing ye call
A "great event" should come to pass,
Than that? Untwine me from the mass
Of deeds which make up life, one deed
Power shall fall short in, or exceed !

II

YOU 'LL love me yet !—and I can tarry
Your love's protracted growing :
June reared that bunch of flowers you carry
From seeds of April's sowing.

I plant a heartfull now—some seed
At least is sure to strike
And yield—what you 'll not pluck, indeed,
Not pluck, but, may be, like !

You 'll look at least on love's remains,
A grave's one violet :
Your look?—that pays a thousand pains.
What 's death?—You 'll love me yet !

4

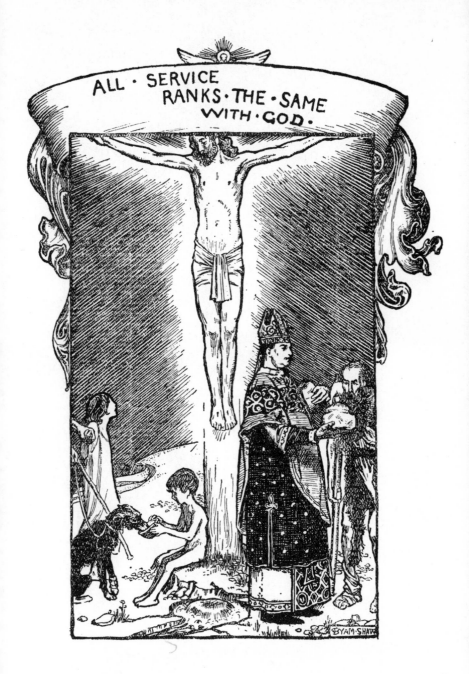

ALL · SERVICE
RANKS · THE · SAME
WITH · GOD ·

BYAM·SHAW

SONGS FROM "PIPPA PASSES"

III

GIVE her but a least excuse to love me!
  When—where—
How—can this arm establish her above me
If fortune fixed her as my lady there,
There already, to eternally reprove me?
(" *Hist*"—*said Kate the queen;*
But "oh—" cried the maiden, binding her tresses,
"*'Tis only a page that carols unseen*
Crumbling your hounds their messes!")

Is she wronged?—To the rescue of her honour,
My heart!
Is she poor?—What costs it to be styled a donor?
Merely an earth's to cleave, a sea's to part!
But that fortune should have thrust allthis upon her!
(" *Nay, list,*"—*bade Kate the queen;*
And still cried the maiden, binding her tresses,
"*'Tis only a page that carols unseen,*
Fitting your hawks their jesses!")

7

SONGS FROM "PIPPA PASSES"

IV

A KING lived long ago,
In the morning of the world,
When earth was nigher heaven than now:
And the king's locks curled
Disparting o'er a forehead full
As the milk-white space 'twixt horn and horn
Of some sacrificial bull—
Only calm as a babe new-born:
For he was got to a sleepy mood,
So safe from all decrepitude,
From age with its bane, so sure gone by,
(The Gods so loved him while he dreamed,)
That, having lived thus long, there seemed
No need the king should ever die.

Among the rocks his city was:
Before his palace, in the sun,
He sate to see his people pass,
And judge them every one
From its threshold of smooth stone.
They haled him many a valley-thief
Caught in the sheep-pens—robber-chief,
Swarthy and shameless—beggar-cheat—
Spy-prowler—or some pirate found
On the sea-sand left aground;
And sometimes clung about his feet,
With bleeding lip and burning cheek,
A woman, bitterest wrong to speak
Of one with sullen thickset brows:
And sometimes from the prison-house
The angry priests a pale wretch brought,
Who through some chink had pushed and pressed,
On knees and elbows, belly and breast,
Worm-like into the temple,—caught
At last there by the very God,
Who ever in the darkness strode

8

BEFORE HIS PALACE, IN THE SUN,
HE SATE TO SEE HIS PEOPLE PASS.

SONGS FROM "PIPPA PASSES"

Backward and forward, keeping watch
O'er his brazen bowls, such rogues to catch!
And these, all and every one,
The king judged, sitting in the sun.

His councillors, on left and right,
Looked anxious up,—but no surprise
Disturbed the king's old smiling eyes,
Where the very blue had turned to white.
'Tis said, a Python scared one day
The breathless city, till he came,
With forky tongue and eyes on flame,
Where the old king sate to judge alway;
But when he saw the sweepy hair,
Girt with a crown of berries rare
Which the God will hardly give to wear
To the maiden who singeth, dancing bare
In the altar-smoke by the pine-torch lights,
At his wondrous forest rites,—
Beholding this, he did not dare,
Approach that threshold in the sun,
Assault the old king smiling there.
Such grace had kings when the world begun!

V

THE year's at the spring,
And day's at the morn:
Morning's at seven;
The hill-side 's dew-pearled:
The lark 's on the wing;
The snail 's on the thorn;
God 's in his heaven—
All 's right with the world!

THE YEAR'S AT THE SPRING.

CAVALIER
TVNES

Marching Along.

I.

KENTISH Sir Byng stood for his King,
Bidding the crop-headed Parliament swing:
And, pressing a troop unable to stoop
And see the rogues flourish and honest folk droop,
Marched them along, fifty-score strong,
Great-hearted gentlemen, singing this song.

CAVALIER TUNES

God for King Charles!   Pym and such carles
To the Devil that prompts 'em their treasonous parles!
Cavaliers, up!   Lips from the cup,
Hands from the pasty, nor bite take nor sup
Till you 're (*Chorus*) *Marching along, fifty-score strong,*
    Great-hearted gentlemen, singing this song.

Hampden to Hell, and his obsequies' knell
Serve Hazelrig, Fiennes, and young Harry as well!
England, good cheer!   Rupert is near!
Kentish and loyalists, keep we not here
   (*Cho.*) *Marching along, fifty-score strong,*
    Great-hearted gentlemen, singing this song?

Then, God for King Charles!   Pym and his snarls
To the Devil that pricks on such pestilent carles!
Hold by the right, you double your might;
So, onward to Nottingham, fresh for the fight,
   (*Cho.*) *March we along, fifty-score strong,*
    Great-hearted gentlemen, singing this song!

II—GIVE A ROUSE

KING CHARLES, and who 'll do him right now?
King Charles, and who 's ripe for fight now?
Give a rouse: here 's, in Hell's despite now,
King Charles!

Who gave me the goods that went since?
Who raised me the house that sank once?
Who helped me to gold I spent since?
Who found me in wine you drank once?
   (*Cho.*) *King Charles, and who 'll do him right now?*
    King Charles, and who 's ripe for fight now?
    Give a rouse: here 's, in Hell's despite now,
    King Charles!

CAVALIER TUNES

To whom used my boy George quaff else,
By the old fool's side that begot him?
For whom did he cheer and laugh else,
While Noll's damned troopers shot him?
      (*Cho.*) *King Charles, and who'll do him right now?*
           King Charles, and who's ripe for fight now?
           Give a rouse : here's, in Hell's despite now,
           King Charles !

CAVALIER TUNES

III—BOOT AND SADDLE

BOOT, saddle, to horse, and away!
Rescue my Castle, before the hot day
Brightens to blue from its silvery gray,
        (*Cho.*) *Boot, saddle, to horse, and away!*

Ride past the suburbs, asleep as you'd say;
Many's the friend there, will listen and pray
"God's luck to gallants that strike up the lay,
        (*Cho.*) "*Boot, saddle, to horse, and away!*"

Forty miles off, like a roebuck at bay,
Flouts Castle Brancepeth the Roundheads' array:
Who laughs, "Good fellows ere this, by my fay,
        (*Cho.*) "*Boot, saddle, to horse, and away?*"

Who? My wife Gertrude; that, honest and gay,
Laughs when you talk of surrendering, "Nay!
"I've better counsellors; what counsel they?
        (*Cho.*) "*Boot, saddle, to horse, and away!*"

MY LAST DUCHESS

FERRARA

THAT'S my last Duchess painted on the wall,
Looking as if she were alive; I call
That piece a wonder, now: Frà Pandolf's hands
Worked busily a day, and there she stands.
Will't please you sit and look at her? I said
"Frà Pandolf" by design, for never read
Strangers like you that pictured countenance,
The depth and passion of its earnest glance,
But to myself they turned (since none puts by
The curtain I have drawn for you, but I)

MY LAST DUCHESS

And seemed as they would ask me, if they durst,
How such a glance came there; so, not the first
Are you to turn and ask thus. Sir, 'twas not
Her husband's presence only, called that spot
Of joy into the Duchess' cheek: perhaps
Frà Pandolf chanced to say "Her mantle laps
"Over my Lady's wrist too much," or "Paint
"Must never hope to reproduce the faint
"Half-flush that dies along her throat"; such stuff
Was courtesy, she thought, and cause enough
For calling up that spot of joy. She had
A heart . . how shall I say? . . too soon made glad,
Too easily impressed; she liked whate'er
She looked on, and her looks went everywhere.
Sir, 'twas all one! My favour at her breast,
The dropping of the daylight in the West,
The bough of cherries some officious fool
Broke in the orchard for her, the white mule
She rode with round the terrace—all and each
Would draw from her alike the approving speech,
Or blush, at least. She thanked men,—good; but thanked
Somehow . . I know not how . . as if she ranked
My gift of a nine hundred years old name
With anybody's gift. Who'd stoop to blame
This sort of trifling? Even had you skill
In speech—(which I have not)—to make your will
Quite clear to such an one, and say "Just this
"Or that in you disgusts me; here you miss,
"Or there exceed the mark"—and if she let
Herself be lessoned so, nor plainly set
Her wits to yours, forsooth, and made excuse,
—E'en then would be some stooping, and I chuse
Never to stoop. Oh, Sir, she smiled, no doubt,
Whene'er I passed her; but who passed without
Much the same smile? This grew; I gave commands;
Then all smiles stopped together. There she stands

MY LAST DUCHESS

As if alive. Will't please you rise? We'll meet
The company below, then. I repeat,
The Count your Master's known munificence
Is ample warrant that no just pretence
Of mine for dowry will be disallowed;
Though his fair daughter's self, as I avowed
At starting, is my object. Nay, we'll go
Together down, Sir! Notice Neptune, tho',
Taming a sea-horse, thought a rarity,
Which Claus of Innsbruck cast in bronze for me.

COUNT GISMOND

COUNT GISMOND

AIX IN PROVENCE

I

CHRIST God, who savest men, save most
  Of men Count Gismond who saved me!
Count Gauthier, when he chose his post,
  Chose time and place and company
To suit it; when he struck at length
My honour 'twas with all his strength.

II

And doubtlessly ere he could draw
  All points to one, he must have schemed!
That miserable morning saw
  Few half so happy as I seemed,
While being dressed in Queen's array
To give our Tourney prize away.

III

I thought they loved me, did me grace
  To please themselves; 'twas all their deed;
God makes, or fair or foul, our face;
  If showing mine so caused to bleed
My cousins' hearts, they should have dropped
A word, and straight the play had stopped.

IV

They, too, so beauteous! Each a queen
  By virtue of her brow and breast;
Not needing to be crowned, I mean,
  As I do. E'en when I was dressed,
Had either of them spoke, instead
Of glancing sideways with still head!

COUNT GISMOND

V

But no : they let me laugh and sing
  My birthday song quite through, adjust
The last rose in my garland, fling
  A last look on the mirror, trust
My arms to each an arm of theirs,
And so descend the castle-stairs—

VI

And come out on the morning troop
  Of merry friends who kissed my cheek,
And called me Queen, and made me stoop
  Under the canopy—(a streak
That pierced it, of the outside sun,
Powdered with gold its gloom's soft dun)—

VII

And they could let me take my state
  And foolish throne amid applause
Of all come there to celebrate
  My Queen's day—Oh, I think the cause
Of much was, they forgot no crowd
Makes up for parents in their shroud !

VIII

Howe'er that be, all eyes were bent
  Upon me, when my cousins cast
Theirs down ; 'twas time I should present
  The victor's crown, but . . there, 'twill last
No long time . . . the old mist again
Blinds me as then it did. How vain !

IX

See ! Gismond's at the gate, in talk
  With his two boys : I can proceed.
Well, at that moment, who should stalk
  Forth boldly (to my face, indeed)

COUNT GISMOND

But Gauthier, and he thundered " Stay !"
And all stayed. " Bring no crowns, I say !"

X

" Bring torches!   Wind the penance-sheet
  " About her!   Let her shun the chaste,
" Or lay herself before their feet!
  " Shall she, whose body I embraced
" A night long, queen it in the day?
" For Honour's sake no crowns, I say !"

XI

I ?   What I answered?   As I live,
  I never fancied such a thing
As answer possible to give.
  What says the body when they spring
Some monstrous torture-engine's whole
Strength on it?   No more says the soul.

XII

Till out strode Gismond ; then I knew
  That I was saved.   I never met
His face before, but, at first view,
  I felt quite sure that God had set
Himself to Satan ; who would spend
A minute's mistrust on the end?

XIII

He strode to Gauthier, in his throat
  Gave him the lie, then struck his mouth
With one back-handed blow that wrote
  In blood men's verdict there.   North, South,
East, West, I looked.   The lie was dead,
And damned, and truth stood up instead.

COUNT GISMOND

XIV

This glads me most, that I enjoyed
   The heart of the joy, with my content
In watching Gismond unalloyed
   By any doubt of the event:
God took that on him—I was bid
Watch Gismond for my part: I did.

XV

Did I not watch him while he let
   His armourer just brace his greaves,
Rivet his hauberk, on the fret
   The while! His foot . . my memory leaves
No least stamp out, nor how anon
He pulled his ringing gauntlets on.

XVI

And e'en before the trumpet's sound
   Was finished, prone lay the false Knight,
Prone as his lie, upon the ground:
   Gismond flew at him, used no sleight
Of the sword, but open-breasted drove,
Cleaving till out the truth he clove.

XVII

Which done, he dragged him to my feet
   And said " Here die, but end thy breath
" In full confession, lest thou fleet
   " From my first, to God's second death!
" Say hast thou lied? " And, " I have lied
" To God and her," he said, and died.

XVIII

Then Gismond, kneeling to me, asked
   —What safe my heart holds, tho' no word

COUNT GISMOND

Could I repeat now, if I tasked
    My powers for ever, to a third
Dear even as you are.   Pass the rest
Until I sank upon his breast.

XIX

Over my head his arm he flung
    Against the world ; and scarce I felt
His sword, that dripped by me and swung,
    A little shifted in its belt,—
For he began to say the while
How South our home lay many a mile.

XX

So 'mid the shouting multitude
    We two walked forth to never more
Return.   My cousins have pursued
    Their life, untroubled as before
I vexed them.   Gauthier's dwelling-place
God lighten !   May his soul find grace !

XXI

Our elder boy has got the clear
    Great brow ; tho' when his brother's black
Full eye shows scorn, it . . . Gismond here ?
    And have you brought my tercel back ?
ı just was telling Adela
How many birds it struck since May.

INCIDENT OF THE FRENCH CAMP

I

YOU know, we French stormed Ratisbon:
    A mile or so away
On a little mound, Napoléon
    Stood on our storming-day;
With neck out-thrust, you fancy how,
    Legs wide, arms locked behind,
As if to balance the prone brow
    Oppressive with its mind.

II

Just as perhaps he mused " My plans
    " That soar, to earth may fall,
" Let once my army-leader Lannes
    " Waver at yonder wall,"—
Out 'twixt the battery-smokes there flew
    A rider, bound on bound
Full-galloping; nor bridle drew
    Until he reached the mound.

III

Then off there flung in smiling joy,
    And held himself erect
By just his horse's mane, a boy:
    You hardly could suspect—
(So tight he kept his lips compressed,
    Scarce any blood came thro')
You looked twice ere you saw his breast
    Was all but shot in two.

IV

" Well," cried he, " Emperor, by God's grace
    " We 've got you Ratisbon!
" The Marshal 's in the market-place,
    " And you 'll be there anon

24

"To see your flag-bird flap his vans
  "Where I, to heart's desire,
"Perched him!" The Chief's eye flashed; his plans
  Soared up again like fire.

V

The Chief's eye flashed; but presently
  Softened itself, as sheathes
A film the mother eagle's eye
  When her bruised eaglet breathes :
"You're wounded!" "Nay," his soldier's pride
  Touched to the quick, he said :
"I'm killed, Sire!" And, his Chief beside,
  Smiling the boy fell dead.

25

SOLILOQUY OF THE SPANISH CLOISTER

I

GR-R-R—there go, my heart's abhorrence!
  Water your damned flower-pots, do!
If hate killed men, Brother Lawrence,
  God's blood, would not mine kill you!
What? your myrtle-bush wants trimming?
  Oh, that rose has prior claims—
Needs its leaden vase filled brimming?
  Hell dry you up with its flames!

II

At the meal we sit together:
  Salve tibi! I must hear
Wise talk of the kind of weather,
  Sort of season, time of year:
Not a plenteous cork-crop: scarcely
  Dare we hope oak-galls, I doubt:
What's the Latin name for "parsley"?
  What's the Greek name for Swine's Snout?

III

Whew! We'll have our platter burnished,
  Laid with care on our own shelf!
With a fire-new spoon we're furnished,
  And a goblet for ourself,
Rinsed like something sacrificial
  Ere 'tis fit to touch our chaps—
Marked with L. for our initial!
  (He, he! There his lily snaps!)

26

SOLILOQUY OF SPANISH CLOISTER

IV

Saint, forsooth! While brown Dolores
    Squats outside the Convent bank,
With Sanchicha, telling stories,
    Steeping tresses in the tank,
Blue-black, lustrous, thick like horsehairs,
    —Can't I see his dead eye glow
Bright, as 'twere a Barbary corsair's?
    (That is, if he'd let it show!)

V

When he finishes refection,
    Knife and fork he never lays
Cross-wise, to my recollection,
    As do I, in Jesu's praise.
I, the Trinity illustrate,
    Drinking watered orange-pulp—
In three sips the Arian frustrate;
    While he drains his at one gulp!

VI

Oh, those melons! If he's able
    We're to have a feast; so nice!
One goes to the Abbot's table,
    All of us get each a slice.
How go on your flowers? None double?
    Not one fruit-sort can you spy?
Strange!—And I, too, at such trouble,
    Keep 'em close-nipped on the sly!

VII

There's a great text in Galatians,
    Once you trip on it, entails
Twenty-nine distinct damnations,
    One sure, if another fails.

If I trip him just a-dying,
    Sure of Heaven as sure can be,
Spin him round and send him flying
    Off to Hell, a Manichee?

VIII

Or, my scrofulous French novel,
    On grey paper with blunt type!
Simply glance at it, you grovel
    Hand and foot in Belial's gripe:
If I double down its pages
    At the woeful sixteenth print,
When he gathers his greengages,
    Ope a sieve and slip it in't?

IX

Or, there's Satan!—one might venture
    Pledge one's soul to him, yet leave
Such a flaw in the indenture
    As he'd miss till, past retrieve,
Blasted lay that rose-acacia
    We're so proud of! *Hy, Zy, Hine* . . .
'St, there's Vespers! *Plena gratiâ*
    Ave, Virgo! Gr-r-r—you swine!

IN A GONDOLA

He sings.

I SEND my heart up to thee, all my heart
    In this my singing!
For the stars help me, and the sea bears part;
    The very night is clinging
Closer to Venice' streets to leave one space
    Above me, whence thy face
May light my joyous heart to thee its dwelling-place

IN A GONDOLA

She speaks.

Say after me, and try to say
My very words, as if each word
Came from you of your own accord,
In your own voice, in your own way:
" This woman's heart, and soul, and brain
" Are mine as much as this gold chain
" She bids me wear; which" (say again)
" I choose to make by cherishing
" A precious thing, or choose to fling
" Over the boat-side, ring by ring."
And yet once more say . . . no word more!
Since words are only words.   Give o'er!
Unless you call me, all the same,
Familiarly by my pet-name
Which, if the Three should hear you call,
And me reply to, would proclaim
At once our secret to them all:
Ask of me, too, command me, blame—
Do break down the partition-wall
'Twixt us, the daylight world beholds
Curtained in dusk and splendid folds.
What 's left but—all of me to take?
I am the Three's; prevent them, slake
Your thirst!   'Tis said, the Arab sage
In practising with gems can loose
Their subtle spirit in his cruce
And leave but ashes: so, sweet mage,
Leave them my ashes when thy use
Sucks out my soul, thy heritage!

He sings.

I

Past we glide, and past, and past!
  What 's that poor Agnese doing
Where they make the shutters fast?
  Grey Zanobi 's just a-wooing

29

IN A GONDOLA

To his couch the purchased bride:
  Past we glide!

II

Past we glide, and past, and past!
  Why's the Pucci Palace flaring
Like a beacon to the blast?
  Guests by hundreds—not one caring
If the dear host's neck were wried:
  Past we glide!

She sings.

I

The Moth's kiss, first!
Kiss me as if you made believe
You were not sure, this eve,
How my face, your flower, had pursed
Its petals up; so, here and there
You brush it, till I grow aware
Who wants me, and wide open burst.

II

The Bee's kiss, now!
Kiss me as if you entered gay
My heart at some noonday,
A bud that dares not disallow
The claim, so all is rendered up,
And passively its shattered cup
Over your head to sleep I bow.

He sings.

I

What are we two?
I am a Jew,
And carry thee, farther than friends can pursue,
To a feast of our tribe,

IN A GONDOLA

Where they need thee to bribe
The devil that blasts them unless he imbibe
Thy . . . Shatter the vision for ever!   And now,
As of old, I am I, Thou art Thou!

II

Say again, what we are?
The sprite of a star,
I lure thee above where the Destinies bar
My plumes their full play
Till a ruddier ray
Than my pale one announce there is withering away
Some . . . Shatter the vision for ever!   And now,
As of old, I am I, Thou art Thou!

He muses.

Oh, which were best, to roam or rest?
The land's lap or the water's breast?
To sleep on yellow millet-sheaves,
Or swim in lucid shallows, just
Eluding water-lily leaves,
An inch from Death's black fingers, thrust
To lock you, whom release he must;
Which life were best on Summer eves?

He speaks, musing.

Lie back; could thought of mine improve you?
From this shoulder let there spring
A wing; from this, another wing;
Wings, not legs and feet, shall move you!
Snow-white must they spring, to blend
With your flesh, but I intend
They shall deepen to the end,
Broader, into burning gold,
Till both wings crescent-wise enfold

31

IN A GONDOLA

Your perfect self, from 'neath your feet
To o'er your head, where, lo, they meet
As if a million sword-blades hurled
Defiance from you to the world!

Rescue me thou, the only real!
And scare away this mad Ideal
That came, nor motions to depart!
Thanks! Now, stay ever as thou art!

Still he muses.

I

What if the Three should catch at last
Thy serenader? While there's cast
Paul's cloak about my head, and fast
Gian pinions me, Himself has past
His stylet thro' my back; I reel;
And . . . is it Thou I feel?

II

They trail me, these three godless knaves,
Past every church that sains and saves,
Nor stop till, where the cold sea raves
By Lido's wet accursed graves,
They scoop mine, roll me to its brink,
And . . . on Thy breast I sink!

She replies, musing.

Dip your arm o'er the boat-side, elbow-deep,
As I do: thus: were Death so unlike Sleep,
Caught this way? Death's to fear from flame, or steel,
Or poison doubtless; but from water—feel!

Go find the bottom! Would you stay me? There!
Now pluck a great blade of that ribbon-grass
To plait in where the foolish jewel was,
I flung away: since you have praised my hair,
'Tis proper to be choice in what I wear.

IN A
GONDOLA

IN A GONDOLA

He speaks.

Row home? must we row home?   Too surely
Know I where its front's demurely
Over the Giudecca piled;
Window just with window mating,
Door on door exactly waiting,
All's the set face of a child:
But behind it, where's a trace
Of the staidness and reserve,
And formal lines without a curve,
In the same child's playing-face?
No two windows look one way
O'er the small sea-water thread
Below them.   Ah, the autumn day
I, passing, saw you overhead!
First, out a cloud of curtain blew,
Then, a sweet cry, and last, came you—
To catch your loory that must needs
Escape just then, of all times then,
To peck a tall plant's fleecy seeds,
And make me happiest of men.
I scarce could breathe to see you reach
So far back o'er the balcony,
(To catch him ere he climbed too high
Above you in the Smyrna peach)
That quick the round smooth cord of gold,
This coiled hair on your head, unrolled,
Fell down you like a gorgeous snake
The Roman girls were wont, of old,
When Rome there was, for coolness' sake
To let lie curling o'er their bosoms.
Dear loory, may his beak retain
Ever its delicate rose stain
As if the wounded lotus-blossoms
Had marked their thief to know again!

IN A GONDOLA

Stay longer yet, for others' sake
Than mine! what should your chamber do?
—With all its rarities that ache
In silence while day lasts, but wake
At night-time and their life renew,
Suspended just to pleasure you
—That brought against their will together
These objects, and, while day lasts, weave
Around them such a magic tether
That they look dumb: your harp, believe,
With all the sensitive tight strings
That dare not speak, now to itself
Breathes slumbrously as if some elf
Went in and out the chords, his wings
Make murmur wheresoe'er they graze,
As an angel may, between the maze
Of midnight palace-pillars, on
And on, to sow God's plagues have gone
Through guilty glorious Babylon.
And while such murmurs flow, the nymph
Bends o'er the harp-top from her shell,
As the dry limpet for the lymph
Come with a tune he knows so well.
And how your statues' hearts must swell!
And how your pictures must descend
To see each other, friend with friend!
Oh, could you take them by surprise,
You'd find Schidone's eager Duke
Doing the quaintest courtesies
To that prim Saint by Haste-thee-Luke:
And, deeper into her rock den,
Bold Castelfranco's Magdalen
You'd find retreated from the ken
Of that robed counsel-keeping Ser—
As if the Tizian thinks of her,
And is not, rather, gravely bent
On seeing for himself what toys

IN A GONDOLA

Are these, his progeny invent,
What litter now the board employs
Whereon he signed a document
That got him murdered!   Each enjoys
Its night so well, you cannot break
The sport up, so, indeed must make
More stay with me, for others' sake.

She speaks.

I

To-morrow, if a harp-string, say,
Is used to tie the jasmine back
That overfloods my room with sweets,
Contrive your Zorzi somehow meets
My Zanze: if the ribbon's black,
The Three are watching; keep away.

II

Your gondola—let Zorzi wreathe
A mesh of water-weeds about
Its prow, as if he unaware
Had struck some quay or bridge-foot stair;
That I may throw a paper out
As you and he go underneath.

There's Zanze's vigilant taper; safe are we!
Only one minute more to-night with me?
Resume your past self of a month ago!
Be you the bashful gallant, I will be
The lady with the colder breast than snow:
Now bow you, as becomes, nor touch my hand
More than I touch yours when I step to land,
And say, All thanks, Siora!—

Heart to heart,
And lips to lips!   Yet once more, ere we part,
Clasp me and make me thine, as mine thou art!

IN A GONDOLA

He is surprised, and stabbed.

It was ordained to be so, Sweet,—and best
Comes now, beneath thine eyes, and on thy breast.
Still kiss me! Care not for the cowards! Care
Only to put aside thy beauteous hair
My blood will hurt! The Three, I do not scorn
To death, because they never lived: but I
Have lived indeed, and so—(yet one more kiss)—can die!

ARTEMIS PROLOGIZES

I AM a Goddess of the ambrosial courts,
And save by Here, Queen of Pride, surpassed
By none whose temples whiten this the world.
Thro' Heaven I roll my lucid moon along;
I shed in Hell o'er my pale people peace;
On Earth, I, caring for the creatures, guard
Each pregnant yellow wolf and fox-bitch sleek,
And every feathered mother's callow brood,
And all that love green haunts and loneliness.
Of men, the chaste adore me, hanging crowns
Of poppies red to blackness, bell and stem,
Upon my image at Athenai here;
And this dead Youth, Asclepios bends above,
Was dearest to me. He my buskined step
To follow thro' the wild-wood leafy ways,
And chase the panting stag, or swift with darts
Stop the swift ounce, or lay the leopard low,
Neglected homage to another God:
Whence Aphrodite, by no midnight smoke
Of tapers lulled, in jealousy dispatched
A noisome lust that, as the gadbee stings,
Possessed his stepdame Phaidra for himself
The son of Theseus her great absent spouse.
Hippolutos exclaiming in his rage

ARTEMIS
    PROLOGIZES.

ARTEMIS PROLOGIZES

Against the miserable Queen, she judged
Life insupportable, and, pricked at heart
An Amazonian stranger's race should dare
To scorn her, perished by the murderous cord :
Yet, ere she perished, blasted in a scroll
The fame of him her swerving made not swerve,
Which Theseus read, returning, and believed,
So, exiled in the blindness of his wrath,
The man without a crime, who, last as first,
Loyal, divulged not to his sire the truth.
Now Theseus from Poseidon had obtained
That of his wishes should be granted Three,
And this he imprecated straight—alive
May ne'er Hippolutos reach other lands !
Poseidon heard, ai ai !   And scarce the prince
Had stepped into the fixed boots of the car,
That gave the feet a stay against the strength
Of the Henetian horses, and around
His body flung the reins, and urged their speed
Along the rocks and shingles of the shore,
When from the gaping wave a monster flung
His obscene body in the coursers' path !
These, mad with terror as the sea-bull sprawled
Wallowing about their feet, lost care of him
That reared them ; and the master-chariot-pole
Snapping beneath their plunges like a reed,
Hippolutos, whose feet were trammelled fast,
Was yet dragged forward by the circling rein
Which either hand directed ; nor was quenched
The frenzy of that flight before each trace,
Wheel-spoke and splinter of the woeful car,
Each boulder-stone, sharp stub, and spiny shell,
Huge fish-bone wrecked and wreathed amid the sands
On that detested beach, was bright with blood
And morsels of his flesh : then fell the steeds
Head-foremost, crashing in their mooned fronts,
Shivering with sweat, each white eye horror-fixed.

41

ARTEMIS PROLOGIZES

His people, who had witnessed all afar,
Bore back the ruins of Hippolutos.
But when his sire, too swoln with pride, rejoiced,
(Indomitable as a man foredoomed)
That vast Poseidon had fulfilled his prayer,
I, in a flood of glory visible,
Stood o'er my dying votary, and deed
By deed revealed, as all took place, the truth.
Then Theseus lay the woefullest of men,
And worthily; but ere the death-veils hid
His face, the murdered prince full pardon breathed
To his rash sire. Whereat Athenai wails.
So I, who ne'er forsake my votaries,
Lest in the cross-way none the honey-cake
Should tender, nor pour out the dog's hot life;
Lest at my fane the priests disconsolate
Should dress my image with some faded poor
Few crowns, made favours of, nor dare object
Such slackness to my worshippers who turn
The trusting heart and loaded hand elsewhere,
As they had climbed Olumpos to report
Of Artemis and nowhere found her throne—
I interposed: and, this eventful night,
While round the funeral pyre the populace
Stood with fierce light on their black robes that blind
Each sobbing head, while yet their hair they clipped
O'er the dead body of their withered prince,
And, in his palace, Theseus prostrated
On the cold hearth, his brow cold as the slab
'Twas bruised on, groaned away the heavy grief—
As the pyre fell, and down the cross logs crashed,
Sending a crowd of sparkles thro' the night,
And the gay fire, elate with mastery,
Towered like a serpent o'er the clotted jars
Of wine, dissolving oils and frankincense,
And splendid gums, like gold,—my potency
Conveyed the perished man to my retreat

WARING

In the thrice venerable forest here.
And this white-bearded Sage who squeezes now
The berried plant, is Phoibos' son of fame,
Asclepios, whom my radiant brother taught
The doctrine of each herb and flower and root,
To know their secret'st virtue and express
The saving soul of all—who so has soothed
With lavers the torn brow and murdered cheeks,
Composed the hair and brought its gloss again,
And called the red bloom to the pale skin back,
And laid the strips and jagged ends of flesh
Even once more, and slacked the sinew's knot
Of every tortured limb—that now he lies
As if mere sleep possessed him underneath
These interwoven oaks and pines.   Oh, cheer,
Divine presenter of the healing rod,
Thy snake, with ardent throat and lulling eye,
Twines his lithe spires around!   I say, much cheer!
Proceed thou with thy wisest pharmacies!
And ye, white crowd of woodland sister-nymphs,
Ply, as the Sage directs, these buds and leaves
That strew the turf around the Twain!   While I
Await, in fitting silence, the event.

WARING

I

I

WHAT'S become of Waring
Since he gave us all the slip,
Chose land-travel or seafaring,
Boots and chest, or staff and scrip,
Rather than pace up and down
Any longer London-town?

WARING

II

Who'd have guessed it from his lip,
Or his brow's accustomed bearing,
On the night he thus took ship,
Or started landward?—little caring
For us, it seems, who supped together,
(Friends of his too, I remember)
And walked home thro' the merry weather,
The snowiest in all December;
I left his arm that night myself
For what's-his-name's, the new prose-poet,
That wrote the book there, on the shelf—
How, forsooth, was I to know it
If Waring meant to glide away
Like a ghost at break of day?
Never looked he half so gay!

III

He was prouder than the Devil:
How he must have cursed our revel!
Ay, and many other meetings,
Indoor visits, outdoor greetings,
As up and down he paced this London,
With no work done, but great works undone,
Where scarce twenty knew his name.
Why not, then, have earlier spoken,
Written, bustled?   Who's to blame
If your silence kept unbroken?
" True, but there were sundry jottings,
" Stray-leaves, fragments, blurrs and blottings,
" Certain first steps were achieved
" Already which "—(is that your meaning?)
" Had well borne out whoe'er believed
" In more to come!"   But who goes gleaning
Hedge-side chance-blades, while full-sheaved
Stand cornfields by him?   Pride, o'erweening

44

WARING

Pride alone, puts forth such claims
O'er the day's distinguished names.

IV

Meantime, how much I loved him,
I find out now I 've lost him :
I, who cared not if I moved him,
Who could so carelessly accost him,
Henceforth never shall get free
Of his ghostly company,
His eyes that just a little wink
As deep I go into the merit
Of this and that distinguished spirit—
His cheeks' raised colour, soon to sink,
As long I dwell on some stupendous
And tremendous (Heaven defend us !)
Monstr'-inform'-ingens-horrend-ous
Demoniaco-seraphic
Penman's latest piece of graphic.
Nay, my very wrist grows warm
With his dragging weight of arm !
E'en so, swimmingly appears,
Thro' one's after-supper musings,
Some lost Lady of old years,
With her beauteous vain endeavour,
And goodness unrepaid as ever ;
The face, accustomed to refusings,
We, puppies that we were . . . Oh never
Surely, nice of conscience, scrupled
Being aught like false, forsooth, to ?
Telling aught but honest truth to ?
What a sin, had we centupled
Its possessor's grace and sweetness !
No ! she heard in its completeness
Truth, for truth 's a weighty matter,
And, truth at issue, we can't flatter !

45

WARING

Well, 'tis done with : she's exempt
From damning us thro' such a sally ;
And so she glides, as down a valley,
Taking up with her contempt,
Past our reach ; and in, the flowers
Shut her unregarded hours.

V

Oh, could I have him back once more,
This Waring, but one half-day more !
Back, with the quiet face of yore,
So hungry for acknowledgment
Like mine ! I'd fool him to his bent !
Feed, should not he, to heart's content?
I'd say, "to only have conceived
"Your great works, tho' they ne'er make progress
"Surpasses all we've yet achieved ! "
I'd lie so, I should be believed.
I'd make such havoc of the claims
Of the day's distinguished names
To feast him with, as feasts an ogress
Her sharp-toothed golden-crowned child !
Or, as one feasts a creature rarely
Captured here, unreconciled
To capture ; and completely gives
Its pettish humours licence, barely
Requiring that it lives.

VI

Ichabod, Ichabod,
The glory is departed !
Travels Waring East away?
Who, of knowledge, by hearsay,
Reports a man upstarted
Somewhere as a God,
Hordes grown European-hearted
Millions of the wild made tame
On a sudden at his fame?

46

WARING

In Vishnu-land what Avatar?
Or who, in Moscow, toward the Czar,
With the demurest of footfalls
Over the Kremlin's pavement, bright
With serpentine and syenite,
Steps, with five other Generals,
That simultaneously take snuff,
For each to have pretext enough
To kerchiefwise unfurl his sash
Which, softness' self, is yet the stuff
To hold fast where a steel chain snaps,
And leave the grand white neck no gash?
Waring, in Moscow, to those rough
Cold northern natures borne, perhaps,
Like the lambwhite maiden dear
From the circle of mute kings
Unable to repress the tear,
Each as his sceptre down he flings,
To Dian's fane at Taurica,
Where now a captive priestess, she alway
Mingles her tender grave Hellenic speech
With theirs, tuned to the hailstone-beaten beach,
As pours some pigeon, from the myrrhy lands
Rapt by the whirlblast to fierce Scythian strands
Where breed the swallows, her melodious cry
Amid their barbarous twitter!
In Russia? Never! Spain were fitter!
Ay, most likely 'tis in Spain
That we and Waring meet again—
Now, while he turns down that cool narrow lane
Into the blackness, out of grave Madrid
All fire and shine—abrupt as when there's slid
Its stiff gold blazing pall
From some black coffin-lid.
Or, best of all,
I love to think
The leaving us was just a feint;

WARING

Back here to London did he slink;
And now works on without a wink
Of sleep, and we are on the brink
Of something great in fresco-paint:
Some garret's ceiling, walls and floor,
Up and down and o'er and o'er
He splashes, as none splashed before
Since great Caldara Polidore:
Or Music means this land of ours
Some favour yet, to pity won
By Purcell from his Rosy Bowers,—
"Give me my so long promised son,
"Let Waring end what I begun!"
Then down he creeps and out he steals
Only when the night conceals
His face—in Kent 'tis cherry-time,
Or, hops are picking; or, at prime
Of March, he wanders as, too happy,
Years ago when he was young,
Some mild eve when woods grew sappy,
And the early moths had sprung
To life from many a trembling sheath
Woven the warm boughs beneath;
While small birds said to themselves
What should soon be actual song,
And young gnats, by tens and twelves,
Made as if they were the throng
That crowd around and carry aloft
The sound they have nursed, so sweet and pure,
Out of the myriad noises soft,
Into a tone that can endure
Amid the noise of a July noon,
When all God's creatures crave their boon,
All at once and all in tune,
And get it, happy as Waring then,
Having first within his ken
What a man might do with men,

WARING

And far too glad, in the even-glow,
To mix with your world he meant to take
Into his hand, he told you, so—
And out of it his world to make,
To contract and to expand
As he shut or oped his hand.
Oh, Waring, what's to really be?
A clear stage and a crowd to see!
Some Garrick—say—out shall not he
The heart of Hamlet's mystery pluck?
Or, where most unclean beasts are rife,
Some Junius—am I right?—shall tuck
His sleeve, and out with flaying-knife!
Some Chatterton shall have the luck
Of calling Rowley into life!
Some one shall somehow run a muck
With this old world, for want of strife
Sound asleep: contrive, contrive
To rouse us, Waring! Who's alive?
Our men scarce seem in earnest now:
Distinguished names!—but 'tis, somehow
As if they played at being names
Still more distinguished, like the games
Of children. Turn our sport to earnest
With a visage of the sternest!
Bring the real times back, confessed
Still better than our very best!

II

I

"WHEN I last saw Waring . . ."
(How all turned to him who spoke—
You saw Waring? Truth or joke?
In land-travel, or sea-faring?)

WARING

II

"We were sailing by Triest,
"Where a day or two we harboured:
"A sunset was in the West,
"When, looking over the vessel's side,
"One of our company espied
"A sudden speck to larboard.
"And, as a sea-duck flies and swims
"At once, so came the light craft up,
"With its sole lateen sail that trims
"And turns (the water round its rims
"Dancing, as round a sinking cup)
"And by us like a fish it curled,
"And drew itself up close beside,
"Its great sail on the instant furled,
"And o'er its planks, a shrill voice cried,
"(A neck as bronzed as a Lascar's)
"'Buy wine of us, you English Brig?
"'Or fruit, tobacco and cigars?
"'A Pilot for you to Triest?
"'Without one, look you ne'er so big,
"'They'll never let you up the bay!
"'We natives should know best.'
"I turned, and 'just those fellows' way,'
"Our captain said, 'The 'long-shore thieves
"'Are laughing at us in their sleeves.'

III

"In truth, the boy leaned laughing back;
"And one, half-hidden by his side
"Under the furled sail, soon I spied,
"With great grass hat, and kerchief black,
"Who looked up, with his kingly throat,
"Said somewhat, while the other shook
"His hair back from his eyes to look
"Their longest at us; then the boat,

RUDEL TO THE LADY OF TRIPOLI

"I know not how, turned sharply round,
"Laying her whole side on the sea
"As a leaping fish does; from the lee
"Into the weather, cut somehow
"Her sparkling path beneath our bow;
"And so went off, as with a bound,
"Into the rose and golden half
"Of the sky, to overtake the sun,
"And reach the shore, like the sea-calf
"Its singing cave; yet I caught one
"Glance ere away the boat quite passed,
"And neither time nor toil could mar
"Those features: so I saw the last
"Of Waring!"—You? Oh, never star
Was lost here, but it rose afar!
Look East, where whole new thousands are!
In Vishnu-land what Avatar?

RUDEL TO THE LADY OF TRIPOLI

I

I KNOW a Mount, the gracious Sun perceives
First when he visits, last, too, when he leaves
The world; and, vainly favoured, it repays
The day-long glory of his steadfast gaze
By no change of its large calm front of snow.
And underneath the Mount, a Flower I know,
He cannot have perceived, that changes ever
At his approach; and, in the lost endeavour
To live his life, has parted, one by one,
With all a flower's true graces, for the grace
Of being but a foolish mimic sun,
With ray-like florets round a disk-like face.

51

RUDEL TO THE LADY OF TRIPOLI

Men nobly call by many a name the Mount,
As over many a land of theirs its large
Calm front of snow like a triumphal targe
Is reared, and still with old names, fresh ones vie,
Each to its proper praise and own account:
Men call the Flower, the Sunflower, sportively.

II

Oh, Angel of the East, one, one gold look
Across the waters to this twilight nook,
—The far sad waters, Angel, to this nook!

III

Dear Pilgrim, art thou for the East indeed?
Go! Saying ever as thou dost proceed,
That I, French Rudel, choose for my device
A sunflower outspread like a sacrifice
Before its idol. See! These inexpert
And hurried fingers could not fail to hurt
The woven picture; 'tis a woman's skill
Indeed; but nothing baffled me, so, ill
Or well, the work is finished. Say, men feed
On songs I sing, and therefore bask the bees
On my flower's breast as on a platform broad:
But, as the flower's concern is not for these
But solely for the sun, so men applaud
In vain this Rudel, he not looking here
But to the East—the East! Go, say this, Pilgrim dear!

THROVGH THE·METIDJA TO·ABD-EL KADR·

BYAM·SHAW·

1842

I

As I ride, as I ride,
With a full heart for my guide,
So its tide rocks my side,
As I ride, as I ride,
That, as I were double-eyed,
He, in whom our Tribes confide,
Is descried, ways untried
As I ride, as I ride.

II

As I ride, as I ride
To our Chief and his Allied,
Who dares chide my heart's pride
As I ride, as I ride?
Or are witnesses denied—
Through the desert waste and wide
Do I glide unespied
As I ride, as I ride?

III

As I ride, as I ride,
When an inner voice has cried,
The sands slide, nor abide
(As I ride, as I ride)

METIDJA TO ABD-EL-KADR

O'er each visioned Homicide
That came vaunting (has he lied?)
To reside—where he died,
As I ride, as I ride.

IV

As I ride, as I ride,
Ne'er has spur my swift horse plied,
Yet his hide, streaked and pied,
As I ride, as I ride,
Shows where sweat has sprung and dried,
—Zebra-footed, ostrich-thighed—
How has vied stride with stride
As I ride, as I ride!

V

As I ride, as I ride,
Could I loose what fate has tied,
Ere I pried, she should hide
As I ride, as I ride,
All that's meant me: satisfied
When the Prophet and the Bride
Stop veins I'd have subside
As I ride, as I ride!

THE PIED·PIPER OF·HAMELIN·

BYAM·SHAW

A CHILD'S STORY, WRITTEN FOR, AND INSCRIBED
TO W. M. THE YOUNGER

I

HAMELIN Town's in Brunswick,
By famous Hanover city;
  The river Weser, deep and wide,
  Washes its wall on the southern side;
  A pleasanter spot you never spied;
But, when begins my ditty,
  Almost five hundred years ago,
  To see the townsfolk suffer so
    From vermin, was a pity.

II

Rats!
They fought the dogs, and killed the cats.
  And bit the babies in the cradles,
And ate the cheeses out of the vats,
  And licked the soup from the cook's own ladles,
Split open the kegs of salted sprats,

55

Made nests inside men's Sunday hats,
And even spoiled the women's chats,
    By drowning their speaking
    With shrieking and squeaking
In fifty different sharps and flats.

III

At last the people in a body
    To the Town Hall came flocking:
" 'Tis clear," cried they, " our Mayor's a noddy;
    " And as for our Corporation—shocking
" To think we buy gowns lined with ermine
" For dolts that can't or won't determine
" What's best to rid us of our vermin!
" You hope, because you're old and obese,
" To find in furry civic robe ease?
" Rouse up, Sirs!   Give your brains a racking
" To find the remedy we're lacking,
" Or, sure as fate, we'll send you packing!"
At this the Mayor and Corporation
Quaked with a mighty consternation.

IV

An hour they sate in council,
    At length the Mayor broke silence:
" For a guilder I'd my ermine gown sell;
    " I wish I were a mile hence!
" It's easy to bid one rack one's brain—
" I'm sure my poor head aches again
" I've scratched it so, and all in vain.
" Oh for a trap, a trap, a trap!"
Just as he said this, what should hap
At the chamber door but a gentle tap?
" Bless us," cried the Mayor, "what's that?"
(With the Corporation as he sat,
Looking little though wondrous fat;

THE PIED PIPER OF HAMELIN

Nor brighter was his eye, nor moister
Than a too-long-opened oyster,
Save when at noon his paunch grew mutinous
For a plate of turtle green and glutinous)
"Only a scraping of shoes on the mat?
"Anything like the sound of a rat
"Makes my heart go pit-a-pat!"

V

"Come in!"—the Mayor cried, looking bigger:
And in did come the strangest figure!
His queer long coat from heel to head
Was half of yellow and half of red;
And he himself was tall and thin,
With sharp blue eyes, each like a pin,
And light loose hair, yet swarthy skin,
No tuft on cheek nor beard on chin,
But lips where smiles went out and in—
There was no guessing his kith and kin!
And nobody could enough admire
The tall man and his quaint attire:
Quoth one: "It's as my great-grandsire,
"Starting up at the Trump of Doom's tone,
"Had walked this way from his painted tomb-stone!"

VI

He advanced to the council-table:
And, "Please your honours," said he, "I'm able,
"By means of a secret charm, to draw
"All creatures living beneath the sun,
"That creep, or swim, or fly, or run,
"After me so as you never saw!
"And I chiefly use my charm
"On creatures that do people harm,
"The mole, and toad, and newt, and viper;
"And people call me the Pied Piper."

57

THE PIED PIPER OF HAMELIN

(And here they noticed round his neck
A scarf of red and yellow stripe,
To match with his coat of the self same cheque;
And at the scarf's end hung a pipe;
And his fingers, they noticed, were ever straying
As if impatient to be playing
Upon this pipe, as low it dangled
Over his vesture so old-fangled.)
" Yet," said he, " poor piper as I am,
" In Tartary I freed the Cham,
" Last June, from his huge swarms of gnats;
" I eased in Asia the Nizam
" Of a monstrous brood of vampyre-bats:
" And, as for what your brain bewilders,
" If I can rid your town of rats
" Will you give me a thousand guilders? "
" One? fifty thousand ! "—was the exclamation
Of the astonished Mayor and Corporation.

VII

Into the street the Piper stept,
   Smiling first a little smile,
As if he knew what magic slept
   In his quiet pipe the while;
Then, like a musical adept,
To blow the pipe his lips he wrinkled,
And green and blue his sharp eyes twinkled
Like a candle flame where salt is sprinkled;
And ere three shrill notes the pipe uttered,
You heard as if an army muttered;
And the muttering grew to a grumbling;
And the grumbling grew to a mighty rumbling;
And out of the houses the rats came tumbling.
Great rats, small rats, lean rats, brawny rats,
Brown rats, black rats, grey rats, tawny rats,

THE PIED PIPER OF HAMELIN

Grave old plodders, gay young friskers,
　　Fathers, mothers, uncles, cousins,
Cocking tails and pricking whiskers,
　　Families by tens and dozens,
Brothers, sisters, husbands, wives—
Followed the Piper for their lives.
From street to street he piped advancing,
And step for step they followed dancing,
Until they came to the river Weser
Wherein all plunged and perished
—Save one who, stout as Julius Cæsar,
Swam across and lived to carry
(As he the manuscript he cherished)
To Rat-land home his commentary,
Which was, "At the first shrill notes of the pipe.
"I heard the sound as of scraping tripe,
"And putting apples, wondrous ripe,
"Into a cider-press's gripe :
"And a moving away of pickle-tub-boards,
"And a leaving ajar of conserve-cupboards,
"And a drawing the corks of train-oil-flasks,
"And a breaking the hoops of butter-casks ;
"And it seemed as if a voice
"(Sweeter far than by harp or by psaltery
"Is breathed) called out, Oh rats, rejoice !
"The world is grown to one vast drysaltery !
"So munch on, crunch on, take your nuncheon,
"Breakfast, supper, dinner, luncheon !
"And just as a bulky sugar-puncheon,
"All ready staved, like a great sun shone
"Glorious scarce an inch before me,
"Just as methought it said, Come, bore me !
"—I found the Weser rolling o'er me."

VIII

You should have heard the Hamelin people
Ringing the bells till they rocked the steeple ;

THE PIED PIPER OF HAMELIN

"Go," cried the Mayor, "and get long poles!
"Poke out the nests and block up the holes!
"Consult with carpenters and builders,
"And leave in our town not even a trace
"Of the rats!"—when suddenly up the face
Of the Piper perked in the market-place,
With a, "First, if you please, my thousand guilders!"

IX

A thousand guilders! The Mayor looked blue;
So did the Corporation too.
For council dinners made rare havock
With Claret, Moselle, Vin-de-Grave, Hock;
And half the money would replenish
Their cellar's biggest butt with Rhenish.
To pay this sum to a wandering fellow
With a gipsy coat of red and yellow!
"Beside," quoth the Mayor with a knowing wink,
"Our business was done at the river's brink;
"We saw with our eyes the vermin sink,
"And what's dead can't come to life, I think.
"So, friend, we're not the folks to shrink
"From the duty of giving you something for drink,
"And a matter of money to put in your poke;
"But, as for the guilders, what we spoke
"Of them, as you very well know, was in joke.
"Beside, our losses have made us thrifty;
"A thousand guilders! Come, take fifty!"

X

The Piper's face fell, and he cried,
"No trifling! I can't wait, beside!
"I've promised to visit by dinner time
"Bagdat, and accept the prime
"Of the Head Cook's pottage, all he's rich in,
"For having left, in the Caliph's kitchen,

THE PIED PIPER OF HAMELIN

" Of a nest of scorpions no survivor—
" With him I proved no bargain-driver,
" With you, don't think I 'll bate a stiver !
" And folks who put me in a passion
" May find me pipe to another fashion."

XI

" How ? " cried the Mayor, " d' ye think I 'll brook
" Being worse treated than a Cook ?
" Insulted by a lazy ribald
" With idle pipe and vesture piebald ?
" You threaten us, fellow ?   Do your worst,
" Blow your pipe there till you burst ! "

XII

Once more he stept into the street ;
    And to his lips again
Laid his long pipe of smooth straight cane ;
    And ere he blew three notes (such sweet
Soft notes as yet musician's cunning
    Never gave the enraptured air)
There was a rustling, that seemed like a bustling
Of merry crowds justling at pitching and hustling,
Small feet were pattering, wooden shoes clattering,
Little hands clapping, and little tongues chattering,
And, like fowls in a farm-yard when barley is scattering
Out came the children running.
All the little boys and girls,
With rosy cheeks and flaxen curls,
And sparkling eyes and teeth like pearls,
Tripping and skipping, ran merrily after
The wonderful music with shouting and laughter.

XIII

The Mayor was dumb, and the Council stood
As if they were changed into blocks of wood,

61

THE PIED PIPER OF HAMELIN

Unable to move a step, or cry
To the children merrily skipping by—
And could only follow with the eye
That joyous crowd at the Piper's back.
But how the Mayor was on the rack,
And the wretched Council's bosom beat,
As the Piper turned from the High Street
To where the Weser rolled its waters
Right in the way of their sons and daughters!
However he turned from South to West,
And to Koppelberg Hill his steps addressed,
And after him the children pressed;
Great was the joy in every breast.
" He never can cross that mighty top!
" He's forced to let the piping drop,
" And we shall see our children stop!"
When, lo, as they reached the mountain's side,
A wondrous portal opened wide,
As if a cavern was suddenly hollowed;
And the Piper advanced and the children followed,
And when all were in to the very last,
The door in the mountain side shut fast.
Did I say, all? No! One was lame,
And could not dance the whole of the way;
And in after years, if you would blame
His sadness, he was used to say,—
" It's dull in our town since my playmates left!
" I can't forget that I'm bereft
" Of all the pleasant sights they see,
" Which the Piper also promised me;
" For he led us, he said, to a joyous land,
" Joining the town and just at hand,
" Where waters gushed and fruit-trees grew,
" And flowers put forth a fairer hue,
" And everything was strange and new;
" The sparrows were brighter than peacocks here,
" And their dogs outran our fallow deer,

THE PIED PIPER OF HAMELIN

" And honey-bees had lost their stings,
" And horses were born with eagles' wings;
" And just as I became assured
" My lame foot would be speedily cured,
" The music stopped and I stood still,
" And found myself outside the Hill,
" Left alone against my will,
" To go now limping as before,
" And never hear of that country more!"

XIV

Alas, alas for Hamelin!
    There came into many a burgher's pate
    A text which says that Heaven's Gate
    Opes to the Rich at as easy rate
As the needle's eye takes a camel in!
The Mayor sent East, West, North, and South
To offer the Piper by word of mouth,
    Wherever it was men's lot to find him,
Silver and gold to his heart's content,
If he 'd only return the way he went,
    And bring the children behind him.
But when they saw 'twas a lost endeavour,
And Piper and dancers were gone for ever,
They made a decree that lawyers never
    Should think their records dated duly
If, after the day of the month and year,
These words did not as well appear,
" And so long after what happened here
    " On the Twenty-second of July,
" Thirteen hundred and Seventy-six ":
And the better in memory to fix
The place of the Children's last retreat,
They called it, the Pied Piper's Street—
Where any one playing on pipe or tabor
Was sure for the future to lose his labour.

63

THE PIED PIPER OF HAMELIN

Nor suffered they Hostelry or Tavern
   To shock with mirth a street so solemn;
But opposite the place of the cavern
   They wrote the story on a column,
And on the Great Church Window painted
The same, to make the world acquainted
How their children were stolen away;
And there it stands to this very day.
And I must not omit to say
That in Transylvania there's a tribe
Of alien people that ascribe
The outlandish ways and dress
On which their neighbours lay such stress,
To their fathers and mothers having risen
Out of some subterraneous prison
Into which they were trepanned
Long time ago in a mighty band
Out of Hamelin town in Brunswick land,
But how or why, they don't understand.

XV

So, Willy, let you and me be wipers
Of scores out with all men—especially pipers:
And, whether they pipe us free, from rats or from mice,
If we've promised them aught, let us keep our promise.

HOW THEY BROVGHT THE GOOD NEWS

FROM GHENT TO AIX

BYAM·SHAW

[16—]

I

I SPRANG to the stirrup, and Joris, and he;
I galloped, Dirck galloped, we galloped all three;
"Good speed!" cried the watch, as the gate-bolts undrew;
"Speed!" echoed the wall to us galloping through;
Behind shut the postern, the lights sank to rest,
And into the midnight we galloped abreast.

II

Not a word to each other; we kept the great pace
Neck by neck, stride by stride, never changing our place;
I turned in my saddle and made its girths tight,
Then shortened each stirrup, and set the pique right,
Rebuckled the cheek-strap, chained slacker the bit,
Nor galloped less steadily Roland a whit.

III

'Twas moonset at starting; but while we drew near
Lokeren, the cocks crew and twilight dawned clear;
At Boom, a great yellow star came out to see;
At Düffeld, 'twas morning as plain as could be;
And from Mecheln church-steeple we heard the half-chime,
So Joris broke silence with, "Yet there is time!"

IV

At Aerschot, up leaped of a sudden the sun,
And against him the cattle stood black every one,
To stare thro' the mist at us galloping past,
And I saw my stout galloper Roland at last,
With resolute shoulders, each butting away
The haze, as some bluff river headland its spray.

V

And his low head and crest, just one sharp ear bent
    back
For my voice, and the other pricked out on his track ;
And one eye's black intelligence,—ever that glance
O'er its white edge at me, his own master, askance !
And the thick heavy spume-flakes which aye and anon
His fierce lips shook upwards in galloping on.

VI

By Hasselt, Dirck groaned ; and cried Joris, " Stay spur !
" Your Roos galloped bravely, the fault's not in her,
" We'll remember at Aix "—for one heard the quick
    wheeze
Of her chest, saw the stretched neck and staggering knees,
And sunk tail, and horrible heave of the flank,
As down on her haunches she shuddered and sank.

VII

So we were left galloping, Joris and I,
Past Looz and past Tongres, no cloud in the sky ;
The broad sun above laughed a pitiless laugh,
'Neath our feet broke the brittle bright stubble like chaff ;
Till over by Dalhem a dome-spire sprang white,
And " Gallop," gasped Joris, " for Aix is in sight ! "

GOOD NEWS FROM GHENT TO AIX

VIII

"How they'll greet us!"—and all in a moment his roan
Rolled neck and croup over, lay dead as a stone;
And there was my Roland to bear the whole weight
Of the news which alone could save Aix from her fate,
With his nostrils like pits full of blood to the brim,
And with circles of red for his eye-sockets' rim.

IX

Then I cast loose my buffcoat, each holster let fall,
Shook off both my jack-boots, let go belt and all,
Stood up in the stirrup, leaned, patted his ear,
Called my Roland his pet-name, my horse without peer;
Clapped my hands, laughed and sang, any noise, bad or
  good,
Till at length into Aix Roland galloped and stood.

X

And all I remember is, friends flocking round
As I sate with his head 'twixt my knees on the ground,
And no voice but was praising this Roland of mine,
As I poured down his throat our last measure of wine,
Which (the burgesses voted by common consent)
Was no more than his due who brought good news from
  Ghent.

PICTOR IGNOTUS

[FLORENCE, 15—]

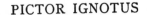

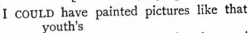

I COULD have painted pictures like that
        youth's
    Ye praise so.   How my soul springs up!
        No bar
Stayed me—ah, thought which saddens
        while it soothes!—
    Never did fate forbid me, star by star,
To outburst on your night with all my gift
    Of fires from God: nor would my flesh
        have shrunk
From seconding my soul, with eyes uplift
    And wide to Heaven, or, straight like
        thunder, sunk
To the centre, of an instant; or around
    Turned calmly and inquisitive, to scan
The license and the limit, space and bound
    Allowed to Truth made visible in Man.
And, like that youth ye praise so, all I saw,
    Over the canvass could my hand have flung,
Each face obedient to its passion's law,
    Each passion clear proclaimed without a tongue;
Whether Hope rose at once in all the blood,
    A-tiptoe for the blessing of embrace,
Or Rapture drooped the eyes, as when her brood
    Pull down the nesting dove's heart to its place,
Or Confidence lit swift the forehead up,
    And locked the mouth fast, like a castle braved,—
O Human faces, hath it spilt, my cup?
    What did ye give me that I have not saved?
Nor will I say I have not dreamed (how well!)
    Of going—I, in each new picture,—forth,
As, making new hearts beat and bosoms swell,
    To Pope or Kaiser, East, West, South or North,

PICTOR IGNOTUS

Bound for the calmly satisfied great State,
  Or glad aspiring little burgh, it went,
Flowers cast upon the car which bore the freight,
  Through old streets named afresh from its event,
Till it reached home, where learned Age should greet
  My face, and Youth, the star not yet distinct
Above his hair, lie yearning at my feet!—
  Oh, thus to live, I and my picture, linked
With love about, and praise, till life should end,
  And then not go to Heaven, but linger here,
Here on my earth, earth's every man my friend,—
  The thought grew frightful, 'twas so wildly dear!
But a voice changed it! Glimpses of such sights
  Have scared me, like the revels thro' a door
Of some strange House of Idols at its rites;
  This world seemed not the world it was before!
Mixed with my loving trusting ones there trooped
  . . . Who summoned those cold faces that begun
To press on me and judge me? Tho' I stooped
  Shrinking, as from the soldiery a nun,
They drew me forth, and spite of me . . enough!
  These buy and sell our pictures, take and give,
Count them for garniture and household-stuff,
  And where they live our pictures needs must live,
And see their faces, listen to their prate,
  Partakers of their daily pettiness,
Discussed of,—" This I love, or this I hate,
  "This likes me more, and this affects me less!"
Wherefore I chose my portion. If at whiles
  My heart sinks, as monotonous I paint
These endless cloisters and eternal aisles
  With the same series, Virgin, Babe, and Saint,
With the same cold, calm, beautiful regard,
  At least no merchant traffics in my heart;
The sanctuary's gloom at least shall ward
  Vain tongues from where my pictures stand apart;
Only prayer breaks the silence of the shrine
  While, blackening in the daily candle-smoke,

69

THE ENGLISHMAN IN ITALY

They moulder on the damp wall's travertine,
  'Mid echoes the light footstep never woke.
So die, my pictures; surely, gently die!
  Oh, youth, men praise so,—holds their praise its worth?
Blown harshly, keeps the trump its golden cry?
  Tastes sweet the water with such specks of earth?

THE ENGLISHMAN IN ITALY

[PIANO DI SORRENTO]

FORTÙ, Fortù, my beloved one,
  Sit here by my side,
On my knees put up both little feet!
  I was sure, if I tried,
I could make you laugh spite of Scirocco:
  Now, open your eyes—
Let me keep you amused till he vanish
  In black from the skies,
With telling my memories over
  As you tell your beads;
All the memories plucked at Sorrento
  —The flowers, or the weeds.

Time for rain! for your long hot dry Autumn
  Had net-worked with brown
The white skin of each grape on the bunches,
  Marked like a quail's crown,
Those creatures you make such account of,
  Whose heads,—specked with white
Over brown like a great spider's back,
  As I told you last night,—
Your mother bites off for her supper;
  Red-ripe as could be.
Pomegranates were chapping and splitting
  In halves on the tree:

70

THE ENGLISHMAN IN ITALY

And betwixt the loose walls of great flintstone,
  Or in the thick dust
On the path, or straight out of the rock side,
  Wherever could thrust
Some burnt sprig of bold hardy rock-flower
  Its yellow face up,
For the prize were great butterflies fighting,
  Some five for one cup.
So, I guessed, ere I got up this morning,
  What change was in store,
By the quick rustle-down of the quail-nets
  Which woke me before
I could open my shutter, made fast
  With a bough and a stone,
And look thro' the twisted dead vine-twigs,
  Sole lattice that's known!
Quick and sharp rang the rings down the net-poles,
  While, busy beneath,
Your priest and his brother tugged at them,
  The rain in their teeth :
And out upon all the flat house-roofs
  Where split figs lay drying,
The girls took the frails under cover :
  Nor use seemed in trying
To get out the boats and go fishing,
  For, under the cliff,
Fierce the black water frothed o'er the blind-rock.
  No seeing our skiff
Arrive about noon from Amalfi,
  —Our fisher arrive,
And pitch down his basket before us,
  All trembling alive
With pink and grey jellies, your sea-fruit,
  —You touch the strange lumps,
And mouths gape there, eyes open, all manner
  Of horns and of humps,
Which only the fisher looks grave at,
  While round him like imps

THE ENGLISHMAN IN ITALY

Cling screaming the children as naked
    And brown as his shrimps;
Himself too as bare to the middle—
    —You see round his neck
The string and its brass coin suspended,
    That saves him from wreck.
But to-day not a boat reached Salerno,
    So back to a man
Came our friends, with whose help in the vineyards
    Grape-harvest began:
In the vat, half-way up in our house-side,
    Like blood the juice spins,
While your brother all bare-legged is dancing
    Till breathless he grins
Dead-beaten, in effort on effort
    To keep the grapes under,
Since still when he seems all but master,
    In pours the fresh plunder
From girls who keep coming and going
    With basket on shoulder,
And eyes shut against the rain's driving,
    Your girls that are older,—
For under the hedges of aloe,
    And where, on its bed
Of the orchard's black mould, the love-apple
    Lies pulpy and red,
All the young ones are kneeling and filling
    Their laps with the snails
Tempted out by this first rainy weather,—
    Your best of regales,
As to-night will be proved to my sorrow,
    When, supping in state,
We shall feast our grape-gleaners (two dozen,
    Three over one plate)
With lasagne so tempting to swallow
    In slippery ropes,
And gourds fried in great purple slices,
    That colour of popes.

72

THE ENGLISHMAN IN ITALY

Meantime, see the grape-bunch they 've brought you,--
 The rain-water slips
O'er the heavy blue bloom on each globe
 Which the wasp to your lips
Still follows with fretful persistence—
 Nay, taste, while awake,
This half of a curd-white smooth cheese-ball,
 That peels, flake by flake,
Like an onion's, each smoother and whiter ;
 Next, sip this weak wine
From the thin green glass flask, with its stopper,
 A leaf of the vine,—
And end with the prickly-pear's red flesh
 That leaves thro' its juice
The stony black seeds on your pearl-teeth
 . . Scirocco is loose !
Hark ! the quick, whistling pelt of the olives
 Which, thick in one's track,
Tempt the stranger to pick up and bite them,
 Tho' not yet half black !
How the old twisted olive trunks shudder !
 The medlars let fall
Their hard fruit, and the brittle great fig-trees
 Snap off, figs and all,—
For here comes the whole of the tempest !
 No refuge, but creep
Back again to my side and my shoulder,
 And listen or sleep.

O how will your country show next week,
 When all the vine-boughs
Have been stripped of their foliage to pasture
 The mules and the cows ?
Last eve, I rode over the mountains ;
 Your brother, my guide,
Soon left me, to feast on the myrtles
 That offered, each side,

THE ENGLISHMAN IN ITALY

Their fruit-balls, black, glossy and luscious,—
  Or strip from the sorbs
A treasure, so rosy and wondrous,
  Of hairy gold orbs!
But my mule picked his sure, sober path out,
  Just stopping to neigh
When he recognised down in the valley
  His mates on their way
With the faggots, and barrels of water;
  And soon we emerged
From the plain, where the woods could scarce follow;
  And still as we urged
Our way, the woods wondered, and left us,
  As up still we trudged
Though the wild path grew wilder each instant,
  And place was e'en grudged
'Mid the rock-chasms, and piles of loose stones
  (Like the loose broken teeth
Of some monster, which climbed there to die
  From the ocean beneath)
Place was grudged to the silver-grey fume-weed
  That clung to the path,
And dark rosemary, ever a-dying,
  That, 'spite the wind's wrath,
So loves the salt rock's face to seaward,—
  And lentisks as staunch
To the stone where they root and bear berries,—
  And . . . what shows a branch
Coral-coloured, transparent, with circlets
  Of pale seagreen leaves—
Over all trode my mule with the caution
  Of gleaners o'er sheaves,
Still, foot after foot like a lady—
  So, round after round,
He climbed to the top of Calvano,
  And God's own profound

THE ENGLISHMAN IN ITALY

Was above me, and round me the mountains,
 And under, the sea,
And within me, my heart to bear witness
 What was and shall be!
Oh heaven, and the terrible crystal!
 No rampart excludes
Your eye from the life to be lived
 In the blue solitudes!
Oh, those mountains, their infinite movement!
 Still moving with you—
For, ever some new head and breast of them
 Thrusts into view
To observe the intruder—you see it
 If quickly you turn
And, before they escape you, surprise them—
 They grudge you should learn
How the soft plains they look on, lean over,
 And love (they pretend)
—Cower beneath them; the flat sea-pine crouches,
 The wild fruit-trees bend,
E'en the myrtle-leaves curl, shrink and shut—
 All is silent and grave—
'Tis a sensual and timorous beauty—
 How fair, but a slave!
So, I turned to the sea,—and there slumbered
 As greenly as ever
Those isles of the siren, your Galli;
 No ages can sever
The Three, nor enable their sister
 To join them,—half way
On the voyage, she looked at Ulysses—
 No farther to-day;
Tho' the small one, just launched on the wave,
 Watches breast-high and steady
From under the rock, her bold sister
 Swum half-way already.

THE ENGLISHMAN IN ITALY

Fortù, shall we sail there together
    And see from the sides
Quite new rocks show their faces—new haunts
    Where the siren abides?
Shall we sail round and round them, close over
    The rocks, tho' unseen,
That ruffle the grey glassy water
    To glorious green?
Then scramble from splinter to splinter,
    Reach land and explore,
On the largest, the strange square black turret
    With never a door,
Just a loop to admit the quick lizards;
    Then, stand there and hear
The birds' quiet singing, that tells us
    What life is, so clear!
The secret they sang to Ulysses,
    When, ages ago,
He heard and he knew this life's secret,
    I hear and I know!

Ah, see! The sun breaks o'er Calvano—
    He strikes the great gloom
And flutters it o'er the mount's summit
    In airy gold fume!
All is over! Look out, see the gypsy,
    Our tinker and smith,
Has arrived, set up bellows and forge,
    And down-squatted forthwith
To his hammering, under the wall there;
    One eye keeps aloof
The urchins that itch to be putting
    His jews'-harps to proof,
While the other, thro' locks of curled wire,
    Is watching how sleek
Shines the hog, come to share in the windfalls
    —An abbot's own cheek!

THE ENGLISHMAN IN ITALY

All is over! Wake up and come out now,
    And down let us go,
And see the fine things got in order
    At Church for the show
Of the Sacrament, set forth this evening;
    To-morrow's the Feast
Of the Rosary's Virgin, by no means
    Of Virgins the least—
As you'll hear in the off-hand discourse
    Which (all nature, no art)
The Dominican brother, these three weeks,
    Was getting by heart.
Not a post nor a pillar but's dizened
    With red and blue papers;
All the roof wave with ribbons, each altar
    A-blaze with long tapers;
But the great masterpiece is the scaffold
    Rigged glorious to hold
All the fiddlers and fifers and drummers,
    And trumpeters bold,
Not afraid of Bellini nor Auber,
    Who, when the priest's hoarse,
Will strike us up something that's brisk
    For the feast's second course.
And then will the flaxen-wigged Image
    Be carried in pomp
Thro' the plain, while in gallant procession
    The priests mean to stomp.
And all round the glad church lie old bottles
    With gunpowder stopped,
Which will be, when the Image re-enters,
    Religiously popped.
And at night from the crest of Calvano
    Great bonfires will hang,
On the plain will the trumpets join chorus
    And more poppers bang!

THE ENGLISHMAN IN ITALY

At all events, come—to the garden,
  As far as the wall,
See me tap with a hoe on the plaster
  Till out there shall fall
A scorpion with wide angry nippers!

  . . . "Such trifles"—you say?
Fortù, in my England at home,
  Men meet gravely to-day
And debate, if abolishing Corn-laws
  Is righteous and wise
—If 'tis proper, Scirocco should vanish
  In black from the skies!

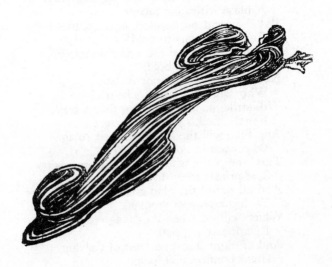

THE LOST LEADER

I

JUST for a handful of silver he left us,
  Just for a riband to stick in his coat—
Found the one gift of which fortune bereft us,
  Lost all the others she lets us devote ;
They, with the gold to give, doled him out silver,
  So much was their's who so little allowed :
How all our copper had gone for his service !
  Rags—were they purple, his heart had been proud !
We that had loved him so, followed him, honoured him,
  Lived in his mild and magnificent eye,
Learned his great language, caught his clear accents,
  Made him our pattern to live and to die !
Shakespeare was of us, Milton was for us,
  Burns, Shelley, were with us,—they watch from their graves !
He alone breaks from the van and the freemen,
  He alone sinks to the rear and the slaves !

II

We shall march prospering,—not thro' his presence ;
  Songs may inspirit us,—not from his lyre ;
Deeds will de done,—while he boasts his quiescence,
  Still bidding crouch whom the rest bade aspire :
Blot out his name, then,—record one lost soul more,
  One task more declined, one more footpath untrod,
One more triumph for devils, and sorrow for angels,
  One wrong more to man, one more insult to God !
Life's night begins : let him never come back to us !
  There would be doubt, hesitation and pain,
Forced praise on our part—the glimmer of twilight,
  Never glad confident morning again !
Best fight on well, for we taught him,—strike gallantly,
  Aim at our heart ere we pierce through his own ;
Then let him receive the new knowledge and wait us,
  Pardoned in Heaven, the first by the throne !

THE LOST MISTRESS

THE LOST MISTRESS

I

ALL's over, then—does truth sound bitter
  As one at first believes?
Hark, 'tis the sparrows' good-night twitter
  About your cottage eaves!

II

And the leaf-buds on the vine are woolly,
  I noticed that, to-day;
One day more bursts them open fully
  —You know the red turns gray.

III

To-morrow we meet the same then, dearest?
  May I take your hand in mine?
Mere friends are we,—well, friends the merest
  Keep much that I'll resign:

IV

For each glance of that eye so bright and black,
  Though I keep with heart's endeavour,—
Your voice, when you wish the snowdrops back,
  Though it stays in my soul for ever!—

V

—Yet I will but say what mere friends say,
  Or only a thought stronger;
I will hold your hand but as long as all may,
  Or so very little longer!

HOME-THOUGHTS FROM ABROAD

I

OH, to be in England
Now that April's there,
And whoever wakes in England
Sees, some morning, unaware,
That the lowest boughs and the brush-wood sheaf
Round the elm-tree bole are in tiny leaf,
While the chaffinch sings on the orchard bough
In England—now!

II

And after April, when May follows,
And the whitethroat builds, and all the swallows—
Hark! where my blossomed pear-tree in the hedge
Leans to the field and scatters on the clover
Blossoms and dewdrops—at the bent spray's edge—
That's the wise thrush; he sings each song twice over,
Lest you should think he never could recapture
The first fine careless rapture!
And though the fields look rough with hoary dew,
All will be gay when noontide wakes anew
The buttercups, the little children's dower,
—Far brighter than this gaudy melon-flower!

HOME-THOUGHTS FROM THE SEA

NOBLY, nobly Cape Saint Vincent to the north-west died
    away;
Sunset ran, one glorious blood-red, reeking into Cadiz Bay;
Bluish mid the burning water, full in face Trafalgar lay;
In the dimmest north-east distance, dawned Gibraltar
    grand and gray;
"Here and here did England help me,—how can I help
    England?"—say,
Whoso turns as I, this evening, turn to God to praise and pray,
While Jove's planet rises yonder, silent over Africa.

THE BISHOP ORDERS HIS TOMB

THE BISHOP ORDERS HIS TOMB AT ST. PRAXED'S CHURCH

[ROME, 15—]

VANITY, saith the preacher, vanity!
Draw round my bed: is Anselm keeping back?
Nephews—sons mine . . . ah God, I know not! Well—
She, men would have to be your mother once,
Old Gandolf envied me, so fair she was!
What's done is done, and she is dead beside,
Dead long ago, and I am Bishop since,
And as she died so must we die ourselves,
And thence ye may perceive the world's a dream.
Life, how and what is it? As here I lie
In this state-chamber, dying by degrees,
Hours and long hours in the dead night, I ask
"Do I live, am I dead?" Peace, peace seems all.
St. Praxed's ever was the church for peace;
And so, about this tomb of mine. I fought
With tooth and nail to save my niche, ye know:
—Old Gandolf cozened me, despite my care;
Shrewd was that snatch from out the corner South
He graced his carrion with, God curse the same!
Yet still my niche is not so cramped but thence
One sees the pulpit o' the epistle-side,
And somewhat of the choir, those silent seats,
And up into the aery dome where live
The angels, and a sunbeam's sure to lurk:
And I shall fill my slab of basalt there,
And 'neath my tabernacle take my rest,
With those nine columns round me, two and two,
The odd one at my feet where Anselm stands:
Peach-blossom marble all, the rare, the ripe
As fresh-poured red wine of a mighty pulse.
—Old Gandolf with his paltry onion-stone,
Put me where I may look at him! True peach,
Rosy and flawless: how I earned the prize!

84

THE BISHOP ORDERS HIS TOMB

Draw close : that conflagration of my church
—What then ? So much was saved if aught were missed !
My sons, ye would not be my death ?   Go dig
The white-grape vineyard where the oil-press stood,
Drop water gently till the surface sinks,
And if ye find . . Ah, God I know not, I ! . . .
Bedded in store of rotten figleaves soft,
And corded up in a tight olive-frail,
Some lump, ah God, of *lapis lazuli*,
Big as a Jew's head cut off at the nape,
Blue as a vein o'er the Madonna's breast . . .
Sons, all have I bequeathed you, villas, all,
That brave Frascati villa with its bath,
So, let the blue lump poise between my knees,
Like God the Father's globe on both his hands
Ye worship in the Jesu Church so gay,
For Gandolf shall not choose but see and burst !
Swift as a weaver's shuttle fleet our years :
Man goeth to the grave, and where is he ?
Did I say basalt for my slab, sons ?   Black—
'Twas ever antique-black I meant !   How else
Shall ye contrast my frieze to come beneath ?
The bas-relief in bronze ye promised me,
Those Pans and Nymphs ye wot of, and perchance
Some tripod, thyrsus, with a vase or so,
The Saviour at his sermon on the mount,
St. Praxed in a glory, and one Pan
Ready to twitch the Nymph's last garment off,
And Moses with the tables . . . but I know
Ye mark me not !   What do they whisper thee,
Child of my bowels, Anselm ?   Ah, ye hope
To revel down my villas while I gasp
Bricked o'er with beggar's mouldy travertine
Which Gandolf from his tomb-top chuckles at !
Nay, boys, ye love me—all of jasper, then !
'Tis jasper ye stand pledged to, lest I grieve
My bath must needs be left behind, alas !

THE BISHOP ORDERS HIS TOMB

One block, pure green as a pistachio-nut,
There's plenty jasper somewhere in the world—
And have I not St. Praxed's ear to pray
Horses for ye, and brown Greek manuscripts,
And mistresses with great smooth marbly limbs?
—That's if ye carve my epitaph aright,
Choice Latin, picked phrase, Tully's every word,
No gaudy ware like Gandolf's second line—
Tully, my masters? Ulpian serves his need!
And then how I shall lie through centuries,
And hear the blessed mutter of the mass,
And see God made and eaten all day long,
And feel the steady candle-flame, and taste
Good strong thick stupifying incense-smoke!
For as I lie here, hours of the dead night,
Dying in state and by such slow degrees,
I fold my arms as if they clasped a crook,
And stretch my feet forth straight as stone can point,
And let the bedclothes for a mortcloth drop
Into great laps and folds of sculptor's-work:
And as yon tapers dwindle, and strange thoughts
Grow, with a certain humming in my ears,
About the life before I lived this life,
And this life too, Popes, Cardinals and Priests,
St. Praxed at his sermon on the mount,
Your tall pale mother with her talking eyes,
And new-found agate urns as fresh as day,
And marble's language, Latin pure, discreet,
—Aha, ELUCESCEBAT quoth our friend?
No Tully, said I, Ulpian at the best!
Evil and brief hath been my pilgrimage.
All *lapis*, all, sons! Else I give the Pope
My villas: will ye ever eat my heart?
Ever your eyes were as a lizard's quick,
They glitter like your mother's for my soul,
Or ye would heighten my impoverished frieze,
Piece out its starved design, and fill my vase

SIBRANDUS SCHAFNABURGENSIS

With grapes, and add a vizor and a Term,
And to the tripod ye would tie a lynx
That in his struggle throws the thyrsus down,
To comfort me on my entablature
Whereon I am to lie till I must ask
"Do I live, am I dead?" There, leave me, there!
For ye have stabbed me with ingratitude
To death—ye wish it—God, ye wish it! Stone—
Gritstone, a-crumble! Clammy squares which sweat
As if the corpse they keep were oozing through—
And no more *lapis* to delight the world!
Well, go! I bless ye. Fewer tapers there,
But in a row : and going, turn your backs
—Ay, like departing altar-ministrants,
And leave me in my church, the church for peace,
That I may watch at leisure if he leers—
Old Gandolf, at me, from his onion-stone,
As still he envied me, so fair she was!

SIBRANDUS SCHAFNABURGENSIS

I

PLAGUE take all your pedants, say I !
    He who wrote what I hold in my hand,
Centuries back was so good as to die,
    Leaving this rubbish to cumber the land ;
This, that was a book in its time,
    Printed on paper and bound in leather,
Last month in the white of a matin-prime
    Just when the birds sang all together.

II

Into the garden I brought it to read,
    And under the arbute and laurustine
Read it, so help me grace in my need,
    From title-page to closing line.

SIBRANDUS SCHAFNABURGENSIS

Chapter on chapter did I count,
  As a curious traveller counts Stonehenge;
Added up the mortal amount;
  And then proceeded to my revenge.

III

Yonder's a plum-tree, with a crevice
  An owl would build in, were he but sage;
For a lap of moss, like a fine pont-levis
  In a castle of the middle age,
Joins to a lip of gum, pure amber;
  When he'd be private, there might he spend
Hours alone in his lady's chamber:
  Into this crevice I dropped our friend.

IV

Splash, went he, as under he ducked,
  —I knew at the bottom rain-drippings stagnate;
Next a handful of blossoms I plucked
  To bury him with, my bookshelf's magnate;
Then I went in-doors, brought out a loaf,
  Half a cheese, and a bottle of Chablis;
Lay on the grass and forgot the oaf
  Over a jolly chapter of Rabelais.

V

Now, this morning, betwixt the moss
  And gum that locked our friend in limbo,
A spider had spun his web across,
  And sate in the midst with arms a-kimbo:
So, I took pity, for learning's sake,
  And, *de profundis, accentibus lætis*,
Cantate! quoth I, as I got a rake,
  And up I fished his delectable treatise.

SIBRANDUS SCHAFNABURGENSIS

VI

Here you have it, dry in the sun,
　With all the binding all of a blister,
And great blue spots where the ink has run,
　And reddish streaks that wink and glister
O'er the page so beautifully yellow—
　Oh, well have the droppings played their tricks!
Did he guess how toadstools grow, this fellow?
　Here's one stuck in his chapter six!

VII

How did he like it when the live creatures
　Tickled and toused and browsed him all over,
And worm, slug, eft, with serious features,
　Came in, each one, for his right of trover;
When the water-beetle with great blind deaf face
　Made of her eggs the stately deposit,
And the newt borrowed just so much of the preface
　As tiled in the top of his black wife's closet.

VIII

All that life, and fun, and romping,
　All that frisking, and twisting, and coupling,
While slowly our poor friend's leaves were swamping,
　And clasps were cracking, and covers suppling!
As if you had carried sour John Knox
　To the play-house at Paris, Vienna, or Munich,
Fastened him into a front-row box,
　And danced off the Ballet with trousers and tunic.

IX

Come, old martyr!　What, torment enough is it?
　Back to my room shall you take your sweet self!
Good bye, mother-beetle; husband-eft, *sufficit!*
　See the snug niche I have made on my shelf:
A.'s book shall prop you up, B.'s shall cover you,
　Here's C. to be grave with, or D. to be gay,
And with E. on each side, and F. right over you,
　Dry-rot at ease till the Judgment-day!

91

THE LABORATORY

BYAM·SHAW·

[ANCIEN REGIME]

I

Now that I, tying thy glass mask tightly,
May gaze thro' these faint smokes curling whitely,
As thou pliest thy trade in this devil's-smithy—
Which is the poison to poison her, prithee?

II

He is with her; and they know that I know
Where they are, what they do: they believe my tears flow
While they laugh, laugh at me, at me fled to the drear
Empty church, to pray God in, for them!—I am here.

III

Grind away, moisten and mash up thy paste,
Pound at thy powder,—I am not in haste!
Better sit thus, and observe thy strange things,
Than go where men wait me and dance at the King's.

THE LABORATORY

IV

That in the mortar—you call it a gum?
Ah, the brave tree whence such gold oozings come!
And yonder soft phial, the exquisite blue,
Sure to taste sweetly,—is that poison too?

V

Had I but all of them, thee and thy treasures,
What a wild crowd of invisible pleasures!
To carry pure death in an earring, a casket,
A signet, a fan-mount, a fillagree-basket!

VI

Soon, at the King's, a mere lozenge to give
And Pauline should have just thirty minutes to live!
But to light a pastille, and Elise, with her head,
And her breast, and her arms, and her hands, should
        drop dead!

VII

Quick—is it finished? The colour's too grim!
Why not soft like the phial's, enticing and dim?
Let it brighten her drink, let her turn it and stir,
And try it and taste, ere she fix and prefer!

VIII

What a drop! She's not little, no minion like me—
That's why she ensnared him: this never will free
The soul from those strong, great eyes,—say, "no!"
To that pulse's magnificent come-and-go.

93

THE LABORATORY

IX

For only last night, as they whispered, I brought
My own eyes to bear. on her so, that I thought
Could I keep them one half minute fixed, she would
    fall,
Shrivelled; she fell not; yet this does it all!

X

Not that I bid you spare her the pain!
Let death be felt and the proof remain;
Brand, burn up, bite into its grace—
He is sure to remember her dying face!

XI

Is it done? Take my mask off! Nay, be not morose,
It kills her, and this prevents seeing it close:
The delicate droplet, my whole fortune's fee—
If it hurts her, beside, can it ever hurt me?

XII

Now, take all my jewels, gorge gold to your fill,
You may kiss me, old man, on my mouth if you will!
But brush this dust off me, lest horror it brings
Ere I know it—next moment I dance at the King's!

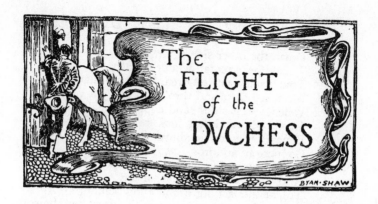

The FLIGHT of the DVCHESS

BYAM·SHAW

I

YOU'RE my friend:
I-was the man the Duke spoke to;
I helped the Duchess to cast off his yoke, too;
So, here's the tale from beginning to end,
My friend!

II

Ours is a great wild country:
If you climb to your castle's top,
I don't see where your eye can stop;
For when you've passed the corn-field country,
Where vineyards leave off, flocks are packed,
And sheep-range leads to cattle-tract,
And cattle-tract to open-chase,
And open-chase to the very base
Of the mountain, where, at a funeral pace,
Round about, solemn and slow,
One by one, row after row,
Up and up the pine-trees go,
So, like black priests up, and so

95

THE FLIGHT OF THE DUCHESS

Down the other side again
To another greater, wilder country,
That's one vast red drear burnt-up plain,
Branched thro' and thro' with many a vein
Whence iron's dug, and copper's dealt;
Look right, look left, look straight before,—
Beneath they mine, above they smelt,
Copper-ore and iron-ore,
And forge and furnace mould and melt,
And so on, more and ever more,
Till, at the last, for a bounding belt,
Comes the salt sand hoar of the great sea shore,
—And the whole is our Duke's country!

III

I was born the day this present Duke was—
(And O, says the song, ere I was old!)
In the castle where the other Duke was—
(When I was hopeful and young, not old!)
I in the Kennel, he in the Bower:
We are of like age to an hour.
My father was Huntsman in that day;
Who has not heard my father say
That, when a boar was brought to bay,
Three times, four times out of five,
With his huntspear he'd contrive
To get the killing-place transfixed,
And pin him true, both eyes betwixt?
And that's why the old Duke had rather
Have lost a salt-pit than my father,
And loved to have him ever in call;
That's why my father stood in the hall
When the old Duke brought his infant out
To show the people, and while they passed
The wondrous bantling round about,
Was first to start at the outside blast

THE FLIGHT OF THE DUCHESS

As the Kaiser's courier blew his horn,
Just a month after the babe was born.
" And," quoth the Kaiser's courier, "since
" The Duke has got an Heir, our Prince
" Needs the Duke's self at his side " :
The Duke looked down and seemed to wince,
But he thought of wars o'er the world wide,
Castles a-fire, men on their march,
The toppling tower, the crashing arch ;
And up he looked, and awhile he eyed
The row of crests and shields and banners,
Of all achievements after all manners,
And " ay," said the Duke with a surly pride.
The more was his comfort when he died
At next year's end, in a velvet suit,
With a gilt glove on his hand, and his foot
In a silken shoe for a leather boot,
Petticoated like a herald,
In a chamber next to an ante-room,
Where he breathed the breath of page and groom.
What he called stink, and they, perfume :
—They should have set him on red Berold,
Mad with pride, like fire to manage !
They should have got his cheek fresh tannage
Such a day as to-day in the merry sunshine !
Had they stuck on his fist a rough-foot merlin !
(Hark, the wind 's on the heath at its game !
Oh for a noble falcon-lanner
To flap each broad wing like a banner,
And turn in the wind, and dance like flame !)
Had they broached a cask of white beer from
    Berlin !
—Or if you incline to prescribe mere wine—
Put to his lips when they saw him pine,
A cup of our own Moldavia fine,
Cotnar, for instance, green as May sorrel,
And ropy with sweet,—we shall not quarrel.

THE FLIGHT OF THE DUCHESS

IV

So, at home, the sick tall yellow Duchess
Was left with the infant in her clutches,
She being the daughter of God knows who:
And now was the time to revisit her tribe,
So, abroad and afar they went, the two,
And let our people rail and gibe
At the empty Hall and extinguished fire,
As loud as we liked, but ever in vain,
Till after long years we had our desire,
And back came the Duke and his mother again.

V

And he came back the pertest little ape
That ever affronted human shape;
Full of his travel, struck at himself—
You'd say, he despised our bluff old ways
—Not he! For in Paris they told the elf
That our rough North land was the Land of Lays,
The one good thing left in evil days;
Since the Mid-Age was the Heroic Time,
And only in wild nooks like ours
Could you taste of it yet as in its prime,
And see true castles, with proper towers,
Young-hearted women, old-minded men,
And manners now as manners were then.
So, all that the old Dukes had been, without knowing it,
This Duke would fain know he was, without being it;
'Twas not for the joy's self, but the joy of his showing it,
Nor for the pride's self, but the pride of our seeing it,
He revived all usages thoroughly worn-out,
The souls of them fumed-forth, the hearts of them torn-
out:
And chief in the chase his neck he perilled,
On a lathy horse, all legs and length,
With blood for bone, all speed, no strength;

THE FLIGHT OF THE DUCHESS

—They should have set him on red Berold,
With the red eye slow consuming in fire,
And the thin stiff ear like an abbey spire!

VI

Well, such as he was, he must marry, we heard:
And out of a convent, at the word,
Came the Lady, in time of spring.
—Oh, old thoughts they cling, they cling!
That day, I know, with a dozen oaths
I clad myself in thick hunting-clothes
Fit for the chase of urox or buffle
In winter-time when you need to muffle;
But the Duke had a mind we should cut a figure,
And so we saw the Lady arrive:
My friend, I have seen a white crane bigger!
She was the smallest lady alive,
Made, in a piece of Nature's madness,
Too small, almost, for the life and gladness
That over-filled her, as some hive
Out of the bears' reach on the high trees
Is crowded with its safe merry bees:
In truth, she was not hard to please!
Up she looked, down she looked, round at the mead,
Straight at the castle, that's best indeed
To look at from outside the walls:
As for us, styled the "serfs and thralls,"
She as much thanked me as if she had said it,
(With her eyes, do you understand?)
Because I patted her horse while I led it;
And Max, who rode on her other hand,
Said, no bird flew past but she enquired
What its true name was, nor ever seemed tired—
If that was an eagle she saw hover,—
If the green and grey bird on the field was the plover.

THE FLIGHT OF THE DUCHESS

When suddenly appeared the Duke,
And as down she sprung, the small foot pointed
On to my hand,—as with a rebuke,
And as if his backbone were not jointed,
The Duke stepped rather aside than forward,
And welcomed her with his grandest smile;
And, mind you, his mother all the while
Chilled in the rear, like a wind to Nor'ward;
And up, like a weary yawn, with its pullies
Went, in a shriek, the rusty portcullis;
And, like a glad sky the north-wind sullies,
The Lady's face stopped its play,
As if her first hair had grown grey—
For such things must begin some one day!

VII

In a day or two she was well again;
As who should say, "You labour in vain!
"This is all a jest against God, who meant
"I should ever be, as I am, content
"And glad in his sight; therefore, glad I will be!"
So, smiling as at first went she.

VIII

She was active, stirring, all fire—
Could not rest, could not tire—
To a stone she had given life!
(I myself loved once, in my day,)
—For a Shepherd's, Miner's, Huntsman's wife,
(I had a wife, I know what I say,)
Never in all the world such an one!
And here was plenty to be done,
And she that could do it, great or small,
She was to do nothing at all.

100

THE FLIGHT OF THE DUCHESS

And, licking her whiskers, out she passed ;
And after her,—making (he hoped) a face
Like Emperor Nero or Sultan Saladin,
Stalked the Duke's self with the austere grace
Of ancient hero or modern paladin,—
From door to staircase—oh, such a solemn
Unbending of the vertebral column !

XII

However, at sunrise our company mustered,
And here was the huntsman bidding unkennel,
And there 'neath his bonnet the pricker blustered,
With feather dank as a bough of wet fennel ;
For the court-yard's four walls were filled with fog
You might cut as an axe chops a log—
Like so much wool for colour and bulkiness ;
And out rode the Duke in a perfect sulkiness,
Since before breakfast, a man feels but queasily,
And a sinking at the lower abdomen
Begins the day with indifferent omen :
And lo, as he looked around uneasily,
The sun ploughed the fog up and drove it asunder
This way and that from the valley under ;
And, looking thro' the court-yard arch,
Down in the valley what should meet him
But a troop of Gypsies on their march,
No doubt with the annual gifts to greet him.

XIII

Now, in your land, Gypsies reach you, only
After reaching all lands beside ;
North they go, south they go, trooping or lonely,
And still, as they travel far and wide,
Catch they and keep now a trace here, a trace there,
That puts you in mind of a place here, a place there :
But with us, I believe they rise out of the ground,
And nowhere else, I take it, are found

THE FLIGHT OF THE DUCHESS

With the earth-tint yet so freshly embrowned;
Born, no doubt, like insects which breed on
The very fruit they are meant to feed on:
For the earth—not a use to which they don't turn it,
The ore that grows in the mountain's womb,
Or the sand in the pits like a honeycomb,
They sift and soften it, bake it and burn it—
Whether they weld you, for instance, a snaffle
With side-bars never a brute can baffle;
Or a lock that's a puzzle of wards within wards;
Or, if your colt's fore-foot inclines to curve inwards,
Horseshoes they'll hammer which turn on a swivel
And won't allow the hoof to shrivel;
Then they cast bells like the shell of the winkle,
That keep a stout heart in the ram with their tinkle:
But the sand—they pinch and pound it like otters;
Commend me to Gypsy glass-makers and potters!
Glasses they'll blow you, crystal-clear,
Where just a faint cloud of rose shall appear,
As if in pure water you dropped and let die
A bruised black-blooded mulberry;
And that other sort, their crowning pride,
With long white threads distinct inside,
Like the lake-flower's fibrous roots which dangle
Loose such a length and never tangle,
Where the bold sword-lily cuts the clear waters,
And the cup-lily couches with all the white daughters:
Such are the works they put their hand to,
And the uses they turn and twist iron and sand to.
And these made the troop which our Duke saw sally
Towards his castle from out of the valley,
Men and women, like new-hatched spiders,
Come out with the morning to greet our riders;
And up they wound till they reached the ditch,
Whereat all stopped save one, a witch,
That I knew, as she hobbled from the group,
By her gait, directly, and her stoop,

THE FLIGHT OF THE DUCHESS

I, whom Jacynth was used to importune
To let that same witch tell us our fortune.
The oldest Gypsy then above ground ;
And, so sure as the autumn season came round,
She paid us a visit for profit or pastime,
And every time, as she swore, for the last time.
And presently she was seen to sidle
Up to the Duke till she touched his bridle,
So that the horse of a sudden reared up
As under its nose the old witch peered up
With her worn-out eyes, or rather eye-holes
Of no use now but to gather brine,
And began a kind of level whine
Such as they used to sing to their viols
When their ditties they go grinding
Up and down with nobody minding :
And, then as of old, at the end of the humming
Her usual presents were forthcoming
—A dog-whistle blowing the fiercest of trebles,
(Just a sea-shore stone holding a dozen fine pebbles),
Or a porcelain mouth-piece to screw on a pipe-end,—
And so she awaited her annual stipend.
But this time, the Duke would scarcely vouchsafe
A word in reply ; and in vain she felt
With twitching fingers at her belt
For the purse of sleek pine-martin pelt,
Ready to put what he gave in her pouch safe,—
Till, either to quicken his apprehension,
Or possibly with an after-intention,
She was come, she said, to pay her duty
To the new Duchess, the youthful beauty.
No sooner had she named his Lady,
Than a shine lit up the face so shady,
And its smirk returned with a novel meaning—
For it struck him, the babe just wanted weaning ;
If one gave her a taste of what life was and sorrow,
She, foolish to-day, would be wiser to-morrow ;

THE FLIGHT OF THE DUCHESS

And who so fit a teacher of trouble
As this sordid crone bent well nigh double?
So, glancing at her wolf-skin vesture,
(If such it was, for they grow so hirsute
That their own fleece serves for natural fur suit)
He was contrasting, 'twas plain from his gesture,
The life of the lady so flower-like and delicate
With the loathsome squalor of this helicat.
I, in brief, was the man the Duke beckoned
From out of the throng, and while I drew near
He told the crone, as I since have reckoned
By the way he bent and spoke into her ear
With circumspection and mystery,
The main of the Lady's history,
Her frowardness and ingratitude;
And for all the crone's submissive attitude
I could see round her mouth the loose plaits tightening
And her brow with assenting intelligence brightening,
As tho' she engaged with hearty good will
Whatever he now might enjoin to fulfil,
And promised the lady a thorough frightening.
And so, just giving her a glimpse
Of a purse, with the air of a man who imps
The wing of the hawk that shall fetch the hernshaw,
He bade me take the Gypsy mother
And set her telling some story or other
Of hill or dale, oak-wood or fernshaw,
To while away a weary hour
For the Lady left alone in her bower,
Whose mind and body craved exertion
And yet shrank from all better diversion.

XIV

Then clapping heel to his horse, the mere curvetter,
Out rode the Duke, and after his hollo
Horses and hounds swept, huntsman and servitor,
And back I turned and bade the crone follow.

THE FLIGHT OF THE DUCHESS

And what makes me confident what's to be told you
Had all along been of this crone's devising,
Is, that, on looking round sharply, behold you,
There was a novelty quick as surprising :
For first, she had shot up a full head in stature,
And her step kept pace with mine nor faltered,
As if age had foregone its usurpature,
And the ignoble mien was wholly altered,
And the face looked quite of another nature,
And the change reached too, whatever the change meant,
Her shaggy wolf-skin cloak's arrangement,
For where its tatters hung loose like sedges,
Gold coins were glittering on the edges,
Like the band-roll strung with tomans
Which proves the veil a Persian woman's :
And under her brow, like a snail's horns newly
Come out as after the rain he paces,
Two unmistakeable eye-points duly
Live and aware looked out of their places.
So we went and found Jacynth at the entry
Of the Lady's chamber standing sentry ;
I told the command and produced my companion,
And Jacynth rejoiced to admit any one,
For since last night, by the same token,
Not a single word had the Lady spoken :
So they went in both to the presence together,
While I in the balcony watched the weather.

XV

And now, what took place at the very first of all,
I cannot tell, as I never could learn it :
Jacynth constantly wished a curse to fall
On that little head of hers and burn it,
If she knew how she came to drop so soundly
Asleep of a sudden and there continue
The whole time sleeping as profoundly
As one of the boars my father would pin you

THE FLIGHT OF THE DUCHESS

'Twixt the eyes where the life holds garrison,
—Jacynth forgive me the comparison!
But where I begin my own narration
Is a little after I took my station
To breathe the fresh air from the balcony,
And, having in those days a falcon eye,
To follow the hunt thro' the open country,
From where the bushes thinlier crested
The hillocks, to a plain where's not one tree :—
When, in a moment, my ear was arrested
By—was it singing, or was it saying,
Or a strange musical instrument playing
In the chamber?—and to be certain
I pushed the lattice, pulled the curtain,
And there lay Jacynth asleep,
Yet as if a watch she tried to keep,
In a rosy sleep along the floor
With her head against the door ;
While in the midst, on the seat of state,
Like a queen the Gypsy woman sate,
With head and face downbent
On the Lady's head and face intent,
For, coiled at her feet like a child at ease,
The Lady sate between her knees
And o'er them the Lady's clasped hands met,
And on those hands her chin was set,
And her upturned face met the face of the crone
Wherein the eyes had grown and grown
As if she could double and quadruple
At pleasure the play of either pupil
—Very like by her hands slow fanning,
As up and down like a gor-crow's flappers
They moved to measure like bell clappers
—I said, is it blessing, is it banning,
Do they applaud you or burlesque you?
Those hands and fingers with no flesh on?
When, just as I thought to spring in to the rescue,

HER UPTURNED FACE MET THE FACE OF THE CRONE.

THE FLIGHT OF THE DUCHESS

At once I was stopped by the Lady's expression :
For it was life her eyes were drinking
From the crone's wide pair above unwinking,
Life's pure fire received without shrinking,
Into the heart and breast whose heaving
Told you no single drop they were leaving—
Life, that filling her, past redundant
Into her very hair, back swerving
Over each shoulder, loose and abundant,
As her head thrown back showed the white throat curving
And the very tresses shared in the pleasure,
Moving to the mystic measure,
Bounding as the bosom bounded.
I stopped short, more and more confounded,
As still her cheeks burned and eyes glistened,
As she listened and she listened,—
When all at once a hand detained me,
And the selfsame contagion gained me,
And I kept time to the wondrous chime,
Making out words and prose and rhyme,
Till it seemed that the music furled
Its wings like a task fulfilled, and dropped
From under the words it first had propped,
And left them midway in the world,
And word took word as hand takes hand,
I could hear at last, and understand,
And when I held the unbroken thread,
The Gypsy said :—

" And so at last we find my tribe,
And so I set thee in the midst,
And to one and all of them describe
What thou saidst and what thou didst,
Our long and terrible journey thro',
And all thou art ready to say and do
In the trials that remain :
I trace them the vein and the other vein

113

THE FLIGHT OF THE DUCHESS

That meet on thy brow and part again,
Making our rapid mystic mark;
And I bid my people prove and probe
Each eye's profound and glorious globe
Till they detect the kindred spark
In those depths so dear and dark,
Like the spots that snap, and burst, and flee,
Circling over the midnight sea.
And on that young round cheek of thine
I made them recognise the tinge,
As when of the costly scarlet wine
They drip so much as will impinge
And spread in a thinnest scale afloat
One thick gold drop from the olive's coat
Over a silver plate whose sheen
Still thro' the mixture shall be seen.
For, so I prove thee, to one and all,
Fit, when my people ope their breast,
To see the sign, and hear the call,
And take the vow, and stand the test
Which adds one more child to the rest—
When the breast is bare, and the arms are wide,
And the world is left outside.
For there is probation to decree,
And many and long must the trials be
Thou shalt victoriously endure,
If that brow is true and those eyes are sure;
Like a jewel-finder's fierce assay
Of the prize he dug from its mountain tomb,—
Let once the vindicating ray
Leap out amid the anxious gloom,
And steel and fire have done their part
And the prize falls on its finder's heart;
So, trial after trial past,
Wilt thou fall at the very last
Breathless, half in trance
With the thrill of the great deliverance,

THE FLIGHT OF THE DUCHESS

Into our arms for evermore;
And thou shalt know, those arms once curled
About thee, what we knew before,
How love is the only good in the world.
Henceforth be loved as heart can love,
Or brain devise, or hand approve!
Stand up, look below,
It is our life at thy feet we throw
To step with into light and joy;
Not a power of life but we 'll employ
To satisfy thy nature's want;
Art thou the tree that props the plant,
Or the climbing plant that seeks the tree—
Canst thou help us, must we help thee?
If any two creatures grew into one,
They would do more than the world has done;
Tho' each apart were never so weak,
Yet vainly thro' the world should ye seek
For the knowledge and the might
Which in such union grew their right:
So, to approach, at least, that end,
And blend,—as much as may be, blend
Thee with us or us with thee,
As climbing-plant or propping-tree,
Shall some one deck thee, over and down,
Up and about, with blossoms and leaves?
Fix his heart's fruit for thy garland crown,
Cling with his soul as the gourd-vine cleaves,
Die on thy boughs and disappear
While not a leaf of thine is sere?
Or is the other fate in store,
And art thou fitted to adore,
To give thy wondrous self away,
And take a stronger nature's sway?
I foresee and I could foretell
Thy future portion, sure and well—
But those passionate eyes speak true, speak true,

And let them say what thou shalt do!
Only, be sure thy daily life,
In its peace, or in its strife,
Never shall be unobserved ;
We pursue thy whole career,
And hope for it, or doubt, or fear,—
Lo, hast thou kept thy path or swerved,
We are beside thee, in all thy ways,
With our blame, with our praise,
Our shame to feel, our pride to show,
Glad, sorry—but indifferent, no!
Whether it is thy lot to go,
For the good of us all, where the haters meet
In the crowded city's horrible street ;
Or thou step alone thro' the morass
Where never sound yet was
Save the dry quick clap of the stork's bill,
For the air is still, and the water still,
When the blue breast of the dipping coot
Dives under, and all again is mute.
So at the last shall come old age,
Decrepit as befits that stage ;
How else wouldst thou retire apart
With the hoarded memories of thy heart,
And gather all to the very least
Of the fragments of life's earlier feast,
Let fall through eagerness to find
The crowning dainties yet behind?
Ponder on the entire past
Laid together thus at last,
When the twilight helps to fuse
The first fresh, with the faded hues,
And the outline of the whole,
As round eve's shades their framework roll,
Grandly fronts for once thy soul :
And then as, 'mid the dark, a gleam
Of yet another morning breaks,

And like the hand which ends a dream,
Death, with the might of his sunbeam
Touches the flesh and the soul awakes,
Then—."

        Ay, then, indeed, something would happen!
But what? For here her voice changed like a bird's;
There grew more of the music and less of the words;
Had Jacynth only been by me to clap pen
To paper and put you down every syllable,
With those clever clerkly fingers,
All that I 've forgotten as well as what lingers
In this old brain of mine that 's but ill able
To give you even this poor version
Of the speech I spoil, as it were, with stammering
—More fault of those who had the hammering
Of prosody into me and syntax,
And did it, not with hobnails but tintacks!
But to return from this excursion,—
Just, do you mark, when the song was sweetest,
The peace most deep and the charm completest,
There came, shall I say, a snap—
And the charm vanished!
And my sense returned, so strangely banished,
And, starting as from a nap,
I knew the crone was bewitching my lady,
With Jacynth asleep; and but one spring made I,
Down from the casement, round to the portal,
Another minute and I had entered,
When the door opened, and more than mortal
Stood, with a face where to my mind centred
All beauties I ever saw or shall see,
The Duchess—I stopped as if struck by palsy.
She was so different, happy and beautiful,
I felt at once that all was best,
And that I had nothing to do, for the rest,
But wait her commands, obey and be dutiful.
Not that, in fact, there was any commanding,

THE FLIGHT OF THE DUCHESS

—I saw the glory of her eye,
And the brow's height and the breast's expanding,
And I was hers to live or to die.
As for finding what she wanted,
You know God Almighty granted
Such little signs should serve his wild creatures
To tell one another all their desires,
So that each knows what its friend requires,
And does its bidding without teachers.
I preceded her ; the crone
Followed silent and alone ;
I spoke to her, but she merely jabbered
In the old style ; both her eyes had slunk
Back to their pits ; her stature shrunk ;
In short, the soul in its body sunk
Like a blade sent home to its scabbard.
We descended, I preceding ;
Crossed the court with nobody heeding ;
All the world was at the chase,
The court-yard like a desert-place,
The stable emptied of its small fry ;
I saddled myself the very palfrey
I remember patting while it carried her,
The day she arrived and the Duke married her.
And, do you know, though it's easy deceiving
Oneself in such matters, I can't help believing
The lady had not forgotten it either,
And knew the poor devil so much beneath her
Would have been only too glad for her service
To dance on hot ploughshares like a Turk dervise,
But unable to pay proper duty where owing it
Was reduced to that pitiful method of showing it :
For though the moment I began setting
His saddle on my own nag of Berold's begetting,
(Not that I meant to be obtrusive)
She stopped me, while his rug was shifting,
By a single rapid finger's lifting,

And, with a gesture kind but conclusive,
And a little shake of the head, refused me,—
I say, although she never used me,
Yet when she was mounted, the Gypsy behind her,
And I ventured to remind her,
I suppose with a voice of less steadiness
Than usual, for my feeling exceeded me,
—Something to the effect that I was in readiness
Whenever God should please she needed me,—
Then, do you know, her face looked down on me
With a look that placed a crown on me,
And she felt in her bosom,—mark, her bosom—
And, as a flower-tree drops its blossom,
Dropped me—ah, had it been a purse
Of silver, my friend, or gold that's worse,
Why, you see, as soon as I found myself
So understood,—that a true heart so may gain
Such a reward,—I should have gone home again,
Kissed Jacynth, and soberly drowned myself!
It was a little plait of hair
Such as friends in a convent make
To wear, each for the other's sake,—
This, see, which at my breast I wear,
Ever did (rather to Jacynth's grudgment),
And ever shall, till the Day of Judgment.
And then,—and then,—to cut short,—this is idle,
These are feelings it is not good to foster,—
I pushed the gate wide, she shook the bridle,
And the palfrey bounded,—and so we lost her!

XVI

When the liquor's out, why clink the cannakin?
I did think to describe you the panic in
The redoubtable breast of our master the mannikin,
And what was the pitch of his mother's yellowness,
How she turned as a shark to snap the spare-rib

THE FLIGHT OF THE DUCHESS

Clean off, sailors say, from a pearl-diving Carib,
When she heard, what she called, the flight of the feloness—
But it seems such child's play
What they said and did with the lady away!
And to dance on, when we've lost the music,
Always made me—and no doubt makes you—sick.
Nay, to my mind, the world's face looked so stern
As that sweet form disappeared thro' the postern,
She that kept it in constant good humour,
It ought to have stopped; there seemed nothing to do more.
But the world thought otherwise and went on,
And my head's one that its spite was spent on:
Thirty years are fled since that morning,
And with them all my head's adorning.
Nor did the old Duchess die outright,
As you expect, of suppressed spite,
The natural end of every adder
Not suffered to empty its poison-bladder:
But she and her son agreed, I take it,
That no one should touch on the story to wake it,
For the wound in the Duke's pride rankled fiery,
So they made no search and small inquiry—
And when fresh Gypsies have paid us a visit, I've
Noticed the couple were never inquisitive,
But told them they're folks the Duke don't want here,
And bade them make haste and cross the frontier.
Brief, the Duchess was gone and the Duke was glad of it
And the old one was in the young one's stead,
And took, in her place, the household's head,
And a blessed time the household had of it!
And were I not, as a man may say, cautious
How I trench, more than needs, on the nauseous,
I could favour you with sundry touches
Of the paint-smutches with which the Duchess
Heightened the mellowness of her cheek's yellowness
(To get on faster) until at last her
Cheek grew to be one master-plaster

THE FLIGHT OF THE DUCHESS

Of mucus and fucus from mere use of ceruse
Till in short she grew from scalp to udder
Just the object to make you shudder!

XVII

You're my friend—
What a thing friendship is, world without end!
How it gives the heart and soul a stir-up,
As if somebody broached you a glorious runlet,
And poured out all lovelily, sparkling, and sunlit,
Our green Moldavia, the streaky syrup,
Cotnar as old as the time of the Druids—
Friendship's as good as that monarch of fluids
To supple a dry brain, fill you its ins-and-outs,—
Gives your Life's hour-glass a shake when the thin sand
    doubts
Whether to run on or stop short, and guarantees
Age is not all made of stark sloth and arrant ease!
I have seen my little Lady once more,
Jacynth, the Gypsy, Berold, and the rest of it,
For to me spoke the Duke, as I told you before;
I always wanted to make a clean breast of it,
And now it is made—why, my heart's-blood, that went
    trickle,
Trickle, but anon, in such muddy dribblets,
Is pumped up brisk now, thro' the main ventricle,
And genially floats me about the giblets!
I'll tell ye what I intend to do:
I must see this fellow his sad life thro'
—He is our Duke after all,
And I, as he says, but a serf and thrall;
My father was born here and I inherit
His fame, a chain he bound his son with,—
Could I pay in a lump I should prefer it,
But there's no mine to blow up and get done with,
So I must stay till the end of the chapter:
For, as to our middle-age-manners-adapter,

121

THE FLIGHT OF THE DUCHESS

Be it a thing to be glad on or sorry on,
One day or other, his head in a morion,
And breast in a hauberk, his heels he'll kick up
Slain by some onslaught fierce of hiccup.
And then, when red doth the sword of our Duke rust,
And its leathern sheath lies o'ergrown with a blue crust,
Then, I shall scrape together my earnings;
For, you see, in the Churchyard Jacynth reposes,
And our children all went the way of the roses—
It's a long lane that knows no turnings—
One needs but little tackle to travel in,
So, just one stout cloak shall I indue,
And for a staff, what beats the javelin
With which his boars my father pinned you?
And then, for a purpose you shall hear presently,
Taking some Cotnar, a tight plump skinfull,
I shall go journeying, who but I, pleasantly?
Sorrow is vain and despondency sinful.
What's a man's age? He must hurry more, that's all,
Cram in a day, what his youth took a year to hold;
When we mind labour, then only, we're too old—
What age had Methusalem when he begat Saul?
And at last, as its haven some buffeted ship sees,
(Come all the way from the north-parts with sperm oil)
I shall get safely out of the turmoil
And arrive one day at the land of the Gypsies
And find my lady, or hear the last news of her
From some old thief and son of Lucifer,
His forehead chapletted green with wreathy hop,
Sunburned all over like an Æthiop:
And when my Cotnar begins to operate
And the tongue of the rogue to run at a proper rate,
And our wine-skin, tight once, shows each flaccid dent,
I shall drop in with—as if by accident—
"You never knew then, how it all ended,
"What fortunes good or bad attended
"The little lady your Queen befriended?"

THE FLIGHT OF THE DUCHESS

—And when that's told me, what's remaining?
This world's too hard for my explaining—
The same wise judge of matters equine
Who still preferred some slim four-year-old
To the big-boned stock of mighty Berold,
And for strong Cotnar drank French weak wine,
He also must be such a Lady's scorner!
Smooth Jacob still robs homely Esau,
Now up, now down, the world's one see-saw!
—So, I shall find out some snug corner
Under a hedge, like Orson the wood-knight,
Turn myself round and bid the world good night;
And sleep a sound sleep till the trumpet's blowing
Wakes me (unless priests cheat us laymen)
To a world where's to be no further throwing
Pearls before swine that can't value them.   Amen.

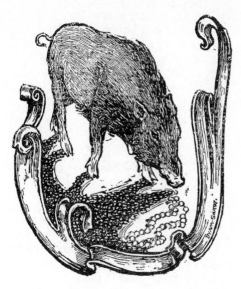

EARTH'S IMMORTALITIES

EARTH'S IMMORTALITIES

FAME

SEE, as the prettiest graves will do in time,
Our poet's wants the freshness of its prime;
Spite of the sexton's browsing horse, the sods
Have struggled thro' its binding osier-rods;
Headstone and half-sunk footstone lean awry,
Wanting the brick-work promised by and by;
How the minute grey lichens, plate o'er plate,
Have softened down the crisp-cut name and date!

LOVE

So, the year's done with!
  (*Love me for ever!*)
All March begun with,
  April's endeavour;
May-wreaths that bound me
  June needs must sever!
Now snows fall round me,
  Quenching June's fever—
  (*Love me for ever!*)

SONG

I

NAY but you, who do not love her,
  Is she not pure gold, my mistress?
Holds earth aught—speak truth—above her?
  Aught like this tress, see, and this tress,
And this last fairest tress of all,
So fair, see, ere I let it fall!

SONG ♡ ♡ "Is she not pure gold, my mistress"

MEETING AT NIGHT

II

Because, you spend your lives in praising;
  To praise, you search the wide world over;
So, why not witness, calmly gazing,
  If earth holds aught—speak truth—above her?
Above this tress, and this I touch
But cannot praise, I love so much!

MEETING AT NIGHT

I

THE grey sea and the long black land;
And the yellow half-moon large and low;
And the startled little waves that leap
In fiery little ringlets from their sleep,
As I gain the cove with pushing prow,
And quench its speed in the slushy sand.

II

Then a mile of warm sea-scented beach;
Three fields to cross till a farm appears;
A tap at the pane, the quick sharp scratch
And blue spurt of a lighted match,
And a voice less loud, thro' its joys and fears,
Than the two hearts beating each to each!

PARTING AT MORNING

ROUND the cape of a sudden came the sea,
And the sun looked over the mountain's rim—
And straight was a path of gold for him,
And the need of a world of men for me.

THE GLOVE

(PETER RONSARD *loquitur*)

" HEIGHO," yawned one day King Francis,
" Distance all value enhances !
" When a man's busy, why, leisure
" Strikes him as wonderful pleasure,—
" 'Faith, and at leisure once is he ?
" Straightway he wants to be busy.
" Here we've got peace ; and aghast I'm
" Caught thinking war the true pastime !
" Is there a reason in metre ?
" Give us your speech, master Peter ! "
I who, if mortal dare say so,
Ne'er am at loss with my Naso,
" Sire," I replied, " joys prove cloudlets :
" Men are the merest Ixions "—
Here the King whistled aloud, " Let's
" . . Heigho . . go look at our lions ! "
Such are the sorrowful chances
If you talk fine to King Francis.

And so, to the courtyard proceeding,
Our company, Francis was leading,
Increased by new followers tenfold
Before he arrived at the penfold ;
Lords, ladies, like clouds which bedizen
At sunset the western horizon.
And Sir De Lorge pressed 'mid the foremost
With the dame he professed to adore most—
Oh, what a face !   One by fits eyed
Her, and the horrible pitside ;
For the penfold surrounded a hollow
Which led where the eye scarce dared follow,
And shelved to the chamber secluded
Where Bluebeard, the great lion, brooded.

THE GLOVE

The King hailed his keeper, an Arab
As glossy and black as a scarab,
And bade him make sport and at once stir
Up and out of his den the old monster.
They opened a hole in the wire-work
Across it, and dropped there a firework,
And fled ; one's heart's beating redoubled ;
A pause, while the pit's mouth was troubled,
The blackness and silence so utter,
By the firework's slow sparkling and sputter ;
Then earth in a sudden contortion
Gave out to our gaze her abortion !
Such a brute ! Were I friend Clement Marot
(Whose experience of nature 's but narrow,
And whose faculties move in no small mist
When he versifies David the Psalmist)
I should study that brute to describe you
Illum Juda Leonem de Tribu !
One's whole blood grew curdling and creepy
To see the black mane, vast and heapy,
The tail in the air stiff and straining,
The wide eyes, nor waxing nor waning,
As over the barrier which bounded
His platform, and us who surrounded
The barrier, they reached and they rested
On the space that might stand him in best stead :
For who knew, he thought, what the amazement,
The eruption of clatter and blaze meant,
And if, in this minute of wonder,
No outlet, 'mid lightning and thunder,
Lay broad, and, his shackles all shivered,
The lion at last was delivered ?
Ay, that was the open sky o'erhead !
And you saw by the flash on his forehead,
By the hope in those eyes wide and steady,
He was leagues in the desert already,

129

THE GLOVE

Driving the flocks up the mountain,
Or catlike couched hard by the fountain
To waylay the date-gathering negress:
So guarded he entrance or egress.
"How he stands!" quoth the King: "we may well swear
"No novice, we've won our spurs elsewhere,
"And so can afford the confession,
"We exercise wholesome discretion
"In keeping aloof from his threshold;
"Once hold you, those jaws want no fresh hold,
"Their first would too pleasantly purloin
"The visitor's brisket or surloin:
"But who's he would prove so fool-hardy?
"Not the best man of Marignan, pardie!"

The sentence no sooner was uttered,
Than over the rails a glove fluttered,
Fell close to the lion, and rested:
The dame 'twas, who flung it and jested
With life so, De Lorge had been wooing
For months past; he sate there pursuing
His suit, weighing out with nonchalance
Fine speeches like gold from a balance.

Sound the trumpet, no true knight's a tarrier!
De Lorge made one leap at the barrier,
Walked straight to the glove,—while the lion
Ne'er moved, kept his far-reaching eye on
The palm-tree-edged desert-spring's sapphire,
And the musky oiled skin of the Kaffir,—
Picked it up, and as calmly retreated,
Leaped back where the lady was seated,
And full in the face of its owner
Flung the glove—

        "Your heart's queen, you dethrone her?
"So should I "—cried the King—"'twas mere vanity,
"Not love, set that task to humanity!"

AND FULL IN THE FACE OF ITS OWNER
FLUNG THE GLOVE—

THE GLOVE

Lords and ladies alike turned with loathing
From such a proved wolf in sheep's clothing.

Not so, I ; for I caught an expression
In her brow's undisturbed self-possession
Amid the Court's scoffing and merriment,—
As if from no pleasing experiment
She rose, yet of pain not much heedful
So long as the process was needful—
As if she had tried in a crucible,
To what "speeches like gold" were reducible,
And, finding the finest prove copper,
Felt the smoke in her face was but proper ;
To know what she had *not* to trust to,
Was worth all the ashes, and dust too.
She went out 'mid hooting and laughter ;
Clement Marot stayed ; I followed after,
And asked, as a grace, what it all meant—
If she wished not the rash deed's recalment ?
"For I "—so I spoke—" am a Poet :
" Human nature,—behoves that I know it ! "

She told me, " Too long had I heard
" Of the deed proved alone by the word :
" For my love,—what De Lorge would not dare !
" With my scorn—what De Lorge could compare !
" And the endless descriptions of death
" He would brave when my lip formed a breath,
" I must reckon as braved, or, of course,
" Doubt his word—and moreover, perforce,
" For such gifts as no lady could spurn,
" Must offer my love in return.
" When I looked on your lion, it brought
" All the dangers at once to my thought,
" Encountered by all sorts of men,
" Before he was lodged in his den,—

133

THE GLOVE

" From the poor slave whose club or bare hands
" Dug the trap, set the snare on the sands,
" With no King and no Court to applaud,
" By no shame, should he shrink, overawed,
" Yet to capture the creature made shift,
" That his rude boys might laugh at the gift,
" To the page who last leaped o'er the fence
" Of the pit, on no greater pretence
" Than to get back the bonnet he dropped,
" Lest his pay for a week should be stopped—
" So, wiser I judged it to make
" One trial what 'death for my sake'
" Really meant, while the power was yet mine,
" Than to wait until time should define
" Such a phrase not so simply as I,
" Who took it to mean just 'to die.'
" The blow a glove gives is but weak—
" Does the mark yet discolour my cheek?
" But when the heart suffers a blow,
" Will the pain pass so soon, do you know?"

I looked, as away she was sweeping,
And saw a youth eagerly keeping
As close as he dared to the doorway:
No doubt that a noble should more weigh
His life than befits a plebeian;
And yet, had our brute been Nemean—
(I judge by a certain calm fervor
The youth stepped with, forward to serve her)
—He'd have scarce thought you did him the worst
      turn
If you whispered "Friend, what you'd get, first
      earn!"
And when, shortly after, she carried
Her shame from the Court, and they married,
To that marriage some happiness, maugre
The voice of the Court, I dared augur.

THE GLOVE

For De Lorge, he made women with men vie,
Those in wonder and praise, these in envy ;
And in short stood so plain a head taller
That he wooed and won . . How do you call her ?
The beauty, that rose in the sequel
To the King's love, who loved her a week well ;
And 'twas noticed he never would honour
De Lorge (who looked daggers upon her)
With the easy commission of stretching
His legs in the service, and fetching
His wife, from her chamber, those straying
Sad gloves she was always mislaying,
While the King took the closet to chat in,—
But of course this adventure came pat in ;
And never the King told the story,
How bringing a glove brought such glory,
But the wife smiled—" His nerves are grown firmer—
" Mine he brings now and utters no murmur ! "

Venienti occurrite morbo !
With which moral I drop my theorbo.

MEN
&
WOMEN

LOVE AMONG THE RVINS

I

WHERE the quiet-coloured end of evening smiles
  Miles and miles
On the solitary pastures where our sheep
  Half-asleep
Tinkle homeward thro' the twilight, stray or stop
  As they crop—

137

LOVE AMONG THE RUINS

II

Was the site once of a city great and gay,
     (So they say)
Of our country's very capital, its prince
     Ages since
Held his court in, gathered councils, wielding far
     Peace or war.

III

Now—the country does not even boast a tree,
     As you see,
To distinguish slopes of verdure, certain rills
     From the hills
Intersect and give a name to, (else they run
     Into one)

IV

Where the domed and daring palace shot its spires
     Up like fires
O'er the hundred-gated circuit of a wall
     Bounding all
Made of marble, men might march on nor be prest,
     Twelve abreast.

V

And such plenty and perfection, see, of grass
     Never was!
Such a carpet as, this summer-time, o'erspreads
     And embeds
Every vestige of the city, guessed alone,
     Stock or stone—

VI

Where a multitude of men breathed joy and woe
     Long ago;

LOVE AMONG THE RUINS

Lust of glory pricked their hearts up, dread of shame
      Struck them tame;
And that glory and that shame alike, the gold
      Bought and sold.

VII

Now,—the single little turret that remains
      On the plains,
By the caper overrooted, by the gourd
      Overscored,
While the patching houseleek's head of blossom winks
      Through the chinks—

VIII

Marks the basement whence a tower in ancient time
      Sprang sublime,
And a burning ring all round, the chariots traced
      As they raced,
And the monarch and his minions and his dames
      Viewed the games.

IX

And I know, while thus the quiet-coloured eve
      Smiles to leave
To their folding, all our many-tinkling fleece
      In such peace,
And the slopes and rills in undistinguished grey
      Melt away—

X

That a girl with eager eyes and yellow hair
      Waits me there
In the turret, whence the charioteers caught soul
      For the goal,   [dumb
When the king looked, where she looks now, breathless,
      Till I come.

LOVE AMONG THE RUINS

XI

But he looked upon the city, every side,
    Far and wide,
All the mountains topped with temples, all the glades'
    Colonnades,
All the causeys, bridges, aqueducts,—and then,
    All the men!

XII

When I do come, she will speak not, she will stand,
    Either hand
On my shoulder, give her eyes the first embrace
    Of my face,
Ere we rush, ere we extinguish sight and speech
    Each on each.

XIII

In one year, they sent a million fighters forth
    South and north,
And they built their gods a brazen pillar high
    As the sky,
Yet reserved a thousand chariots in full force—
    Gold, of course.

XIV

Oh, heart! oh, blood that freezes, blood that burns!
    Earth's returns
For whole centuries of folly, noise and sin!
    Shut them in,
With their triumphs and their glories and the rest.
    Love is best!

A LOVERS' QUARREL

A LOVERS' QUARREL

I

OH, what a dawn of day!
How the March sun feels like May!
    All is blue again
    After last night's rain,
And the South dries the hawthorn-spray.
    Only, my Love 's away!
I 'd as lief that the blue were grey.

II

Runnels, which rillets swell,
Must be dancing down the dell
    With a foamy head
    On the beryl bed
Paven smooth as a hermit's cell;
    Each with a tale to tell,
Could my Love but attend as well.

III

Dearest, three months ago!
When we lived blocked-up with snow,—
    When the wind would edge
    In and in his wedge,
In, as far as the point could go—
    Not to our ingle, though,
Where we loved each the other so!

IV

Laughs with so little cause!
We devised games out of straws.
    We would try and trace
    One another's face
In the ash, as an artist draws;
    Free on each other's flaws,
How we chattered like two church daws!

A LOVERS' QUARREL

V

What 's in the " Times "?—a scold
At the emperor deep and cold ;
    He has taken a bride
    To his gruesome side,
That 's as fair as himself is bold :
    There they sit ermine-stoled,
And she powders her hair with gold.

VI

Fancy the Pampas' sheen !
Miles and miles of gold and green
    Where the sun-flowers blow
    In a solid glow,
And to break now and then the screen—
    Black neck and eyeballs keen,
Up a wild horse leaps between !

VII

Try, will our table turn ?
Lay your hands there light, and yearn
    Till the yearning slips
    Thro' the finger tips
In a fire which a few discern,
    And a very few feel burn,
And the rest, they may live and learn !

VIII

Then we would up and pace,
For a change, about the place,
    Each with arm o'er neck.
    'Tis our quarter-deck,
We are seamen in woeful case.
    Help in the ocean-space !
Or, if no help, we 'll embrace.

A LOVERS' QUARREL

IX

See, how she looks now, drest
In a sledging-cap and vest!
    'Tis a huge fur cloak—
    Like a reindeer's yoke
Falls the lappet along the breast:
    Sleeves for her arms to rest,
Or to hang, as my Love likes best.

X

Teach me to flirt a fan
As the Spanish ladies can,
    Or I tint your lip
    With a burnt stick's tip
And you turn into such a man!
    Just the two spots that span
Half the bill of the young male swan.

XI

Dearest, three months ago
When the mesmeriser Snow
    With his hand's first sweep
    Put the earth to sleep,
'Twas a time when the heart could show
    All—how was earth to know,
'Neath the mute hand's to-and-fro!

XII

Dearest, three months ago
When we loved each other so,
    Lived and loved the same
    Till an evening came
When a shaft from the Devil's bow
    Pierced to our ingle-glow,
And the friends were friend and foe!

A LOVERS' QUARREL

XIII

Not from the heart beneath—
'Twas a bubble born of breath,
  Neither sneer nor vaunt,
  Nor reproach nor taunt.
See a word, how it severeth!
  Oh, power of life and death
In the tongue, as the Preacher saith!

XIV

Woman, and will you cast
For a word, quite off at last,
  Me, your own, your you,—
  Since, as Truth is true,
I was you all the happy past—
  Me do you leave aghast
With the memories we amassed?

XV

Love, if you knew the light
That your soul casts in my sight,
  How I look to you
  For the pure and true,
And the beauteous and the right,—
  Bear with a moment's spite
When a mere mote threats the white!

XVI

What of a hasty word?
Is the fleshly heart not stirred
  By a worm's pin-prick
  Where its roots are quick?
See the eye, by a fly's-foot blurred—
  Ear, when a straw is heard
Scratch the brain's coat of curd!

144

A LOVERS' QUARREL

XVII

Foul be the world or fair,
More or less, how can I care?
    'Tis the world the same
    For my praise or blame,
And endurance is easy there.
    Wrong in the one thing rare—
Oh, it is hard to bear!

XVIII

Here's the spring back or close,
When the almond-blossom blows;
    We shall have the word
    In that minor third
There is none but the cuckoo knows.
    Heaps of the guelder-rose!
I must bear with it, I suppose.

XIX

Could but November come,
Were the noisy birds struck dumb,
    At the warning slash
    Of his driver's-lash—
I would laugh like the valiant Thumb
    Facing the castle glum
And the giant's fee-faw-fum!

XX

Then, were the world well stript
Of the gear wherein equipped
    We can stand apart,
    Heart dispense with heart
In the sun, with the flowers unnipped,—
    Oh, the world's hangings ripped,
We were both in a bare-walled crypt!

145

A LOVERS' QUARREL

XXI

Each in the crypt would cry
" But one freezes here! and why?
    When a heart as chill
    At my own would thrill
Back to life, and its fires out-fly?
    Heart, shall we live or die?
The rest, . . . settle it by and by!"

XXII

So, she 'd efface the score,
And forgive me as before.
    Just at twelve o'clock
    I shall hear her knock
In the worst of a storm's uproar—
    I shall pull her through the door—
I shall have her for evermore!

EVELYN HOPE

I

BEAUTIFUL Evelyn Hope is dead
    Sit and watch by her side an hour.
That is her book-shelf, this her bed;
    She plucked that piece of geranium-flower,
Beginning to die too, in the glass.
    Little has yet been changed, I think—
The shutters are shut, no light may pass
    Save two long rays thro' the hinge's chink.

II

Sixteen years old when she died!
    Perhaps she had scarcely heard my name—
It was not her time to love: beside,
    Her life had many a hope and aim,

EVELYN HOPE

Duties enough and little cares,
  And now was quiet, now astir—
Till God's hand beckoned unawares,
  And the sweet white brow is all of her.

III

Is it too late then, Evelyn Hope?
  What, your soul was pure and true,
The good stars met in your horoscope,
  Made you of spirit, fire and dew—
And just because I was thrice as old,
  And our paths in the world diverged so wide,
Each was nought to each, must I be told?
  We were fellow mortals, nought beside?

IV

No, indeed! for God above
  Is great to grant, as mighty to make,
And creates the love to reward the love,—
  I claim you still, for my own love's sake!
Delayed it may be for more lives yet,
  Through worlds I shall traverse, not a few—
Much is to learn and much to forget
  Ere the time be come for taking you.

V

But the time will come,—at last it will,
  When, Evelyn Hope, what meant, I shall say,
In the lower earth, in the years long still,
  That body and soul so pure and gay?
Why your hair was amber, I shall divine,
  And your mouth of your own geranium's red—
And what you would do with me, in fine,
  In the new life come in the old one's stead.

147

EVELYN HOPE

VI

I have lived, I shall say, so much since then,
　Given up myself so many times,
Gained me the gains of various men,
　Ransacked the ages, spoiled the climes;
Yet one thing, one, in my soul's full scope,
　Either I missed or itself missed me—
And I want and find you, Evelyn Hope!
　What is the issue? let us see!

VII

I loved you, Evelyn, all the while;
　　My heart seemed full as it could hold—
There was place and to spare for the frank young
　　　smile
　　And the red young mouth and the hair's young
　　　gold.
　　So, hush,—I will give you this leaf to keep—
　　　See, I shut it inside the sweet cold hand.
　　There, that is our secret! go to sleep;
　　　You will wake, and remember, and under-
　　　stand.

UP AT A VILLA—DOWN IN THE CITY

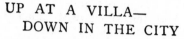

UP AT A VILLA— DOWN IN THE CITY

(AS DISTINGUISHED BY AN ITALIAN PERSON OF QUALITY)

I

HAD I but plenty of money, money enough
and to spare,
The house for me, no doubt, were a house in
the city-square.
Ah, such a life, such a life, as one leads at the
window there!

II

Something to see, by Bacchus, something to
hear, at least!
There, the whole day long, one's life is a perfect
feast;
While up at a villa one lives, I maintain it, no
more than a beast.

III

Well now, look at our villa! stuck like the horn of a bull
Just on a mountain's edge as bare as the creature's skull,
Save a mere shag of a bush with hardly a leaf to pull!
—I scratch my own, sometimes, to see if the hair's turned
wool.

IV

But the city, oh the city—the square with the houses! Why?
They are stone-faced, white as a curd, there's something to
take the eye!
Houses in four straight lines, not a single front awry!
You watch who crosses and gossips, who saunters, who
hurries by:

UP AT A VILLA—DOWN IN THE CITY

Green blinds, as a matter of course, to draw when the sun
gets high ;
And the shops with fanciful signs which are painted
properly.

V

What of a villa ?   Though winter be over in March by rights,
'Tis May perhaps ere the snow shall have withered well off
the heights :
You 've the brown ploughed land before, where the oxen
steam and wheeze,
And the hills over-smoked behind by the faint grey olive
trees.

VI

Is it better in May, I ask you ? you 've summer all at once ;
In a day he leaps complete with a few strong April suns !
'Mid the sharp short emerald wheat, scarce risen three
fingers well,
The wild tulip, at end of its tube, blows out its great red bell,
Like a thin clear bubble of blood, for the children to pick
and sell.

VII

Is it ever hot in the square ?   There 's a fountain to spout
and splash !
In the shade it sings and springs ; in the shine such foam-
bows flash
On the horses with curling fish-tails, that prance and paddle
and pash
Round the lady atop in the conch—fifty gazers do not abash,
Though all that she wears is some weeds round her waist
in a sort of sash !

VIII

All the year long at the villa, nothing 's to see though you
linger,
Except yon cypress that points like Death's lean lifted
forefinger.

UP AT A VILLA—DOWN IN THE CITY

Some think fireflies pretty, when they mix in the corn and
    mingle,
Or thrid the stinking hemp till the stalks of it seem a-tingle.
Late August or early September, the stunning cicala is shrill,
And the bees keep their tiresome whine round the resinous
    firs on the hill.
Enough of the seasons,—I spare you the months of the
    fever and chill.

IX

Ere opening your eyes in the city, the blessed church-bells
    begin :
No sooner the bells leave off, than the diligence rattles in :
You get the pick of the news, and it costs you never a pin.
By and by there's the travelling doctor gives pills, lets
    blood, draws teeth ;
Or the Pulcinello-trumpet breaks up the market beneath.
At the post-office such a scene-picture—the new play,
    piping hot !
And a notice how, only this morning, three liberal thieves
    were shot.
Above it, behold the archbishop's most fatherly of rebukes,
And beneath, with his crown and his lion, some little new
    law of the Duke's !
Or a sonnet with flowery marge, to the Reverend Don So-
    and-so
Who is Dante, Boccaccio, Petrarca, Saint Jerome, and Cicero,
"And moreover," (the sonnet goes rhyming,) "the skirts of
    St. Paul has reached,
Having preached us those six Lent-lectures more unctuous
    than ever he preached."
Noon strikes,—here sweeps the procession ! our Lady
    borne smiling and smart
With a pink gauze gown all spangles, and seven swords
    stuck in her heart !
Bang, whang, whang, goes the drum, *tootle-te-tootle* the fife ;
No keeping one's haunches still : it's the greatest pleasure
    in life.

UP AT A VILLA—DOWN IN THE CITY

X

But bless you, it's dear—it's dear!—fowls, wine, at double
the rate.
They have clapped a new tax upon salt, and what oil pays
passing the gate
It's a horror to think of. And so, the villa for me, not the
city!
Beggars can scarcely be choosers—but still—ah, the pity,
the pity!
Look, two and two go the priests, then the monks with
cowls and sandals,
And the penitents dressed in white shirts, a-holding the
yellow candles.
One, he carries a flag up straight, and another a cross with
handles,
And the Duke's guard brings up the rear, for the better
prevention of scandals.
Bang, whang, whang, goes the drum, *tootle-te-tootle* the fife.
Oh, a day in the city-square, there
is no such pleasure in life!

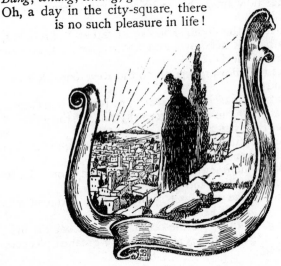

A WOMAN'S LAST WORD

A WOMAN'S LAST WORD

I

LET'S contend no more, Love,
 Strive nor weep—
All be as before, Love,
 —Only sleep!

II

What so wild as words are?
 —I and thou
In debate, as birds are,
 Hawk on bough!

III

See the creature stalking
 While we speak—
Hush and hide the talking,
 Cheek on cheek!

IV

What so false as truth is,
 False to thee?
Where the serpent's tooth is
 Shun the tree—

V

Where the apple reddens
 Never pry—
Lest we lose our Edens,
 Eve and I!

153

A WOMAN'S LAST WORD

VI

Be a god and hold me
  With a charm—
Be a man and fold me
  With thine arm !

VII

Teach me, only teach, Love !
  As I ought
I will speak thy speech, Love,
  Think thy thought—

VIII

Meet, if thou require it,
  Both demands,
Laying flesh and spirit
  In thy hands !

IX

That shall be to-morrow
  Not to-night :
I must bury sorrow
  Out of sight.

X

—Must a little weep, Love,
  —Foolish me !
And so fall asleep, Love,
  Loved by thee.

FRA LIPPO LIPPI

FRA LIPPO LIPPI

I AM poor brother Lippo, by your leave!
You need not clap your torches to my face.
Zooks, what's to blame? you think you see a monk!
What, it's past midnight, and you go the rounds,
And here you catch me at an alley's end
Where sportive ladies leave their doors ajar.
The Carmine's my cloister: hunt it up,
Do,—harry out, if you must show your zeal,
Whatever rat, there, haps on his wrong hole,
And nip each softling of a wee white mouse,
Weke, weke, that's crept to keep him company!
Aha, you know your betters? Then, you'll take
Your hand away that's fiddling on my throat,
And please to know me likewise. Who am I?
Why, one, sir, who is lodging with a friend
Three streets off—he's a certain . . . how d'ye call?
Master—a . . . Cosimo of the Medici,
In the house that caps the corner. Boh! you were best!
Remember and tell me, the day you're hanged,
How you affected such a gullet's-gripe!
But you, sir, it concerns you that your knaves
Pick up a manner nor discredit you.
Zooks, are we pilchards, that they sweep the streets
And count fair prize what comes into their net?
He's Judas to a tittle, that man is!
Just such a face! why, sir, you make amends.
Lord, I'm not angry! Bid your hangdogs go
Drink out this quarter-florin to the health
Of the munificent House that harbours me
(And many more beside, lads! more beside!)
And all's come square again. I'd like his face—
His, elbowing on his comrade in the door
With the pike and lantern,—for the slave that holds
John Baptist's head a-dangle by the hair

FRA LIPPO LIPPI

With one hand ("look you, now," as who should say)
And his weapon in the other, yet unwiped!
It's not your chance to have a bit of chalk,
A wood-coal or the like? or you should see!
Yes, I'm the painter, since you style me so.
What, brother Lippo's doings, up and down,
You know them and they take you? like enough!
I saw the proper twinkle in your eye—
'Tell you I liked your looks at very first.
Let's sit and set things straight now, hip to haunch.
Here's spring come, and the nights one makes up bands
To roam the town and sing out carnival,
And I've been three weeks shut within my mew,
A-painting for the great man, saints and saints
And saints again. I could not paint all night—
Ouf! I leaned out of window for fresh air.
There came a hurry of feet and little feet,
A sweep of lute-strings, laughs, and whifts of song,—
Flower o' the broom,
Take away love, and our earth is a tomb!
Flower o' the quince,
I let Lisa go, and what good 's in life since?
Flower o' the thyme—and so on. Round they went.
Scarce had they turned the corner when a titter,
Like the skipping of rabbits by moonlight,—three slim
          shapes—
And a face that looked up . . . zooks, sir, flesh and blood,
That's all I'm made of! Into shreds it went,
Curtain and counterpane and coverlet,
All the bed furniture—a dozen knots,
There was a ladder! down I let myself,
Hands and feet, scrambling somehow, and so dropped,
And after them. I came up with the fun
Hard by St. Laurence, hail fellow, well met,—
Flower o' the rose,
If I've been merry, what matter who knows?
And so as I was stealing back again

FRA LIPPO LIPPI
I am poor brother Lippo, by your leave!

FRA LIPPO LIPPI

To get to bed and have a bit of sleep
Ere I rise up to-morrow and go work
On Jerome knocking at his poor old breast
With his great round stone to subdue the flesh,
You snap me of the sudden. Ah, I see!
Though your eye twinkles still, you shake your head—
Mine's shaved,—a monk, you say—the sting's in that!
If Master Cosimo announced himself,
Mum's the word naturally; but a monk!
Come, what am I a beast for? tell us, now!
I was a baby when my mother died
And father died and left me in the street.
I starved there, God knows how, a year or two
On fig-skins, melon-parings, rinds and shucks,
Refuse and rubbish. One fine frosty day
My stomach being empty as your hat,
The wind doubled me up and down I went.
Old Aunt Lapaccia trussed me with one hand,
(Its fellow was a stinger as I knew)
And so along the wall, over the bridge,
By the straight cut to the convent. Six words, there,
While I stood munching my first bread that month:
"So, boy, you're minded," quoth the good fat father
Wiping his own mouth, 'twas refection-time,—
"To quit this very miserable world?
Will you renounce" . . . The mouthful of bread? thought
    I;
By no means! Brief, they made a monk of me;
I did renounce the world, its pride and greed,
Palace, farm, villa, shop and banking-house,
Trash, such as these poor devils of Medici
Have given their hearts to—all at eight years old.
Well, sir, I found in time, you may be sure,
'Twas not for nothing—the good bellyful,
The warm serge and the rope that goes all round,
And day-long blessed idleness beside!
"Let's see what the urchin's fit for"—that came next.

159

FRA LIPPO LIPPI

Not overmuch their way, I must confess.
Such a to-do! they tried me with their books.
Lord, they'd have taught me Latin in pure waste!
Flower o' the clove,
All the Latin I construe is, "amo" I love!
But, mind you, when a boy starves in the streets
Eight years together, as my fortune was,
Watching folk's faces to know who will fling
The bit of half-stripped grape-bunch he desires,
And who will curse or kick him for his pains—
Which gentleman processional and fine,
Holding a candle to the Sacrament
Will wink and let him lift a plate and catch
The droppings of the wax to sell again,
Or holla for the Eight and have him whipped,—
How say I?—nay, which dog bites, which lets drop
His bone from the heap of offal in the street!
—The soul and sense of him grow sharp alike,
He learns the look of things, and none the less
For admonitions from the hunger-pinch.
I had a store of such remarks, be sure,
Which, after I found leisure, turned to use:
I drew men's faces on my copy-books,
Scrawled them within the antiphonary's marge,
Joined legs and arms to the long music-notes,
Found nose and eyes and chin for A.s and B.s,
And made a string of pictures of the world
Betwixt the ins and outs of verb and noun,
On the wall, the bench, the door. The monks looked black
"Nay," quoth the Prior, "turn him out, d'ye say?
In no wise. Lose a crow and catch a lark.
What if at last we get our man of parts,
We Carmelites, like those Camaldolese
And Preaching Friars, to do our church up fine
And put the front on it that ought to be!"
And hereupon they bade me daub away.
Thank you! my head being crammed, their walls a blank,

FRA·LIPPO·LIPPI·

"a·face·that·looked·up"

FRA LIPPO LIPPI

Never was such prompt disemburdening.
First, every sort of monk, the black and white,
I drew them, fat and lean : then, folks at church,
From good old gossips waiting to confess
Their cribs of barrel-droppings, candle-ends,—
To the breathless fellow at the altar-foot,
Fresh from his murder, safe and sitting there
With the little children round him in a row
Of admiration, half for his beard and half
For that white anger of his victim's son
Shaking a fist at him with one fierce arm,
Signing himself with the other because of Christ
(Whose sad face on the cross sees only this
After the passion of a thousand years)
Till some poor girl, her apron o'er her head
Which the intense eyes looked through, came at eve
On tip-toe, said a word, dropped in a loaf,
Her pair of ear-rings and a bunch of flowers
The brute took growling, prayed, and then was gone.
I painted all, then cried " 'tis ask and have—
Choose, for more 's ready ! "—laid the ladder flat,
And showed my covered bit of cloister-wall.
The monks closed in a circle and praised loud
Till checked, (taught what to see and not to see,
Being simple bodies) "that 's the very man !
Look at the boy who stoops to pat the dog !
That woman 's like the Prior's niece who comes
To care about his asthma : it 's the life ! "
But there my triumph's straw-fire flared and funked—
Their betters took their turn to see and say :
The Prior and the learned pulled a face
And stopped all that in no time.   " How ? what 's here ?
Quite from the mark of painting, bless us all !
Faces, arms, legs and bodies like the true
As much as pea and pea ! it 's devil's-game !
Your business is not to catch men with show,
With homage to the perishable clay,

FRA LIPPO LIPPI

But lift them over it, ignore it all,
Make them forget there's such a thing as flesh.
Your business is to paint the souls of men—
Man's soul, and it's a fire, smoke . . no it's not . .
It's vapour done up like a new-born babe—
(In that shape when you die it leaves your mouth)
It's . . well, what matters talking, it's the soul!
Give us no more of body than shows soul.
Here's Giotto, with his Saint a-praising God!
That sets you praising,—why not stop with him?
Why put all thoughts of praise out of our heads
With wonder at lines, colours, and what not?
Paint the soul, never mind the legs and arms!
Rub all out, try at it a second time.
Oh, that white smallish female with the breasts,
She's just my niece . . . Herodias, I would say,—
Who went and danced and got men's heads cut off—
Have it all out!" Now, is this sense, I ask?
A fine way to paint soul, by painting body
So ill, the eye can't stop there, must go further
And can't fare worse! Thus, yellow does for white
When what you put for yellow's simply black,
And any sort of meaning looks intense
When all beside itself means and looks nought.
Why can't a painter lift each foot in turn,
Left foot and right foot, go a double step,
Make his flesh liker and his soul more like,
Both in their order? Take the prettiest face,
The Prior's niece . . . patron-saint—is it so pretty
You can't discover if it means hope, fear,
Sorrow or joy? won't beauty go with these?
Suppose I've made her eyes all right and blue,
Can't I take breath and try to add life's flash,
And then add soul and heighten them threefold?
Or say there's beauty with no soul at all—
(I never saw it—put the case the same—)
If you get simple beauty and nought else,

FRA LIPPO LIPPI

You get about the best thing God invents,—
That's somewhat. And you'll find the soul you have
     missed,
Within yourself when you return Him thanks!
"Rub all out!" well, well, there's my life, in short,
And so the thing has gone on ever since.
I'm grown a man no doubt, I've broken bounds—
You should not take a fellow eight years old
And make him swear to never kiss the girls—
I'm my own master, paint now as I please—
Having a friend, you see, in the Corner-house!
Lord, it's fast holding by the rings in front—
Those great rings serve more purposes than just
To plant a flag in, or tie up a horse!
And yet the old schooling sticks—the old grave eyes
Are peeping o'er my shoulder as I work,
The heads shake still—"It's Art's decline, my son!
You're not of the true painters, great and old:
Brother Angelico's the man, you'll find:
Brother Lorenzo stands his single peer.
Fag on at flesh, you'll never make the third!"
Flower o' the pine,
You keep your mistr . . . manners, and I'll stick to mine!
I'm not the third, then: bless us, they must know!
Don't you think they're the likeliest to know,
They, with their Latin? so I swallow my rage,
Clench my teeth, suck my lips in tight, and paint
To please them—sometimes do, and sometimes don't,
For, doing most, there's pretty sure to come
A turn—some warm eve finds me at my saints—
A laugh, a cry, the business of the world—
(*Flower o' the peach,*
Death for us all, and his own life for each!)
And my whole soul revolves, the cup runs o'er,
The world and life's too big to pass for a dream,
And I do these wild things in sheer despite,
And play the fooleries you catch me at,

FRA LIPPO LIPPI

In pure rage! the old mill-horse, out at grass
After hard years, throws up his stiff heels so,
Although the miller does not preach to him
The only good of grass is to make chaff.
What would men have? Do they like grass or no—
May they or mayn't they? all I want's the thing
Settled for ever one way: as it is,
You tell too many lies and hurt yourself.
You don't like what you only like too much,
You do like what, if given you at your word,
You find abundantly detestable.
For me, I think I speak as I was taught—
I always see the Garden and God there
A-making man's wife—and, my lesson learned,
The value and significance of flesh,
I can't unlearn ten minutes afterward.

    You understand me: I'm a beast, I know.
But see, now—why, I see as certainly
As that the morning-star's about to shine,
What will hap some day. We've a youngster here
Comes to our convent, studies what I do,
Slouches and stares and lets no atom drop—
His name is Guidi—he'll not mind the monks—
They call him Hulking Tom, he lets them talk—
He picks my practice up—he'll paint apace,
I hope so—though I never live so long,
I know what's sure to follow. You be judge!
You speak no Latin more than I, belike—
However, you're my man, you've seen the world
—The beauty and the wonder and the power,
The shapes of things, their colours, lights and shades,
Changes, surprises,—and God made it all!
—For what? do you feel thankful, ay or no,
For this fair town's face, yonder river's line,
The mountain round it and the sky above,
Much more the figures of man, woman, child,
These are the frame to? What's it all about?

FRA LIPPO LIPPI

To be passed o'er, despised? or dwelt upon,
Wondered at? oh, this last of course, you say.
But why not do as well as say,—paint these
Just as they are, careless what comes of it?
God's works—paint anyone, and count it crime
To let a truth slip. Don't object, "His works
Are here already—nature is complete:
Suppose you reproduce her—(which you can't)
There's no advantage! you must beat her, then."
For, don't you mark, we're made so that we love
First when we see them painted, things we have passed
Perhaps a hundred times nor cared to see;
And so they are better, painted—better to us,
Which is the same thing. Art was given for that—
God uses us to help each other so,
Lending our minds out. Have you noticed, now,
Your cullion's hanging face? A bit of chalk,
And trust me but you should, though! How much
        more,
If I drew higher things with the same truth!
That were to take the Prior's pulpit-place,
Interpret God to all of you! oh, oh,
It makes me mad to see what men shall do
And we in our graves! This world's no blot for us,
Nor blank—it means intensely, and means good:
To find its meaning is my meat and drink.
"Ay, but you don't so instigate to prayer"
Strikes in the Prior! "when your meaning's plain
It does not say to folks—remember matins—
Or, mind you fast next Friday." Why, for this
What need of art at all? A skull and bones,
Two bits of stick nailed cross-wise, or, what's best,
A bell to chime the hour with, does as well.
I painted a St. Laurence six months since
At Prato, splashed the fresco in fine style.
"How looks my painting, now the scaffold's down?"
I ask a brother: "Hugely," he returns—

FRA LIPPO LIPPI

" Already not one phiz of your three slaves
That turn the Deacon off his toasted side,
But 's scratched and prodded to our heart's content,
The pious people have so eased their own
When coming to say prayers there in a rage.
We get on fast to see the bricks beneath.
Expect another job this time next year,
For pity and religion grow i' the crowd—
Your painting serves its purpose!"   Hang the fools!

—That is—you'll not mistake an idle word
Spoke in a huff by a poor monk, God wot,
Tasting the air this spicy night which turns
The unaccustomed head like Chianti wine!
Oh, the church knows! don't misreport me, now!
It's natural a poor monk out of bounds
Should have his apt word to excuse himself:
And hearken how I plot to make amends.
I have bethought me: I shall paint a piece
. . . There's for you!   Give me six months, then go, see
Something in Sant' Ambrogio's . . . (bless the nuns!
They want a cast of my office) I shall paint
God in the midst, Madonna and her babe,
Ringed by a bowery, flowery angel-brood,
Lilies and vestments and white faces, sweet
As puff on puff of grated orris-root
When ladies crowd to church at midsummer.
And then in the front, of course a saint or two—
Saint John, because he saves the Florentines,
Saint Ambrose, who puts down in black and white
The convent's friends and gives them a long day,
And Job, I must have him there past mistake,
The man of Uz, (and Us without the z,
Painters who need his patience).   Well, all these
Secured at their devotions, up shall come
Out of a corner when you least expect,
As one by a dark stair into a great light

FRA LIPPO LIPPI

Music and talking, who but Lippo! I!—
Mazed, motionless and moon-struck—I'm the man
Back I shrink—what is this I see and hear?
I, caught up with my monk's things by mistake,
My old serge gown and rope that goes all round,
I, in this presence, this pure company!
Where's a hole, where's a corner for escape?
Then steps a sweet angelic slip of a thing
Forward, puts out a soft palm—"Not so fast!"
—Addresses the celestial presence, "nay—
He made you and devised you, after all,
Though he's none of you!   Could Saint John there,
    draw—
His camel-hair make up a painting-brush?
We come to brother Lippo for all that,
Iste perfecit opus!"   So, all smile—
I shuffle sideways with my blushing face
Under the cover of a hundred wings
Thrown like a spread of kirtles when you're gay
And play hot cockles, all the doors being shut,
Till, wholly unexpected, in there pops
The hothead husband!   Thus I scuttle off
To some safe bench behind, not letting go
The palm of her, the little lily thing
That spoke the good word for me in the nick,
Like the Prior's niece . . . Saint Lucy, I would say.
And so all's saved for me, and for the church
A pretty picture gained.   Go, six months hence!
Your hand, sir, and good bye: no lights, no lights!
The street's hushed, and I know my own way back—
Don't fear me!   There's the grey beginning.   Zooks!

A TOCCATA OF GALUPPI'S

I

OH, Galuppi, Baldassaro, this is very sad to find!
I can hardly misconceive you ; it would prove me deaf and
blind ;
But although I give you credit, 'tis with such a heavy
mind !

II

Here you come with your old music, and here's all the
good it brings.
What, they lived once thus at Venice, where the merchants
were the kings,
Where St. Mark's is, where the Doges used to wed the sea
with rings ?

III

Ay, because the sea's the street there ; and 'tis arched by
. . . what you call
. . . Shylock's bridge with houses on it, where they kept
the carnival !
I was never out of England—it's as if I saw it all !

170

A TOCCATA OF GALUPPI'S

IV

Did young people take their pleasure when the sea was
warm in May?
Balls and masks begun at midnight, burning ever to mid-
day,
When they made up fresh adventures for the morrow, do
you say?

V

Was a lady such a lady, cheeks so round and lips so red,—
On her neck the small face buoyant, like a bell-flower on
its bed,
O'er the breast's superb abundance where a man might
base his head?

VI

Well (and it was graceful of them) they 'd break talk off
and afford
—She, to bite her mask's black velvet, he to finger on his
sword,
While you sat and played Toccatas, stately at the
clavichord?

VII

What? Those lesser thirds so plaintive, sixths diminished,
sigh on sigh,
Told them something? Those suspensions, those solu-
tions—" Must we die?"
Those commiserating sevenths—" Life might last! we can
but try!"

VIII

" Were you happy?"—" Yes."—" And are you still as
happy?"—"Yes—And you?"
—" Then more kisses "—" Did *I* stop them, when a million
seemed so few?"
Hark—the dominant's persistence, till it must be answered to!

A TOCCATA OF GALUPPI'S

IX

So an octave struck the answer. Oh, they praised you, I
dare say !
" Brave Galuppi ! that was music ! good alike at grave and
gay !
I can always leave off talking, when I hear a master play."

X

Then they left you for their pleasure : till in due time, one
by one,
Some with lives that came to nothing, some with deeds as
well undone,
Death came tacitly and took them where they never see
the sun.

XI

But when I sit down to reason,—think to take my stand
nor swerve
Till I triumph o'er a secret wrung from nature's close
reserve,
In you come with your cold music, till I creep thro' every
nerve.

XII

Yes, you, like a ghostly cricket, creaking where a house
was burned—
" Dust and ashes, dead and done with, Venice spent what
Venice earned !
The soul, doubtless, is immortal—where a soul can be dis-
cerned.

XIII

"Yours for instance, you know physics, something of geology,
Mathematics are your pastime ; souls shall rise in their
degree ;
Butterflies may dread extinction,—you 'll not die, it cannot
be !

BY THE FIRE-SIDE

XIV

"As for Venice and its people, merely born to bloom and
drop,
Here on earth they bore their fruitage, mirth and folly
were the crop.
What of soul was left, I wonder, when the kissing had to
stop?

XV

"Dust and ashes!" So you creak it, and I want the heart
to scold.
Dear dead women, with such hair, too—what's become of
all the gold
Used to hang and brush their bosoms; I feel chilly and
grown old.

BY THE FIRE-SIDE

I

How well I know what I mean to do
  When the long dark Autumn evenings come,
And where, my soul, is thy pleasant hue?
  With the music of all thy voices, dumb
In life's November too!

II

I shall be found by the fire, suppose,
  O'er a great wise book as beseemeth age,
While the shutters flap as the cross-wind blows,
  And I turn the page, and I turn the page,
Not verse now, only prose!

173

BY THE FIRE-SIDE

III

Till the young ones whisper, finger on lip,
  "There he is at it, deep in Greek—
Now or never, then, out we slip
  To cut from the hazels by the creek
A mainmast for our ship."

IV

I shall be at it indeed, my friends!
  Greek puts already on either side
Such a branch-work forth, as soon extends
  To a vista opening far and wide,
And I pass out where it ends.

V

The outside-frame like your hazel-trees—
  But the inside-archway narrows fast,
And a rarer sort succeeds to these,
  And we slope to Italy at last
And youth, by green degrees.

VI

I follow wherever I am led,
  Knowing so well the leader's hand—
Oh, woman-country, wooed, not wed,
  Loved all the more by earth's male-lands,
Laid to their hearts instead!

VII

Look at the ruined chapel again
  Half way up in the Alpine gorge.
Is that a tower, I point you plain,
  Or is it a mill or an iron forge
Breaks solitude in vain?

174

BY THE FIRE-SIDE

VIII

A turn, and we stand in the heart of things ;
 The woods are round us, heaped and dim ;
From slab to slab how it slips and springs,
 The thread of water single and slim,
Thro' the ravage some torrent brings !

IX

Does it feed the little lake below ?
 That speck of white just on its marge
Is Pella ; see, in the evening glow
 How sharp the silver spear-heads charge
When Alp meets Heaven in snow.

X

On our other side is the straight-up rock ;
 And a path is kept 'twixt the gorge and it
By boulder-stones where lichens mock
 The marks on a moth, and small ferns fit
Their teeth to the polished block.

XI

Oh, the sense of the yellow mountain flowers,
 And the thorny balls, each three in one,
The chestnuts throw on our path in showers,
 For the drop of the woodland fruit 's begun,
These early November hours—

XII

That crimson the creeper's leaf across
 Like a splash of blood, intense, abrupt,
O'er a shield, else gold from rim to boss,
 And lay it for show on the fairy-cupped
Elf-needled mat of moss,

175

BY THE FIRE-SIDE

XIII

By the rose-flesh mushrooms, undivulged
  Last evening—nay, in to-day's first dew
Yon sudden coral nipple bulged
  Where a freaked, fawn-coloured, flaky crew
Of toad-stools peep indulged.

XIV

And yonder, at foot of the fronting ridge
  That takes the turn to a range beyond,
Is the chapel reached by the one-arched bridge
  Where the water is stopped in a stagnant pond
Danced over by the midge.

XV

The chapel and bridge are of stone alike,
  Blackish grey and mostly wet ;
Cut hemp-stalks steep in the narrow dyke.
  See here again, how the lichens fret
And the roots of the ivy strike !

XVI

Poor little place, where its one priest comes
  On a festa-day, if he comes at all,
To the dozen folk from their scattered homes,
  Gathered within that precinct small
By the dozen ways one roams—

XVII

To drop from the charcoal-burners' huts,
  Or climb from the hemp-dressers' low shed,
Leave the grange where the woodman stores his nuts,
  Or the wattled cote where the fowlers spread
Their gear on the rock's bare juts.

BY THE FIRE-SIDE

XVIII

It has some pretension too, this front,
   With its bit of fresco half-moon-wise
Set over the porch, art's early wont—
   'Tis John in the Desert, I surmise,
But has borne the weather's brunt—

XIX

Not from the fault of the builder, though,
   For a pent-house properly projects
Where three carved beams make a certain show,
   Dating—good thought of our architect's—
'Five, six, nine, he lets you know.

XX

And all day long a bird sings there,
   And a stray sheep drinks at the pond at times
The place is silent and aware;
   It has had its scenes, its joys and crimes,
But that is its own affair.

XXI

My perfect wife, my Leonor,
   Oh, heart my own, oh, eyes, mine too,
Whom else could I dare look backward for,
   With whom beside should I dare pursue
The path grey heads abhor?

XXII

For it leads to a crag's sheer edge with them;
   Youth, flowery all the way, there stops—
Not they; age threatens and they contemn,
   Till they reach the gulf wherein youth drops,
One inch from our life's safe hem!

BY THE FIRE-SIDE

XXIII

With me, youth led—I will speak now,
No longer watch you as you sit
Reading by fire-light, that great brow
And the spirit-small hand propping it
Mutely—my heart knows how—

XXIV

When, if I think but deep enough,
You are wont to answer, prompt as rhyme;
And you, too, find without a rebuff
The response your soul seeks many a time
Piercing its fine flesh-stuff—

XXV

My own, confirm me! If I tread
This path back, is it not in pride
To think how little I dreamed it led
To an age so blest that by its side
Youth seems the waste instead!

XXVI

My own, see where the years conduct!
At first, 'twas something our two souls
Should mix as mists do: each is sucked
Into each now; on, the new stream rolls,
Whatever rocks obstruct.

XXVII

Think, when our one soul understands
The great Word which makes all things new—
When earth breaks up and Heaven expands—
How will the change strike me and you
In the House not made with hands?

BY THE FIRE-SIDE

XXVIII

Oh, I must feel your brain prompt mine,
　Your heart anticipate my heart,
You must be just before, in fine,
　See and make me see, for your part,
New depths of the Divine!

XXIX

But who could have expected this,
　When we two drew together first
Just for the obvious human bliss,
　To satisfy life's daily thirst
With a thing men seldom miss?

XXX

Come back with me to the first of all,
　Let us lean and love it over again—
Let us now forget and then recall,
　Break the rosary in a pearly rain,
And gather what we let fall!

XXXI

What did I say?—that a small bird sings
　All day long, save when a brown pair
Of hawks from the wood float with wide wings
　Strained to a bell: 'gainst the noon-day glare
You count the streaks and rings.

XXXII

But at afternoon or almost eve
　'Tis better; then the silence grows
To that degree, you half believe
　It must get rid of what it knows,
Its bosom does so heave.

BY THE FIRE-SIDE

XXXIII

Hither we walked, then, side by side,
  Arm in arm and cheek to cheek,
And still I questioned or replied,
  While my heart, convulsed to really speak,
Lay choking in its pride.

XXXIV

Silent the crumbling bridge we cross,
  And pity and praise the chapel sweet,
And care about the fresco's loss,
  And wish for our souls a like retreat,
And wonder at the moss.

XXXV

Stoop and kneel on the settle under—
  Look through the window's grated square:
Nothing to see! for fear of plunder,
  The cross is down and the altar bare,
As if thieves don't fear thunder.

XXXVI

We stoop and look in through the grate,
  See the little porch and rustic door,
Read duly the dead builder's date,
  Then cross the bridge we crossed before,
Take the path again—but wait!

XXXVII

Oh moment, one and infinite!
  The water slips o'er stock and stone;
The west is tender, hardly bright.
  How grey at once is the evening grown—
One star, the chrysolite!

BY THE FIRE-SIDE

XXXVIII

We two stood there with never a third,
    But each by each, as each knew well.
The sights we saw and the sounds we heard,
    The lights and the shades made up a spell
Till the trouble grew and stirred.

XXXIX

Oh, the little more, and how much it is!
    And the little less, and what worlds away!
How a sound shall quicken content to bliss,
    Or a breath suspend the blood's best play,
And life be a proof of this!

XL

Had she willed it, still had stood the screen
    So slight, so sure, 'twixt my love and her.
I could fix her face with a guard between,
    And find her soul as when friends confer,
Friends—lovers that might have been.

XLI

For my heart had a touch of the woodland time,
    Wanting to sleep now over its best.
Shake the whole tree in the summer-prime,
    But bring to the last leaf no such test.
"Hold the last fast!" says the rhyme.

XLII

For a chance to make your little much,
    To gain a lover and lose a friend,
Venture the tree and a myriad such,
    When nothing you mar but the year can mend!
But a last leaf—fear to touch.

181

BY THE FIRE-SIDE

XLIII

Yet should it unfasten itself and fall
   Eddying down till it find your face
At some slight wind—(best chance of all!)
   Be your heart henceforth its dwelling-place
You trembled to forestall!

XLIV

Worth how well, those dark grey eyes,
   —That hair so dark and dear, how worth
That a man should strive and agonise,
   And taste a very hell on earth
For the hope of such a prize!

XLV

Oh, you might have turned and tried a man,
   Set him a space to weary and wear,
And prove which suited more your plan,
   His best of hope or his worst despair,
Yet end as he began.

XLVI

But you spared me this, like the heart you are,
   And filled my empty heart at a word.
If you join two lives, there is oft a scar,
   They are one and one, with a shadowy third;
One near one is too far.

XLVII

A moment after, and hands unseen
   Were hanging the night around us fast.
But we knew that a bar was broken between
   Life and life; we were mixed at last
In spite of the mortal screen.

BY THE FIRE-SIDE

XLVIII

The forests had done it ; there they stood—
　　We caught for a second the powers at play :
They had mingled us so, for once and for good,
　　Their work was done—we might go or stay,
They relapsed to their ancient mood.

XLIX

How the world is made for each of us !
　　How all we perceive and know in it
Tends to some moment's product thus,
　　When a soul declares itself—to wit,
By its fruit—the thing it does !

L

Be Hate that fruit or Love that fruit,
　　It forwards the General Deed of Man,
And each of the Many helps to recruit
　　The life of the race by a general plan,
Each living his own, to boot.

LI

I am named and known by that hour's feat,
　　There took my station and degree.
So grew my own small life complete
　　As nature obtained her best of me—
One born to love you, sweet !

LII

And to watch you sink by the fire-side now
　　Back again, as you mutely sit
Musing by fire-light, that great brow
　　And the spirit-small hand propping it
Yonder, my heart knows how !

BY THE FIRE-SIDE

LIII

So the earth has gained by one man more,
    And the gain of earth must be Heaven's gain too,
And the whole is well worth thinking o'er
    When the autumn comes: which I mean to do
One day, as I said before.

ANY WIFE TO ANY HUSBAND

I

My love, this is the bitterest, that thou
Who art all truth and who dost love me now
    As thine eyes say, as thy voice breaks to say—
Should'st love so truly and could'st love me still
A whole long life through, had but love its will,
    Would death that leads me from thee brook delay!

II

I have but to be by thee, and thy hand
Would never let mine go, thy heart withstand
    The beating of my heart to reach its place.
When should I look for thee and feel thee gone?
When cry for the old comfort and find none?
    Never, I know! Thy soul is in thy face.

III

Oh, I should fade—'tis willed so! might I save,
Gladly I would, whatever beauty gave
    Joy to thy sense, for that was precious too.
It is not to be granted. But the soul
Whence the love comes, all ravage leaves that whole;
    Vainly the flesh fades—soul makes all things new.

184

ANY WIFE TO ANY HUSBAND

IV

And 'twould not be because my eye grew dim
Thou could'st not find the love there, thanks to Him
 Who never is dishonoured in the spark
He gave us from his fire of fires, and bade
Remember whence it sprang nor be afraid
 While that burns on, though all the rest grow dark.

V

So, how thou would'st be perfect, white and clean
Outside as inside, soul and soul's demesne
 Alike, this body given to show it by!
Oh, three-parts through the worst of life's abyss,
What plaudits from the next world after this,
 Could'st thou repeat a stroke and gain the sky!

VI

And is it not the bitterer to think
That, disengage our hands and thou wilt sink
 Although thy love was love in very deed?
I know that nature! Pass a festive day
Thou dost not throw its relic-flower away
 Nor bid its music's loitering echo speed.

VII

Thou let'st the stranger's glove lie where it fell;
If old things remain old things all is well,
 For thou art grateful as becomes man best:
And hadst thou only heard me play one tune,
Or viewed me from a window, not so soon
 With thee would such things fade as with the rest.

ANY WIFE TO ANY HUSBAND

VIII

I seem to see ! we meet and part : 'tis brief:
The book I opened keeps a folded leaf,
   The very chair I sat on, breaks the rank ;
That is a portrait of me on the wall—
Three lines, my face comes at so slight a call ;
   And for all this, one little hour 's to thank.

IX

But now, because the hour through years was fixed,
Because our inmost beings met and mixed,
   Because thou once hast loved me—wilt thou dare
Say to thy soul and Who may list beside,
" Therefore she is immortally my bride,
   Chance cannot change that love, nor time impair.

X

" So, what if in the dusk of life that 's left,
I, a tired traveller, of my sun bereft,
   Look from my path when, mimicking the same,
The fire-fly glimpses past me, come and gone?
—Where was it till the sunset ? where anon
   It will be at the sunrise ! what 's to blame ? "

XI

Is it so helpful to thee ? canst thou take
The mimic up, nor, for the true thing's sake,
   Put gently by such efforts at a beam ?
Is the remainder of the way so long
Thou need'st the little solace, thou the strong ?
   Watch out thy watch, let weak ones doze and
      dream!

ANY WIFE TO ANY HUSBAND

XII

" —Ah, but the fresher faces! Is it true,"
Thou 'lt ask, " some eyes are beautiful and new?
   Some hair,—how can one choose but grasp such
      wealth ?
And if a man would press his lips to lips
Fresh as the wilding hedge-rose-cup there slips
   The dew-drop out of, must it be by stealth?

XIII

" It cannot change the love kept still for Her,
Much more than, such a picture to prefer
   Passing a day with, to a room's bare side.
The painted form takes nothing she possessed,
Yet while the Titian's Venus lies at rest
   A man looks. Once more, what is there to chide?"

XIV

So must I see, from where I sit and watch,
My own self sell myself, my hand attach
   Its warrant to the very thefts from me—
Thy singleness of soul that made me proud,
Thy purity of heart I loved aloud,
   Thy man's truth I was bold to bid God see!

XV

Love so, then, if thou wilt! Give all thou canst
Away to the new faces—disentranced—
   (Say it and think it) obdurate no more,
Re-issue looks and words from the old mint—
Pass them afresh, no matter whose the print
   Image and superscription once they bore!

ANY WIFE TO ANY HUSBAND

XVI

Re-coin thyself and give it them to spend,—
It all comes to the same thing at the end,
  Since mine thou wast, mine art, and mine shalt be,
Faithful or faithless, sealing up the sum
Or lavish of my treasure, thou must come
  Back to the heart's place here I keep for thee!

XVII

Only, why should it be with stain at all?
Why must I, 'twixt the leaves of coronal,
  Put any kiss of pardon on thy brow?
Why need the other women know so much
And talk together, " Such the look and such
  The smile he used to love with, then as now!"

XVIII

Might I die last and shew thee!   Should I find
Such hardship in the few years left behind,
  If free to take and light my lamp, and go
Into thy tomb, and shut the door and sit
Seeing thy face on those four sides of it
  The better that they are so blank, I know!

XIX

Why, time was what I wanted, to turn o'er
Within my mind each look, get more and more
  By heart each word, too much to learn at first,
And join thee all the fitter for the pause
'Neath the low door-way's lintel.   That were cause
  For lingering, though thou calledst, if I durst!

ANY WIFE TO ANY HUSBAND

And yet thou art the nobler of us two.
What dare I dream of, that thou canst not do,
   Outstripping my ten small steps with one stride?
I 'll say then, here 's a trial and a task—
Is it to bear?—if easy, I 'll not ask—
   Though love fail, I can trust on in thy pride.

Pride?—when those eyes forestall the life behind
The death I have to go through!—when I find,
   Now that I want thy help most, all of thee!
What did I fear?   Thy love shall hold me fast
Until the little minute's sleep is past
   And I wake saved.—And yet, it will not be!

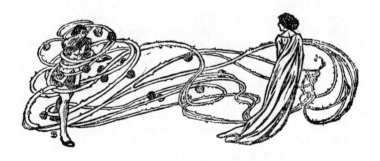

AN EPISTLE

AN EPISTLE

CONTAINING THE STRANGE MEDICAL EXPERIENCE OF KARSHISH, THE ARAB PHYSICIAN

KARSHISH, the picker-up of learning's crumbs,
The not-incurious in God's handiwork
(This man's-flesh He hath admirably made,
Blown like a bubble, kneaded like a paste,
To coop up and keep down on earth a space
That puff of vapour from His mouth, man's soul)
—To Abib, all-sagacious in our art,
Breeder in me of what poor skill I boast,
Like me inquisitive how pricks and cracks
Befall the flesh through too much stress and strain,
Whereby the wily vapour fain would slip
Back and rejoin its source before the term,—
And aptest in contrivance, under God,
To baffle it by deftly stopping such :—
The vagrant Scholar to his Sage at home
Sends greeting (health and knowledge, fame with peace)
Three samples of true snake-stone—rarer still,
One of the other sort, the melon-shaped,
(But fitter, pounded fine, for charms than drugs)
And writeth now the twenty-second time.

My journeyings were brought to Jericho,
Thus I resume.   Who studious in our art
Shall count a little labour unrepaid?
I have shed sweat enough, left flesh and bone
On many a flinty furlong of this land.
Also the country-side is all on fire
With rumours of a marching hitherward—
Some say Vespasian cometh, some, his son.
A black lynx snarled and pricked a tufted ear ;
Lust of my blood inflamed his yellow balls :
I cried and threw my staff and he was gone.

AN EPISTLE

Twice have the robbers stripped and beaten me,
And once a town declared me for a spy,
But at the end, I reach Jerusalem,
Since this poor covert where I pass the night,
This Bethany, lies scarce the distance thence
A man with plague-sores at the third degree
Runs till he drops down dead.   Thou laughest here!
'Sooth, it elates me, thus reposed and safe,
To void the stuffing of my travel-scrip
And share with thee whatever Jewry yields.
A viscid choler is observable
In tertians, I was nearly bold to say,
And falling-sickness hath a happier cure
Than our school wots off: there's a spider here
Weaves no web, watches on the ledge of tombs,
Sprinkled with mottles on an ash-grey back;
Take five and drop them . . . but who knows his mind,
The Syrian run-a-gate I trust this to?
His service payeth me a sublimate
Blown up his nose to help the ailing eye.
Best wait: I reach Jerusalem at morn,
There set in order my experiences,
Gather what most deserves and give thee all—
Or I might add, Judea's gum-tragacanth
Scales off in purer flakes, shines clearer-grained,
Cracks 'twixt the pestle and the porphyry,
In fine exceeds our produce.   Scalp-disease
Confounds me, crossing so with leprosy—
Thou hadst admired one sort I gained at Zoar—
But zeal outruns discretion.   Here I end.

   Yet stay: my Syrian blinketh gratefully,
Protesteth his devotion is my price—
Suppose I write what harms not, though he steal?
I half resolve to tell thee, yet I blush,
What set me off a-writing first of all.
An itch I had, a sting to write, a tang!

AN EPISTLE

For, be it this town's barrenness—or else
The Man had something in the look of him—
His case has struck me far more than 'tis worth.
So, pardon if—(lest presently I lose
In the great press of novelty at hand
The care and pains this somehow stole from me)
I bid thee take the thing while fresh in mind,
Almost in sight—for, wilt thou have the truth?
The very man is gone from me but now,
Whose ailment is the subject of discourse.
Thus then, and let thy better wit help all.

'Tis but a case of mania—subinduced
By epilepsy, at the turning-point
Of trance prolonged unduly some three days,
When by the exhibition of some drug
Or spell, exorcisation, stroke of art
Unknown to me and which 'twere well to know,
The evil thing out-breaking all at once
Left the man whole and sound of body indeed,—
But, flinging, so to speak, life's gates too wide,
Making a clear house of it too suddenly,
The first conceit that entered pleased to write
Whatever it was minded on the wall
So plainly at that vantage, as it were,
(First come, first served) that nothing subsequent
Attaineth to erase the fancy-scrawls
Which the returned and new-established soul
Hath gotten now so thoroughly by heart
That henceforth she will read or these or none.
And first—the man's own firm conviction rests
That he was dead (in fact they buried him)
That he was dead and then restored to life
By a Nazarene physician of his tribe:
—'Sayeth, the same bade " Rise," and he did rise.
" Such cases are diurnal," thou wilt cry.
Not so this figment!—not, that such a fume,

AN EPISTLE

Instead of giving way to time and health,
Should eat itself into the life of life,
As saffron tingeth flesh, blood, bones and all!
For see, how he takes up the after-life. ˙
The man—it is one Lazarus a Jew,
Sanguine, proportioned, fifty years of age,
The body's habit wholly laudable,
As much, indeed, beyond the common health
As he were made and put aside to shew.
Think, could we penetrate by any drug
And bathe the wearied soul and worried flesh,
And bring it clear and fair, by three days sleep!
Whence has the man the balm that brightens all?
This grown man eyes the world now like a child.
Some elders of his tribe, I should premise,
Led in their friend, obedient as a sheep,
To bear my inquisition.   While they spoke,
Now sharply, now with sorrow,—told the case,—
He listened not except I spoke to him,
But folded his two hands and let them talk,
Watching the flies that buzzed : and yet no fool.
And that's a sample how his years must go.
Look if a beggar, in fixed middle-life,
Should find a treasure, can he use the same
With straightened habits and with tastes starved small,
And take at once to his impoverished brain
The sudden element that changes things,
—That sets the undreamed-of rapture at his hand,
And puts the cheap old joy in the scorned dust?
Is he not such an one as moves to mirth—
Warily parsimonious, when 's no need,
Wasteful as drunkenness at undue times?
All prudent counsel as to what befits
The golden mean, is lost on such an one.
The man's fantastic will is the man's law.
So here—we 'll call the treasure knowledge, say—
Increased beyond the fleshly faculty—

AN EPISTLE

Heaven opened to a soul while yet on earth,
Earth forced on a soul's use while seeing Heaven.
The man is witless of the size, the sum,
The value in proportion of all things,
Or whether it be little or be much.
Discourse to him of prodigious armaments
Assembled to besiege his city now,
And of the passing of a mule with gourds—
'Tis one!   Then take it on the other side,
Speak of some trifling fact—he will gaze rapt
With stupor at its very littleness—
(Far as I see) as if in that indeed
He caught prodigious import, whole results ;
And so will turn to us the bystanders
In ever the same stupor (note this point)
That we too see not with his opened eyes !
Wonder and doubt come wrongly into play,
Preposterously, at cross purposes.
Should his child sicken unto death,—why, look
For scarce abatement of his cheerfulness,
Or pretermission of his daily craft—
While a word, gesture, glance, from that same child
At play or in the school or laid asleep,
Will start him to an agony of fear,
Exasperation, just as like ! demand
The reason why—"'tis but a word," object—
" A gesture "— he regards thee as our lord
Who lived there in the pyramid alone,
Looked at us, dost thou mind, when being young
We both would unadvisedly recite
Some charm's beginning, from that book of his,
Able to bid the sun throb wide and burst
All into stars, as suns grown old are wont.
Thou and the child have each a veil alike
Thrown o'er your heads from under which ye both
Stretch your blind hands and trifle with a match
Over a mine of Greek fire, did ye know !

AN EPISTLE

He holds on firmly to some thread of life—
(It is the life to lead perforcedly)
Which runs across some vast distracting orb
Of glory on either side that meagre thread,
Which, conscious of, he must not enter yet—
The spiritual life around the earthly life!
The law of that is known to him as this—
His heart and brain move there, his feet stay here.
So is the man perplext with impulses
Sudden to start off crosswise, not straight on,
Proclaiming what is Right and Wrong across—
And not along—this black thread through the
    blaze—
"It should be" balked by "here it cannot be."
And oft the man's soul springs into his face
As if he saw again and heard again
His sage that bade him "Rise" and he did rise.
Something—a word, a tick of the blood within
Admonishes—then back he sinks at once
To ashes, that was very fire before,
In sedulous recurrence to his trade
Whereby he earneth him the daily bread—
And studiously the humbler for that pride,
Professedly the faultier that he knows
God's secret, while he holds the thread of life.
Indeed the especial marking of the man
Is prone submission to the Heavenly will—
Seeing it, what it is, and why it is.
'Sayeth, he will wait patient to the last
For that same death which will restore his being
To equilibrium, body loosening soul
Divorced even now by premature full growth:
He will live, nay, it pleaseth him to live
So long as God please, and just how God please.
He even seeketh not to please God more
(Which meaneth, otherwise) than as God please.
Hence I perceive not he affects to preach

AN EPISTLE

The doctrine of his sect whate'er it be—
Make proselytes as madmen thirst to do.
How can he give his neighbour the real ground,
His own conviction? ardent as he is—
Call his great truth a lie, why still the old
" Be it as God please " reassureth him.
I probed the sore as thy disciple should—
" How, beast," said I, " this stolid carelessness
Sufficeth thee, when Rome is on her march
To stamp out like a little spark thy town,
Thy tribe, thy crazy tale and thee at once ? "
He merely looked with his large eyes on me.
The man is apathetic, you deduce?
Contrariwise he loves both old and young,
Able and weak—affects the very brutes
And birds—how say I ? flowers of the field—
As a wise workman recognises tools
In a master's workshop, loving what they make.
Thus is the man as harmless as a lamb :
Only impatient, let him do his best,
At ignorance and carelessness and sin—
An indignation which is promptly curbed.
As when in certain travels I have feigned
To be an ignoramus in our art
According to some preconceived design,
And happed to hear the land's practitioners
Steeped in conceit sublimed by ignorance,
Prattle fantastically on disease,
Its cause and cure—and I must hold my peace !

Thou wilt object—why have I not ere this
Sought out the sage himself, the Nazarene
Who wrought this cure, enquiring at the source,
Conferring with the frankness that befits ?
Alas ! it grieveth me, the learned leech
Perished in a tumult many years ago,
Accused,—our learning's fate,—of wizardry,

AN EPISTLE

Rebellion, to the setting up a rule
And creed prodigious as described to me.
His death which happened when the earthquake fell
(Prefiguring, as soon appeared, the loss
To occult learning in our lord the sage
That lived there in the pyramid alone)
Was wrought by the mad people—that's their wont—
On vain recourse, as I conjecture it,
To his tried virtue, for miraculous help—
How could he stop the earthquake? That's their way!
The other imputations must be lies:
But take one—though I loathe to give it thee,
In mere respect to any good man's fame!
(And after all our patient Lazarus
Is stark mad—should we count on what he says?
Perhaps not—though in writing to a leech
'Tis well to keep back nothing of a case.)
This man so cured regards the curer then,
As—God forgive me—who but God himself,
Creator and Sustainer of the world,
That came and dwelt in flesh on it awhile!
—'Sayeth that such an One was born and lived,
Taught, healed the sick, broke bread at his own house,
Then died, with Lazarus by, for aught I know,
And yet was . . . what I said nor choose repeat,
And must have so avouched himself, in fact,
In hearing of this very Lazarus
Who saith—but why all this of what he saith?
Why write of trivial matters, things of price
Calling at every moment for remark?
I noticed on the margin of a pool
Blue-flowering borage, the Aleppo sort,
Aboundeth, very nitrous. It is strange!

Thy pardon for this long and tedious case,
Which, now that I review it, needs must seem
Unduly dwelt on, prolixly set forth.

AN EPISTLE

Nor I myself discern in what is writ
Good cause for the peculiar interest
And awe indeed this man has touched me with.
Perhaps the journey's end, the weariness
Had wrought upon me first. I met him thus—
I crossed a ridge of short sharp broken hills
Like an old lion's cheek-teeth. Out there came
A moon made like a face with certain spots
Multiform, manifold, and menacing:
Then a wind rose behind me. So we met
In this old sleepy town at unaware,
The man and I. I send thee what is writ.
Regard it as a chance, a matter risked
To this ambiguous Syrian—he may lose,
Or steal, or give it thee with equal good.
Jerusalem's repose shall make amends
For time this letter wastes, thy time and mine,
Till when, once more thy pardon and farewell!

  The very God! think, Abib; dost thou think?
So, the All-Great, were the All-Loving too—
So, through the thunder comes a human voice
Saying, "O heart I made, a heart beats here!
Face, my hands fashioned, see it in myself.
Thou hast no power nor may'st conceive of mine,
But love I gave thee, with Myself to love,
And thou must love me who have died for thee!"
The madman saith He said so: it is strange.

MESMERISM

♡ ♡

I

ALL I believed is true!
I am able yet
All I want to get
By a method as strange as new:
Dare I trust the same to you?

II

If at night, when doors are shut,
And the wood-worm picks,
And the death-watch ticks,
And the bar has a flag of smut,
And a cat's in the water-butt—

III

And the socket floats and flares,
And the house-beams groan,
And a foot unknown
Is surmised on the garret-stairs,
And the locks slip unawares—

MESMERISM

IV

And the spider, to serve his ends,
    By a sudden thread,
    Arms and legs outspread,
On the table's midst descends,
Comes to find, God knows what friends!—

V

If since eve drew in, I say,
    I have sate and brought
    (So to speak) my thought
To bear on the woman away,
Till I felt my hair turn grey—

VI

Till I seemed to have and hold
    In the vacancy
    'Twixt the wall and me,
From the hair-plait's chestnut-gold
To the foot in its muslin fold—

VII

Have and hold, then and there,
    Her, from head to foot,
    Breathing and mute,
Passive and yet aware,
In the grasp of my steady stare—

VIII

Hold and have, there and then,
    All her body and soul
    That completes my Whole,
All that women add to men,
In the clutch of my steady ken—

MESMERISM

IX

Having and holding, till
    I imprint her fast
    On the void at last
As the sun does whom he will
By the calotypist's skill—

X

Then,—if my heart's strength serve,
    And through all and each
    Of the veils I reach
To her soul and never swerve,
Knitting an iron nerve—

XI

Commanding that to advance
    And inform the shape
    Which has made escape
And before my countenance
Answers me glance for glance—

XII

I, still with a gesture fit
    Of my hands that best
    Do my soul's behest,
Pointing the power from it,
While myself do steadfast sit—

XIII

Steadfast and still the same
    On my object bent
    While the hands gave vent
To my ardour and my aim
And break into very flame—

MESMERISM

XIV

Then, I reach, I must believe,
    Not her soul in vain,
    For to me again
It reaches, and past retrieve
Is wound in the toils I weave—

XV

And must follow as I require,
    As befits a thrall,
    Bringing flesh and all,
Essence and earth-attire,
To the source of the tractile fire—

XVI

Till the house called hers, not mine,
    With a growing weight
    Seems to suffocate
If she break not its leaden line
And escape from its close confine—

XVII

Out of doors into the night!
    On to the maze
    Of the wild wood-ways,
Not turning to left or right
From the pathway, blind with sight—

XVIII

Making thro' rain and wind
    O'er the broken shrubs,
    'Twixt the stems and stubs,
With a still composed strong mind,
Not a care for the world behind—

MESMERISM

XIX

Swifter and still more swift,
    As the crowding peace
    Doth to joy increase
In the wide blind eyes uplift,
Thro' the darkness and the drift!

XX

While I—to the shape, I too
    Feel my soul dilate
    Nor a whit abate
And relax not a gesture due
As I see my belief come true—

XXI

For there! have I drawn or no
    Life to that lip?
    Do my fingers dip
In a flame which again they throw
On the cheek that breaks a-glow?

XXII

Ha! was the hair so first?
    What, unfilleted,
    Made alive, and spread
Through the void with a rich outburst,
Chestnut gold-interspersed!

XXIII

Like the doors of a casket-shrine,
    See, on either side,
    Her two arms divide
Till the heart betwixt makes sign,
Take me, for I am thine!

MESMERISM

Now—now—the door is heard
  Hark! the stairs and near—
  Nearer—and here—
Now! and at call the third
She enters without a word.

XXV

On doth she march and on
  To the fancied shape—
  It is past escape
Herself, now—the dream is done
And the shadow and she are one.

XXVI

First I will pray. Do Thou
  That ownest the soul,
  Yet wilt grant control
To another nor disallow
For a time, restrain me now!

XXVII

I admonish me while I may,
  Not to squander guilt,
  Since require Thou wilt
At my hand its price one day!
What the price is, who can say?

A SERENADE AT THE VILLA

I

THAT was I, you heard last night
  When there rose no moon at all,
Nor, to pierce the strained and tight
  Tent of heaven, a planet small:
Life was dead, and so was light.

II

Not a twinkle from the fly,
  Not a glimmer from the worm.
When the crickets stopped their cry,
  When the owls forbore a term,
You heard music; that was I.

III

Earth turned in her sleep with pain,
  Sultrily suspired for proof:
In at heaven and out again,
  Lightning!—where it broke the roof,
Bloodlike, some few drops of rain.

IV

What they could my words expressed,
  O my love, my all, my one!
Singing helped the verses best,
  And when singing's best was done,
To my lute I left the rest.

V

So wore night; the east was grey,
  White the broad-faced hemlock flowers;
Soon would come another day;
  Ere its first of heavy hours
Found me, I had past away.

A SERENADE AT THE VILLA

VI

What became of all the hopes,
   Words and song and lute as well?
Say, this struck you—"When life gropes
   Feebly for the path where fell
Light last on the evening slopes,

VII

"One friend in that path shall be
   To secure my steps from wrong;
One to count night day for me,
   Patient through the watches long,
Serving most with none to see."

VIII

Never say—as something bodes—
   "So the worst has yet a worse!
When life halts 'neath double loads,
   Better the task-master's curse
Than such music on the roads!

IX

"When no moon succeeds the sun,
   Nor can pierce the midnight's tent
Any star, the smallest one,
   While some drops, where lightning went,
Show the final storm begun—

X

"When the fire-fly hides its spot,
   When the garden-voices fail
In the darkness thick and hot,—
   Shall another voice avail,
That shape be where those are not?

MY STAR

XI

" Has some plague a longer lease
 Proffering its help uncouth?
Can't one even die in peace?
 As one shuts one's eyes on youth,
Is that face the last one sees?"

XII

Oh, how dark your villa was,
 Windows fast and obdurate!
How the garden grudged me grass
 Where I stood—the iron gate
Ground its teeth to let me pass!

MY STAR

ALL that I know
 Of a certain star,
Is, it can throw
 (Like the angled spar)
Now a dart of red,
 Now a dart of blue,
Till my friends have said
 They would fain see, too,
My star that dartles the red and the blue!
Then it stops like a bird,—like a flower, hangs furled;
 They must solace themselves with the Saturn above it.
What matter to me if their star is a world?
 Mine has opened its soul to me; therefore I love it.

INSTANS TYRANNVS

I

Of the million or two, more or less,
I rule and possess,
One man, for some cause undefined,
Was least to my mind.

II

I struck him, he grovelled of course—
For, what was his force?
I pinned him to earth with my weight
And persistence of hate—
And he lay, would not moan, would not curse,
As if lots might be worse.

III

" Were the object less mean, would he stand
At the swing of my hand!
For obscurity helps him and blots
The hole where he squats."
So I set my five wits on the stretch
To inveigle the wretch.
All in vain! gold and jewels I threw,
Still he couched there perdue.
I tempted his blood and his flesh,
Hid in roses my mesh,
Choicest cates and the flagon's best spilth—
Still he kept to his filth!

208

INSTANS TYRANNUS

IV

Had he kith now or kin, were access
To his heart, if I press—
Just a son or a mother to seize—
No such booty as these!
Were it simply a friend to pursue
'Mid my million or two,
Who could pay me in person or pelf
What he owes me himself.
No! I could not but smile through my chafe—
For the fellow lay safe
As his mates do, the midge and the nit,
—Through minuteness, to wit.

V

Then a humour more great took its place
At the thought of his face,
The droop, the low cares of the mouth,
The trouble uncouth
'Twixt the brows, all that air one is fain
To put out of its pain—
And, no, I admonished myself,
" Is one mocked by an elf,
Is one baffled by toad or by rat?
The gravamen's in that!
How the lion, who crouches to suit
His back to my foot,
Would admire that I stand in debate!
But the Small is the Great
If it vexes you,—that is the thing!
Toad or rat vex the King?
Though I waste half my realm to unearth
Toad or rat, 'tis well worth!"

VI

So I soberly laid my last plan
To extinguish the man.

INSTANS TYRANNUS

Round his creep-hole,—with never a break
Ran my fires for his sake;
Over-head, did my thunders combine
With my under-ground mine:
Till I looked from my labour content
To enjoy the event.

VII

When sudden . . . how think ye, the end?
Did I say "without friend"?
Say rather, from marge to blue marge
The whole sky grew his targe
With the sun's self for visible boss,
While an Arm ran across
Which the earth heaved beneath like a breast
Where the wretch was safe prest!
Do you see? just my vengeance complete,
The man sprang to his feet,
Stood erect, caught at God's skirts, and prayed!
—So, *I* was afraid!

A PRETTY WOMAN

A PRETTY WOMAN

I

THAT fawn-skin-dappled hair of hers,
    And the blue eye
    Dear and dewy,
And that infantine fresh air of hers!

II

To think men cannot take you, Sweet,
    And enfold you,
    Ay, and hold you,
And so keep you what they make you, Sweet!

III

You like us for a glance, you know—
    For a word's sake,
    Or a sword's sake,
All 's the same, whate'er the chance, you know.

IV

And in turn we make you ours, we say—
    You and youth too,
    Eyes and mouth too,
All the face composed of flowers, we say.

V

All 's our own, to make the most of, Sweet—
    Sing and say for,
    Watch and pray for,
Keep a secret or go boast of, Sweet.

VI

But for loving, why, you would not, Sweet,
    Though we prayed you,
    Paid you, brayed you
In a mortar—for you could not, Sweet.

A PRETTY WOMAN

VII

So, we leave the sweet face fondly there—
    Be its beauty
    Its sole duty!
Let all hope of grace beyond, lie there!

VIII

And while the face lies quiet there,
    Who shall wonder
    That I ponder
A conclusion?   I will try it there.

IX

As,—why must one, for the love forgone,
    Scout mere liking?
    Thunder-striking
Earth,—the heaven, we looked above for, gone!

X

Why with beauty, needs there money be—
    Love with liking?
    Crush the fly-king
In his gauze, because no honey bee?

XI

May not liking be so simple-sweet,
    If love grew there
    'Twould undo there
All that breaks the cheek to dimples sweet?

XII

Is the creature too imperfect, say?
    Would you mend it
    And so end it?
Since not all addition perfects aye!

XIII

Or is it of its kind, perhaps,
    Just perfection—
    Whence, rejection
Of a grace not to its mind, perhaps?

A PRETTY WOMAN

XIV

Shall we burn up, tread that face at once
    Into tinder,
    And so hinder
Sparks from kindling all the place at once?

XV

Or else kiss away one's soul on her?
    Your love-fancies!—
    A sick man sees
Truer, when his hot eyes roll on her!

XVI

Thus the craftsman thinks to grace the rose,—
    Plucks a mould-flower
    For his gold flower,
Uses fine things that efface the rose.

XVII

Rosy rubies make its cup more rose,
    Precious metals
    Ape the petals,—
Last, some old king locks it up, morose!

XVIII

Then, how grace a rose?   I know a way!
    Leave it rather.
    Must you gather?
Smell, kiss, wear it—at last, throw away!

CHILDE ROLAND

"CHILDE ROLAND TO THE DARK TOWER CAME"

(See Edgar's Song in "Lear")

I

My first thought was, he lied in every word,
  That hoary cripple, with malicious eye
  Askance to watch the working of his lie
On mine, and mouth scarce able to afford
Suppression of the glee that pursed and scored
  Its edge at one more victim gained thereby.

II

What else should he be set for, with his staff?
  What, save to waylay with his lies, ensnare
  All travellers that might find him posted there,
And ask the road? I guessed what skull-like laugh
Would break, what crutch 'gin write my epitaph
  For pastime in the dusty thoroughfare,

III

If at his counsel I should turn aside
  Into that ominous tract which, all agree,
  Hides the Dark Tower. Yet acquiescingly
I did turn as he pointed ; neither pride
Nor hope rekindling at the end descried,
  So much as gladness that some end should be.

IV

For, what with my whole world-wide wandering,
  What with my search drawn out thro' years, my hope
  Dwindled into a ghost not fit to cope
With that obstreperous joy success would bring,—
I hardly tried now to rebuke the spring
  My heart made, finding failure in its scope.

CHILDE ROLAND
TO THE
DARK TOWER CAME

CHILDE ROLAND

V

As when a sick man very near to death
  Seems dead indeed, and feels begin and end
  The tears and takes the farewell of each friend,
And hears one bid the other go, draw breath
Freelier outside, ("since all is o'er," he saith,
  "And the blow fall'n no grieving can amend")

VI

While some discuss if near the other graves
  Be room enough for this, and when a day
  Suits best for carrying the corpse away,
With care about the banners, scarves and staves,—
And still the man hears all, and only craves
  He may not shame such tender love and stay.

VII

Thus I had so long suffered in this quest,
  Heard failure prophesied so oft, been writ
  So many times among "The Band"—to wit,
The knights who to the Dark Tower's search addressed
Their steps—that just to fail as they, seemed best,
  And all the doubt was now—should I be fit.

VIII

So, quiet as despair, I turned from him,
  That hateful cripple, out of his highway
  Into the path he pointed.   All the day
Had been a dreary one at best, and dim
Was settling to its close, yet shot one grim
  Red leer to see the plain catch its estray.

IX

For mark! no sooner was I fairly found
  Pledged to the plain, after a pace or two,
  Than pausing to throw backward a last view

CHILDE ROLAND

To the safe road, 'twas gone! grey plain all round!
Nothing but plain to the horizon's bound.
  I might go on; nought else remained to do.

X

So on I went. I think I never saw
  Such starved ignoble nature; nothing throve:
  For flowers—as well expect a cedar grove!
But cockle, spurge, according to their law
Might propagate their kind, with none to awe,
  You'd think: a burr had been a treasure-trove.

XI

No! penury, inertness, and grimace,
  In some strange sort, were the land's portion. "See
  Or shut your eyes"—said Nature peevishly—
"It nothing skills: I cannot help my case:
The Judgment's fire alone can cure this place,
  Calcine its clods and set my prisoners free."

XII

If there pushed any ragged thistle-stalk
  Above its mates, the head was chopped—the bents
  Were jealous else. What made those holes and rents
In the dock's harsh swarth leaves—bruised as to baulk
All hope of greenness? 'tis a brute must walk
  Pashing their life out, with a brute's intents.

XIII

As for the grass, it grew as scant as hair
  In leprosy—thin dry blades pricked the mud
  Which underneath looked kneaded up with blood.
One stiff blind horse, his every bone a-stare,
Stood stupefied, however he came there—
  Thrust out past service from the devil's stud!

CHILDE ROLAND

XIV

Alive? he might be dead for all I know,
  With that red gaunt and colloped neck a-strain,
  And shut eyes underneath the rusty mane.
Seldom went such grotesqueness with such woe:
I never saw a brute I hated so—
  He must be wicked to deserve such pain.

XV

I shut my eyes and turned them on my heart.
  As a man calls for wine before he fights,
  I asked one draught of earlier, happier sights
Ere fitly I could hope to play my part.
Think first, fight afterwards—the soldier's art:
  One taste of the old times sets all to rights!

XVI

Not it! I fancied Cuthbert's reddening face
  Beneath its garniture of curly gold,
  Dear fellow, till I almost felt him fold
An arm in mine to fix me to the place,
That way he used.   Alas! one night's disgrace!
  Out went my heart's new fire and left it cold.

XVII

Giles, then, the soul of honoúr—there he stands
  Frank as ten years ago when knighted first.
  What honest men should dare (he said) he durst.
Good—but the scene shifts—faugh! what hangman's hands
Pin to his breast a parchment? his own bands
  Read it.   Poor traitor, spit upon and curst!

XVIII

Better this present than a past like that—
  Back therefore to my darkening path again.
  No sound, no sight as far as eye could strain.

CHILDE ROLAND

Will the night send a howlet or a bat?
I asked: when something on the dismal flat
 Came to arrest my thoughts and change their train.

XIX

A sudden little river crossed my path
 As unexpected as a serpent comes.
 No sluggish tide congenial to the glooms—
This, as it frothed by, might have been a bath
For the fiend's glowing hoof—to see the wrath
 Of its black eddy bespate with flakes and spumes.

XX

So petty yet so spiteful! all along,
 Low scrubby alders kneeled down over it;
 Drenched willows flung them headlong in a fit
Of mute despair, a suicidal throng:
The river which had done them all the wrong,
 Whate'er that was, rolled by, deterred no whit.

XXI

Which, while I forded,—good saints, how I feared
 To set my foot upon a dead man's cheek,
 Each step, or feel the spear I thrust to seek
For hollows, tangled in his hair or beard!
—It may have been a water-rat I speared,
 But, ugh! it sounded like a baby's shriek.

XXII

Glad was I when I reached the other bank.
 Now for a better country. Vain presage!
 Who were the strugglers, what war did they wage
Whose savage trample thus could pad the dank
Soil to a plash? toads in a poisoned tank,
 Or wild cats in a red-hot iron cage—

CHILDE ROLAND

XXIII

The fight must so have seemed in that fell cirque.
  What kept them there, with all the plain to choose?
  No foot-print leading to that horrid mews,
None out of it: mad brewage set to work
Their brains, no doubt, like galley-slaves the Turk
  Pits for his pastime, Christians against Jews.

XXIV

And more than that—a furlong on—why, there!
  What bad use was that engine for, that wheel,
  Or brake, not wheel—that harrow fit to reel
Men's bodies out like silk? with all the air
Of Tophet's tool, on earth left unaware,
  Or brought to sharpen its rusty teeth of steel.

XXV

Then came a bit of stubbed ground, once a wood,
  Next a marsh, it would seem, and now mere earth
  Desperate and done with; (so a fool finds mirth,
Makes a thing and then mars it, till his mood
Changes and off he goes!) within a rood
  Bog, clay and rubble, sand and stark black dearth.

XXVI

Now blotches rankling, coloured gay and grim,
  Now patches where some leanness of the soil's
  Broke into moss or substances like boils;
Then came some palsied oak, a cleft in him
Like a distorted mouth that splits its rim
  Gaping at death, and dies while it recoils.

XXVII

And just as far as ever from the end!
  Nought in the distance but the evening, nought
  To point my footstep further! At the thought,

221

CHILDE ROLAND

A great black bird, Apollyon's bosom-friend,
Sailed past, nor beat his wide wing dragon-penned
   That brushed my cap—perchance the guide I sought.

XXVIII

For looking up, aware I somehow grew,
  'Spite of the dusk, the plain had given place
  All round to mountains—with such name to grace
Mere ugly heights and heaps now stol'n in view.
How thus they had surprised me,—solve it, you!
  How to get from them was no plainer case.

XXIX

Yet half I seemed to recognise some trick
  Of mischief happened to me, God knows when—
  In a bad dream perhaps. Here ended, then,
Progress this way. When, in the very nick
Of giving up, one time more, came a click
  As when a trap shuts—you're inside the den!

XXX

Burningly it came on me all at once,
  This was the place! those two hills on the right
  Crouched like two bulls locked horn in horn in fight—
While to the left, a tall scalped mountain . . . Dunce,
Fool, to be dozing at the very nonce,
  After a life spent training for the sight!

XXXI

What in the midst lay but the Tower itself?
  The round squat turret, blind as the fool's heart,
  Built of brown stone, without a counterpart
In the whole world. The tempest's mocking elf
Points to the shipman thus the unseen shelf
  He strikes on, only when the timbers start.

CHILDE ROLAND

XXXII

Not see? because of night perhaps?—Why, day
  Came back again for that! before it left,
  The dying sunset kindled through a cleft:
The hills, like giants at a hunting, lay—
Chin upon hand, to see the game at bay,—
  "Now stab and end the creature—to the heft!"

XXXIII

Not hear? when noise was everywhere? it tolled
  Increasing like a bell. Names in my ears,
  Of all the lost adventurers my peers,—
How such a one was strong, and such was bold,
And such was fortunate, yet each of old
  Lost, lost! one moment knelled the woe of years.

XXXIV

There they stood, ranged along the hill-sides—met
  To view the last of me, a living frame
  For one more picture! in a sheet of flame
I saw them and I knew them all. And yet
Dauntless the slug-horn to my lips I set
  And blew. "*Childe Roland to the Dark Tower came.*"

RESPECTABILITY

I

DEAR, had the world in its caprice
  Deigned to proclaim " I know you both,
  Have recognised your plighted troth,
Am sponsor for you—live in peace!"—
How many precious months and years
  Of youth had passed, that speed so fast,
  Before we found it out at last,
The world, and what it fears?

II

How much of priceless life were spent
  With men that every virtue decks,
  And women models of their sex,
Society's true ornament,—
Ere we dared wander, nights like this,
  Thro' wind and rain, and watch the Seine,
  And feel the Boulevart break again
To warmth and light and bliss?

III

I know! the world proscribes not love;
  Allows my finger to caress
  Your lip's contour and downiness,
Provided it supply a glove.
The world's good word!—the Institute!
  Guizot receives Montalembert!
  Eh? down the court three lampions flare—
Put forward your best foot!

I

So far as our story approaches the end,
  Which do you pity the most of us three?
My friend, or the mistress of my friend
  With her wanton eyes, or me?

II

My friend was already too good to lose,
  And seemed in the way of improvement yet,
When she crossed his path with her hunting-noose
  And over him drew her net.

III

When I saw him tangled in her toils,
  A shame, said I, if she adds just him
To her nine-and-ninety other spoils,
  The hundredth, for a whim!

IV

And before my friend be wholly hers,
  How easy to prove to him, I said,
An eagle's the game her pride prefers,
  Though she snaps at the wren instead!

A LIGHT WOMAN

So I gave her eyes my own eyes to take,
  My hand sought hers as in earnest need,
And round she turned for my noble sake,
  And gave me herself indeed.

The eagle am I, with my fame in the world,
  The wren is he, with his maiden face.
—You look away and your lip is curled?
  Patience, a moment's space!

For see—my friend goes shaking and white;
  He eyes me as the basilisk:
I have turned, it appears, his day to night,
  Eclipsing his sun's disc.

And I did it, he thinks, as a very thief:
  "Though I love her—that he comprehends—
One should master one's passions, (love, in chief)
  And be loyal to one's friends!"

And she,—she lies in my hand as tame
  As a pear hung basking over a wall;
Just a touch to try and off it came;
  'Tis mine,—can I let it fall?

With no mind to eat it, that's the worst!
  Were it thrown in the road, would the case assist?
'Twas quenching a dozen blue-flies' thirst
  When I gave its stalk a twist.

A LIGHT WOMAN

XI

And I,—what I seem to my friend, you see—
  What I soon shall seem to his love, you guess.
What I seem to myself, do you ask of me?
  No hero, I confess.

XII

'Tis an awkward thing to play with souls,
  And matter enough to save one's own.
Yet think of my friend, and the burning coals
  He played with for bits of stone!

XIII

One likes to show the truth for the truth;
  That the woman was light is very true:
But suppose she says,—never mind that youth—
  What wrong have I done to you?

XIV

Well, any how, here the story stays,
  So far at least as I understand;
And, Robert Browning, you writer of plays,
  Here's a subject made to your hand!

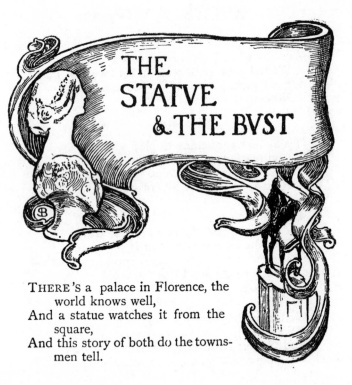

THE STATVE & THE BVST

THERE'S a palace in Florence, the
  world knows well,
And a statue watches it from the
  square,
And this story of both do the towns-
  men tell.

Ages ago, a lady there,
At the farthest window facing the east
Asked, "Who rides by with the royal air?"

The brides-maids' prattle around her ceased;
She leaned forth, one on either hand;
They saw how the blush of the bride increased—

They felt by its beats her heart expand—
As one at each ear and both in a breath
Whispered, "The Great-Duke Ferdinand."

THE STATUE AND THE BUST

That selfsame instant, underneath,
The Duke rode past in his idle way,
Empty and fine like a swordless sheath.

Gay he rode, with a friend as gay,
Till he threw his head back—" Who is she? "
—" A Bride the Riccardi brings home to-day."

Hair in heaps laid heavily
Over a pale brow spirit-pure—
Carved like the heart of the coal-black tree,

Crisped like a war-steed's encolure—
Which vainly sought to dissemble her eyes
Of the blackest black our eyes endure.

And lo, a blade for a knight's emprise
Filled the fine empty sheath of a man,—
The Duke grew straightway brave and wise.

He looked at her, as a lover can ;
She looked at him, as one who awakes,—
The past was a sleep, and her life began.

As love so ordered for both their sakes,
A feast was held that selfsame night
In the pile which the mighty shadow makes.

(For Via Larga is three-parts light,
But the Palace overshadows one,
Because of a crime which may God requite !

To Florence and God the wrong was done,
Through the first republic's murder there
By Cosimo and his cursed son.)

THE STATUE AND THE BUST

The Duke (with the statue's face in the square)
Turned in the midst of his multitude
At the bright approach of the bridal pair.

Face to face the lovers stood
A single minute and no more,
While the bridegroom bent as a man subdued—

Bowed till his bonnet brushed the floor—
For the Duke on the lady a kiss conferred,
As the courtly custom was of yore.

In a minute can lovers exchange a word?
If a word did pass, which I do not think,
Only one out of the thousand heard.

That was the bridegroom.   At day's brink
He and his bride were alone at last
In a bed-chamber by a taper's blink.

Calmly he said that her lot was cast,
That the door she had passed was shut on her
Till the final catafalk repassed.

The world meanwhile, its noise and stir,
Through a certain window facing the east
She might watch like a convent's chronicler.

Since passing the door might lead to a feast,
And a feast might lead to so much beside,
He, of many evils, chose the least.

" Freely I choose too," said the bride—
" Your window and its world suffice."
So replied the tongue, while the heart replied—

THE STATUE AND THE BUST

" If I spend the night with that devil twice,
May his window serve as my loop of hell
Whence a damned soul looks on Paradise !

" I fly to the Duke who loves me well,
Sit by his side and laugh at sorrow
Ere I count another ave-bell.

" 'Tis only the coat of a page to borrow,
And tie my hair in a horse-boy's trim,
And I save my soul—but not to-morrow "—

(She checked herself and her eye grew dim)—
" My father tarries to bless my state :
I must keep it one day more for him.

" Is one day more so long to wait ?
Moreover the Duke rides past, I know—
We shall see each other, sure as fate."

She turned on her side and slept.   Just so !
So we resolve on a thing and sleep.
So did the lady, ages ago.

That night the Duke said, " Dear or cheap
As the cost of this cup of bliss may prove
To body or soul, I will drain it deep."

And on the morrow, bold with love,
He beckoned the bridegroom (close on call,
As his duty bade, by the Duke's alcove)

And smiled " ' Twas a very funeral
Your lady will think, this feast of ours,—
A shame to efface, whate'er befall !

THE STATUE AND THE BUST

"What if we break from the Arno bowers,
And let Petraja, cool and green,
Cure last night's fault with this morning's flowers?"

The bridegroom, not a thought to be seen
On his steady brow and quiet mouth,
Said, "Too much favour for me so mean!

"Alas! my lady leaves the south.
Each wind that comes from the Apennine
Is a menace to her tender youth.

"No way exists, the wise opine,
If she quits her palace twice this year,
To avert the flower of life's decline."

Quoth the Duke, "A sage and a kindly fear.
Moreover Petraja is cold this spring—
Be our feast to-night as usual here!"

And then to himself—"Which night shall bring
Thy bride to her lover's embraces, fool—
Or I am the fool, and thou art his king!

"Yet my passion must wait a night, nor cool—
For to-night the Envoy arrives from France,
Whose heart I unlock with thyself, my tool.

"I need thee still and might miss perchance.
To-day is not wholly lost, beside,
With its hope of my lady's countenance—

"For I ride—what should I do but ride?
And passing her palace, if I list,
May glance at its window—well betide!"

THE STATUE AND THE BUST

So said, so done: nor the lady missed
One ray that broke from the ardent brow,
Nor a curl of the lips where the spirit kissed.

Be sure that each renewed the vow,
No morrow's sun should arise and set
And leave them then as it left them now.

But next day passed, and next day yet,
With still fresh cause to wait once more
Ere each leaped over the parapet.

And still, as love's brief morning wore,
With a gentle start, half smile, half sigh,
They found love not as it seemed before.

They thought it would work infallibly,
But not in despite of heaven and earth—
The rose would blow when the storm passed by.

Meantime they could profit in winter's dearth
By winter's fruits that supplant the rose:
The world and its ways have a certain worth!

And to press a point while these oppose
Were a simple policy—best wait,
And lose no friends and gain no foes

Meanwhile, worse fates than a lover's fate,
Who daily may ride and lean and look
Where his lady watches behind the grate!

And she—she watched the square like a book
Holding one picture and only one,
Which daily to find she undertook.

THE STATUE AND THE BUST

When the picture was reached the book was done,
And she turned from it all night to scheme
Of tearing it out for herself next sun.

Weeks grew months, years—gleam by gleam
The glory dropped from youth and love,
And both perceived they had dreamed a dream,

Which hovered as dreams do, still above,—
But who can take a dream for truth?
Oh, hide our eyes from the next remove!

One day as the lady saw her youth
Depart, and the silver thread that streaked
Her hair, and, worn by the serpent's tooth,

The brow so puckered, the chin so peaked,—
And wondered who the woman was,
So hollow-eyed and haggard-cheeked,

Fronting her silent in the glass—
" Summon here," she suddenly said,
" Before the rest of my old self pass,

" Him, the Carver, a hand to aid,
Who moulds the clay no love will change,
And fixes a beauty never to fade.

" Let Robbia's craft so apt and strange
Arrest the remains of young and fair,
And rivet them while the seasons range.

" Make me a face on the window there
Waiting as ever, mute the while,
My love to pass below in the square!

THE STATUE AND THE BUST

" And let me think that it may beguile
Dreary days which the dead must spend
Down in their darkness under the aisle—

" To say,—' What matters at the end?
I did no more while my heart was warm,
Than does that image, my pale-faced friend.'

" Where is the use of the lip's red charm,
The heaven of hair, the pride of the brow,
And the blood that blues the inside arm—

Unless we turn, as the soul knows how,
The earthly gift to an end divine?
A lady of clay is as good, I trow."

But long ere Robbia's cornice, fine
With flowers and fruits which leaves enlace,
Was set where now is the empty shrine—

(With, leaning out of a bright blue space,
As a ghost might from a chink of sky,
The passionate pale lady's face—

Eyeing ever with earnest eye
And quick-turned neck at its breathless stretch,
Some one who ever passes by—)

The Duke sighed like the simplest wretch
In Florence, " So, my dream escapes!
Will its record stay?"   And he bade them fetch

Some subtle fashioner of shapes—
" Can the soul, the will, die out of a man
Ere his body find the grave that gapes?

THE STATUE AND THE BUST

THAT MEN MAY ADMIRE

"John of Douay shall work my plan,
Mould me on horseback here aloft,
Alive—(the subtle artisan!)

"In the very square I cross so oft!
That men may admire, when future suns
Shall touch the eyes to a purpose soft,

"While the mouth and the brow are brave in bronze—
Admire and say, 'When he was alive,
How he would take his pleasure once!'

"And it shall go hard but I contrive
To listen meanwhile and laugh in my tomb
At indolence which aspires to strive."

So! while these wait the trump of doom,
How do their spirits pass, I wonder,
Nights and days in the narrow room?

Still, I suppose, they sit and ponder
What a gift life was, ages ago,
Six steps out of the chapel yonder.

THE STATUE AND THE BUST

Surely they see not God, I know,
Nor all that chivalry of His,
The soldier-saints who, row on row,

Burn upward each to his point of bliss—
Since, the end of life being manifest,
He had cut his way thro' the world to this.

I hear your reproach—" But delay was best,
For their end was a crime!"—Oh, a crime will do
As well, I reply, to serve for a test,

As a virtue golden through and through,
Sufficient to vindicate itself
And prove its worth at a moment's view.

Must a game be played for the sake of pelf?
Where a button goes, 'twere an epigram
To offer the stamp of the very Guelph.

The true has no value beyond the sham.
As well the counter as coin, I submit,
When your table's a hat, and your prize, a dram.

Stake your counter as boldly every whit,
Venture as truly, use the same skill,
Do your best, whether winning or losing it,

If you choose to play—is my principle!
Let a man contend to the uttermost
For his life's set prize, be it what it will!

The counter our lovers staked was lost
As surely as if it were lawful coin:
And the sin I impute to each frustrate ghost

THE STATUE AND THE BUST

Was, the unlit lamp and the ungirt loin
Though the end in sight was a crime, I say.
You of the virtue, (we issue join)
How strive you? *De te, fabula!*

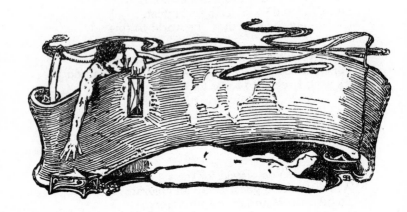

LOVE IN A LIFE

I

ROOM after room,
I hunt the house through
We inhabit together.
Heart, fear nothing, for, heart, thou shalt find her,
Next time, herself!—not the trouble behind her
Left in the curtain, the couch's perfume!
As she brushed it, the cornice-wreath blossomed anew,—
Yon looking-glass gleamed at the wave of her feather.

LIFE IN A LOVE

II

Yet the day wears,
And door succeeds door;
I try the fresh fortune—
Range the wide house from the wing to the centre.
Still the same chance! she goes out as I enter.
Spend my whole day in the quest,—who cares?
But 'tis twilight, you see,—with such suites to explore,
Such closets to search, such alcoves to importune!

LIFE IN A LOVE

ESCAPE me?
Never—
Beloved!
While I am I, and you are you,
   So long as the world contains us both,
   Me the loving and you the loth,
While the one eludes, must the other pursue.
My life is a fault at last, I fear—
   It seems too much like a fate, indeed!
   Though I do my best I shall scarce succeed—
But what if I fail of my purpose here?
It is but to keep the nerves at strain,
   To dry one's eyes and laugh at a fall,
And baffled, get up to begin again,—
   So the chace takes up one's life, that's all.
While, look but once from your farthest bound,
   At me so deep in the dust and dark,
No sooner the old hope drops to ground
   Than a new one, straight to the self-same mark,
      I shape me—
      Ever
      Removed!

HOW IT STRIKES A CONTEMPORARY

I ONLY knew one poet in my life:
And this, or something like it, was his way.

You saw go up and down Valladolid,
A man of mark, to know next time you saw.
His very serviceable suit of black
Was courtly once and conscientious still,
And many might have worn it, though none did:
The cloak that somewhat shone and shewed the threads
Had purpose, and the ruff, significance.
He walked and tapped the pavement with his cane,
Scenting the world, looking it full in face,
An old dog, bald and blindish, at his heels.
They turned up, now, the alley by the church,
That leads no whither; now, they breathed themselves
On the main promenade just at the wrong time.
You 'd come upon his scrutinising hat,
Making a peaked shade blacker than itself
Against the single window spared some house
Intact yet with its mouldered Moorish work,—
Or else surprise the ferrel of his stick
Trying the mortar's temper 'tween the chinks
Of some new shop a-building, French and fine.
He stood and watched the cobbler at his trade,
The man who slices lemons into drink,
The coffee-roaster's brazier, and the boys
That volunteer to help him turn its winch.
He glanced o'er books on stalls with half an eye,
And fly-leaf ballads on the vendor's string,
And broad-edge bold-print posters by the wall.
He took such cognisance of men and things,
If any beat a horse, you felt he saw ;
If any cursed a woman, he took note ;

240

HOW IT STRIKES A CONTEMPORARY

Yet stared at nobody,—they stared at him,
And found, less to their pleasure than surprise,
He seemed to know them and expect as much.
So, next time that a neighbour's tongue was loosed,
It marked the shameful and notorious fact,
We had among us, not so much a spy,
As a recording chief-inquisitor,
The town's true master if the town but knew!
We merely kept a Governor for form,
While this man walked about and took account
Of all thought, said, and acted, then went home,
And wrote it fully to our Lord the King
Who has an itch to know things, He knows why,
And reads them in His bed-room of a night.
Oh, you might smile! there wanted not a touch,
A tang of . . . well, it was not wholly ease
As back into your mind the man's look came—
Stricken in years a little,—such a brow
His eyes had to live under!—clear as flint
On either side the formidable nose
Curved, cut, and coloured, like an eagle's claw.
Had he to do with A.'s surprising fate?
When altogether old B. disappeared
And young C. got his mistress,—was 't our friend,
His letter to the King, that did it all?
What paid the bloodless man for so much pains?
Our Lord the King has favourites manifold,
And shifts his ministry some once a month;
Our city gets new Governors at whiles,—
But never word or sign, that I could hear,
Notified to this man about the streets
The King's approval of those letters conned
The last thing duly at the dead of night.
Did the man love his office? frowned our Lord,
Exhorting when none heard—"Beseech me not!
Too far above my people,—beneath Me!
I set the watch,—how should the people know?

HOW IT STRIKES A CONTEMPORARY

Forget them, keep Me all the more in mind!"
Was some such understanding 'twixt the Two?

I found no truth in one report at least—
That if you tracked him to his home, down lanes
Beyond the Jewry, and as clean to pace,
You found he ate his supper in a room
Blazing with lights, four Titians on the wall,
And twenty naked girls to change his plate!
Poor man, he lived another kind of life
In that new, stuccoed, third house by the bridge,
Fresh-painted, rather smart than otherwise!
The whole street might o'erlook him as he sat,
Leg crossing leg, one foot on the dog's back,
Playing a decent cribbage with his maid
(Jacynth, you 're sure her name was) o'er the cheese
And fruit, three red halves of starved winter-pears,
Or treat of radishes in April! nine—
Ten, struck the church clock, straight to bed went he.

My father, like the man of sense he was,
Would point him out to me a dozen times;
"St—St," he 'd whisper, "the Corregidor!"
I had been used to think that personage
Was one with lacquered breeches, lustrous belt,
And feathers like a forest in his hat,
Who blew a trumpet and proclaimed the news,
Announced the bull-fights, gave each church its turn,
And memorized the miracle in vogue!
He had a great observance from us boys—
I was in error; that was not the man.

I 'd like now, yet had haply been afraid,
To have just looked, when this man came to die,
And seen who lined the clean gay garret's sides
And stood about the neat low truckle-bed,
With the heavenly manner of relieving guard.

RVMOVR

BYAM·SHAW

'I·FOVND·NO
TRVTH·IN
ONE·REPORT
AT·LEAST·'

HOW IT STRIKES A CONTEMPORARY

Here had been, mark, the general-in-chief,
Thro' a whole campaign of the world's life and death,
Doing the King's work all the dim day long,
In his old coat, and up to his knees in mud,
Smoked like a herring, dining on a crust,—
And now the day was won, relieved at once!
No further show or need for that old coat,
You are sure, for one thing! Bless us, all the while
How sprucely we are dressed out, you and I!
A second, and the angels alter that.
Well, I could never write a verse,—could you?
Let's to the Prado and make the most of time.

A · DECENT · GAME · OF · CRIBBAGE
WITH · HIS · MAID

RYAM · SHA

THE LAST RIDE TOGETHER

I

I SAID—Then, dearest, since 'tis so,
Since now at length my fate I know,
Since nothing all my love avails,
Since all my life seemed meant for, fails,
    Since this was written and needs must be—
My whole heart rises up to bless
Your name in pride and thankfulness!
Take back the hope you gave,—I claim
Only a memory of the same,
—And this beside, if you will not blame,
    Your leave for one more last ride with me.

II

My mistress bent that brow of hers,
Those deep dark eyes where pride demurs
When pity would be softening through,
Fixed me a breathing-while or two
    With life or death in the balance—Right!
The blood replenished me again:
My last thought was at least not vain.
I and my mistress, side by side
Shall be together, breathe and ride,
So one day more am I deified.
    Who knows but the world may end to-night?

III

Hush! if you saw some western cloud
All billowy-bosomed, over-bowed
By many benedictions—sun's
And moon's and evening-star's at once—
    And so, you, looking and loving best,
Conscious grew, your passion drew
Cloud, sunset, moonrise, star-shine too

246

THE
LAST RIDE·TOGETHER

THE LAST RIDE TOGETHER

Down on you, near and yet more near,
Till flesh must fade for heaven was here!—
Thus leant she and lingered—joy and fear!
   Thus lay she a moment on my breast.

IV

Then we began to ride. My soul
Smoothed itself out, a long-cramped scroll
Freshening and fluttering in the wind.
Past hopes already lay behind.
   What need to strive with a life awry?
Had I said that, had I done this,
So might I gain, so might I miss.
Might she have loved me? just as well
She might have hated,—who can tell?
Where had I been now if the worst befell?
   And here we are riding, she and I.

V

Fail I alone, in words and deeds?
Why, all men strive and who succeeds?
We rode; it seemed my spirit flew,
Saw other regions, cities new,
   As the world rushed by on either side.
I thought, All labour, yet no less
Bear up beneath their unsuccess.
Look at the end of work, contrast
The pretty Done the Undone vast,
This present of theirs with the hopeful past!
   I hoped she would love me. Here we ride.

VI

What hand and brain went ever paired?
What heart alike conceived and dared?
What act proved all its thought had been?
What will but felt the fleshly screen?

THE LAST RIDE TOGETHER

We ride and I see her bosom heave.
There's many a crown for who can reach.
Ten lines, a statesman's life in each!
The flag stuck on a heap of bones,
A soldier's doing! what atones?
They scratch his name on the Abbey-stones.
My riding is better, by their leave.

VII

What does it all mean, poet? well,
Your brain's beat into rhythm—you tell
What we felt only; you expressed
You hold things beautiful the best,
And pace them in rhyme so, side by side.
'Tis something, nay 'tis much—but then,
Have you yourself what's best for men?
Are you—poor, sick, old ere your time—
Nearer one whit your own sublime
Than we who never have turned a rhyme?
Sing, riding's a joy! For me, I ride.

VIII

And you, great sculptor—so you gave
A score of years to art, her slave,
And that's your Venus—whence we turn
To yonder girl that fords the burn!
You acquiesce and shall I repine?
What, man of music, you, grown grey
With notes and nothing else to say,
Is this your sole praise from a friend,
"Greatly his opera's strains intend,
"But in music we know how fashions end!"
I gave my youth—but we ride, in fine.

IX

Who knows what's fit for us? Had fate
Proposed bliss here should sublimate

THE LAST RIDE TOGETHER

My being; had I signed the bond—
Still one must lead some life beyond,
   —Have a bliss to die with, dim-descried.
This foot once planted on the goal,
This glory-garland round my soul,
Could I descry such?   Try and test!
I sink back shuddering from the quest—
Earth being so good, would Heaven seem best?
   Now, Heaven and she are beyond this ride.

X

And yet—she has not spoke so long!
What if Heaven be, that, fair and strong
At life's best, with our eyes upturned
Whither life's flower is first discerned,
   We, fixed so, ever should so abide?
What if we still ride on, we two,
With life for ever old yet new,
Changed not in kind but in degree,
The instant made eternity,—
And Heaven just prove that I and she
   Ride, ride together, for ever ride?

I

IT was roses, roses, all the way,
  With myrtle mixed in my path like mad.
The house-roofs seemed to heave and sway,
  The church-spires flamed, such flags they had,
A year ago on this very day!

II

The air broke into a mist with bells,
  The old walls rocked with the crowds and cries.
Had I said, " Good folks, mere noise repels—
  But give me your sun from yonder skies ! "
They had answered, " And afterward, what else ? "

III

Alack, it was I who leaped at the sun,
  To give it my loving friends to keep.
Nought man could do, have I left undone
  And you see my harvest, what I reap
This very day, now a year is run.

THE PATRIOT

IV

There's nobody on the house-tops now—
   Just a palsied few at the windows set—
For the best of the sight is, all allow,
   At the Shambles' Gate—or, better yet,
By the very scaffold's foot, I trow.

V

I go in the rain, and, more than needs,
   A rope cuts both my wrists behind,
And I think, by the feel, my forehead bleeds,
   For they fling, whoever has a mind,
Stones at me for my year's misdeeds.

VI

Thus I entered Brescia, and thus I go!
   In such triumphs, people have dropped down dead.
"Thou, paid by the World,—what dost thou owe
   Me?" God might have questioned: but now instead
'Tis God shall requite! I am safer so.

MASTER HUGUES OF SAXE-GOTHA

I

HIST, but a word, fair and soft!
  Forth and be judged, Master Hugues!
Answer the question I've put you so oft—
  What do you mean by your mountainous fugues?
See, we're alone in the loft,

II

I, the poor organist here,
  Hugues, the composer of note—
Dead, though, and done with, this many a year—
  Let's have a colloquy, something to quote,
Make the world prick up its ear!

III

See, the church empties a-pace.
  Fast they extinguish the lights—
Hallo, there, sacristan! five minutes' grace!
  Here's a crank pedal wants setting to rights,
Baulks one of holding the base.

IV

See, our huge house of the sounds
  Hushing its hundreds at once,
Bids the last loiterer back to his bounds
  —Oh, you may challenge them, not a response
Get the church saints on their rounds!

V

(Saints go their rounds, who shall doubt?
  —March, with the moon to admire,
Up nave, down chancel, turn transept about,
  Supervise all betwixt pavement and spire,
Put rats and mice to the rout—

MASTER HUGUES OF SAXE-GOTHA

VI

Aloys and Jurien and Just—
   Order things back to their place,
Have a sharp eye lest the candlesticks rust,
   Rub the church plate, darn the sacrament lace,
Clear the desk velvet of dust.)

VII

Here's your book, younger folks shelve!
   Played I not off-hand and runningly,
Just now, your masterpiece, hard number twelve?
   Here's what should strike,—could one handle it
Help the axe, give it a helve!   [cunningly.

VIII

Page after page as I played,
   Every bar's rest where one wipes
Sweat from one's brow, I looked up and surveyed
   O'er my three claviers, yon forest of pipes
Whence you still peeped in the shade.

IX

Sure you were wishful to speak,
   You, with brow ruled like a score,
Yes, and eyes buried in pits on each cheek,
   Like two great breves as they wrote them of yore
Each side that bar, your straight beak!

X

Sure you said—" Good, the mere notes!
   Still, couldst thou take my intent,
Know what procured me our Company's votes—
   Masters being lauded and sciolists shent,
Parted the sheep from the goats!"

MASTER HUGUES OF SAXE-GOTHA

XI

Well then, speak up, never flinch!
  Quick, ere my candle's a snuff
—Burnt, do you see? to its uttermost inch—
  I believe in you, but that's not enough.
Give my conviction a clinch!

XII

First you deliver your phrase
  —Nothing propound, that I see,
Fit in itself for much blame or much praise—
  Answered no less, where no answer needs be:
Off start the Two on their ways!

XIII

Straight must a Third interpose,
  Volunteer needlessly help—
In strikes a Fourth, a Fifth thrusts in his nose,
  So the cry's open, the kennel's a-yelp,
Argument's hot to the close!

XIV

One dissertates, he is candid—
  Two must discept,—has distinguished!
Three helps the couple, if ever yet man did:
  Four protests, Five makes a dart at the thing wished—
Back to One, goes the case bandied!

XV

One says his say with a difference—
  More of expounding, explaining!
All now is wrangle, abuse, and vociferance—
  Now there's a truce, all's subdued, self-restraining—
Five, though, stands out all the stiffer hence.

256

MASTER HUGUES OF SAXE-GOTHA

XVI

One is incisive, corrosive—
   Two retorts, nettled, curt, crepitant—
Three makes rejoinder, expansive, explosive—
   Four overbears them all, strident and strepitant—
Five . . . O Danaides, O Sieve!

XVII

Now, they ply axes and crowbars—
   Now, they prick pins at a tissue
Fine as a skene of the casuist Escobar's
   Worked on the bone of a lie. To what issue?
Where is our gain at the Two-bars?

XVIII

Est fuga, volvitur rota!
   On we drift. Where looms the dim port?
One, Two, Three, Four, Five, contribute their quota—
   Something is gained, if one caught but the import—
Show it us, Hugues of Saxe-Gotha!

XIX

What with affirming, denying,
   Holding, risposting, subjoining,
All's like . . . it's like . . . for an instance I'm trying . . .
   There! See our roof, its gilt moulding and groining
Under those spider-webs lying!

XX

So your fugue broadens and thickens,
   Greatens and deepens and lengthens,
Till one exclaims—" But where's music, the dickens?
   Blot ye the gold, while your spider-web strengthens,
Blacked to the stoutest of tickens?"

MASTER HUGUES OF SAXE-GOTHA

XXI

I for man's effort am zealous.
 Prove me such censure 's unfounded!
Seems it surprising a lover grows jealous—
 Hopes 'twas for something his organ-pipes sounded,
Tiring three boys at the bellows?

XXII

Is it your moral of Life?
 Such a web, simple and subtle,
Weave we on earth here in impotent strife,
 Backward and forward each throwing his shuttle,
Death ending all with a knife?

XXIII

Over our heads Truth and Nature—
 Still our life's zigzags and dodges,
Ins and outs weaving a new legislature—
 God's gold just shining its last where that lodges,
Palled beneath Man's usurpature!

XXIV

So we o'ershroud stars and roses,
 Cherub and trophy and garland.
Nothings grow something which quietly closes
 Heaven's earnest eye,—not a glimpse of the far land
Gets through our comments and glozes.

XXV

Ah, but traditions, inventions,
 (Say we and make up a visage)
So many men with such various intentions
 Down the past ages must know more than this age!
Leave the web all its dimensions!

MASTER HUGUES OF SAXE-GOTHA

XXVI

Who thinks Hugues wrote for the deaf?
  Proved a mere mountain in labour?
Better submit—try again—what's the clef?
  'Faith, it's no trifle for pipe and for tabor—
Four flats—the minor in F.

XXVII

Friend, your fugue taxes the finger.
  Learning it once, who would lose it?
Yet all the while a misgiving will linger—
  Truth's golden o'er us although we refuse it—
Nature, thro' dust-clouds we fling her!

XXVIII

Hugues! I advise *meâ pœnâ*
  (Counterpoint glares like a Gorgon)
Bid One, Two, Three, Four, Five, clear the arena!
  Say the word, straight I unstop the Full-Organ,
Blare out the *mode Palestrina.*

XXIX

While in the roof, if I'm right there—
  . . . Lo, you, the wick in the socket!
Hallo, you sacristan, show us a light there!
  Down it dips, gone like a rocket!
What, you want, do you, to come unawares,
Sweeping the church up for first morning-prayers,
And find a poor devil at end of his cares
At the foot of your rotten-planked rat-riddled stairs?
  Do I carry the moon in my pocket?

259

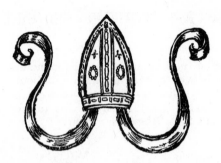

BISHOP BLOUGRAM'S APOLOGY

No more wine? then we'll push back chairs
    and talk.
A final glass for me, tho': cool, i' faith!
We ought to have our Abbey back, you see.
It's different, preaching in basilicas,
And doing duty in some masterpiece
Like this of brother Pugin's, bless his heart!
I doubt if they're half baked, those chalk rosettes,
Ciphers and stucco-twiddlings everywhere;
It's just like breathing in a lime-kiln: eh?
These hot long ceremonies of our church
Cost us a little—oh, they pay the price,
You take me—amply pay it! Now, we'll talk.

So, you despise me, Mr Gigadibs.
No deprecation,—nay, I beg you, sir!
Beside 'tis our engagement: don't you know,
I promised, if you'd watch a dinner out,
We'd see truth dawn together?—truth that peeps
Over the glass's edge when dinner's done,
And body gets its sop and holds its noise
And leaves soul free a little. Now's the time—
'Tis break of day! You do despise me then.
And if I say, "despise me,"—never fear—
I know you do not in a certain sense—
Not in my arm-chair for example: here

BISHOP BLOUGRAM'S APOLOGY

I well imagine you respect my place
(Status, *entourage*, worldly circumstance)
Quite to its value—very much indeed
—Are up to the protesting eyes of you
In pride at being seated here for once—
You'll turn it to such capital account!
When somebody, through years and years to come,
Hints of the bishop,—names me—that's enough—
"Blougram? I knew him"—(into it you slide)
"Dined with him once, a Corpus Christi Day,
All alone, we two—he's a clever man—
And after dinner,—why, the wine you know,—
Oh, there was wine, and good!—what with the wine . . .
'Faith, we began upon all sorts of talk!
He's no bad fellow, Blougram—he had seen
Something of mine he relished—some review—
He's quite above their humbug in his heart,
Half-said as much, indeed—the thing's his trade—
I warrant, Blougram's sceptical at times—
How otherwise? I liked him, I confess!"
Che ch'è, my dear sir, as we say at Rome,
Don't you protest now! It's fair give and take;
You have had your turn and spoken your home-truths—
The hand's mine now, and here you follow suit.

Thus much conceded, still the first fact stays—
You do despise me; your ideal of life
Is not the bishop's—you would not be I—
You would like better to be Goethe, now,
Or Buonaparte—or, bless me, lower still,
Count D'Orsay,—so you did what you preferred,
Spoke as you thought, and, as you cannot help,
Believed or disbelieved, no matter what,
So long as on that point, whate'er it was,
You loosed your mind, were whole and sole yourself.
—That, my ideal never can include,
Upon that element of truth and worth

BISHOP BLOUGRAM'S APOLOGY

Never be based! for say they make me Pope
(They can't—suppose it for our argument)
Why, there I'm at my tether's end—I've reached
My height, and not a height which pleases you.
An unbelieving Pope won't do, you say.
It's like those eerie stories nurses tell,
Of how some actor played Death on a stage
With pasteboard crown, sham orb, and tinselled dart,
And called himself the monarch of the world,
Then going in the tire-room afterward
Because the play was done, to shift himself,
Got touched upon the sleeve familiarly
The moment he had shut the closet door
By Death himself.   Thus God might touch a Pope
At unawares, ask what his baubles mean,
And whose part he presumed to play just now?
Best be yourself, imperial, plain and true!

So, drawing comfortable breath again,
You weigh and find whatever more or less
I boast of my ideal realised
Is nothing in the balance when opposed
To your ideal, your grand simple life,
Of which you will not realise one jot.
I am much, you are nothing; you would be all,
I would be merely much—you beat me there.

No, friend, you do not beat me,—hearken why.
The common problem, yours, mine, every one's,
Is not to fancy what were fair in life
Provided it could be,—but, finding first
What may be, then find how to make it fair
Up to our means—a very different thing!
No abstract intellectual plan of life
Quite irrespective of life's plainest laws,
But one, a man, who is man and nothing more,
May lead within a world which (by your leave)

BISHOP BLOUGRAM'S APOLOGY

Is Rome or London—not Fool's-paradise,
Embellish Rome, idealise away,
Make Paradise of London if you can,
You're welcome, nay, you're wise.

                                A simile!
We mortals cross the ocean of this world
Each in his average cabin of a life—
The best's not big, the worst yields elbow-room.
Now for our six months' voyage—how prepare?
You come on shipboard with a landsman's list
Of things he calls convenient—so they are!
An India screen is pretty furniture,
A piano-forte is a fine resource,
All Balzac's novels occupy one shelf,
The new edition fifty volumes long;
And little Greek books with the funny type
They get up well at Leipsic fill the next—
Go on! slabbed marble, what a bath it makes!
And Parma's pride, the Jerome, let us add!
'Twere pleasant could Correggio's fleeting glow
Hang full in face of one where'er one roams,
Since he more than the others brings with him
Italy's self,—the marvellous Modenese!
Yet 'twas not on your list before, perhaps.
—Alas! friend, here's the agent . . . is't the name?
The captain, or whoever's master here—
You see him screw his face up; what's his cry
Ere you set foot on shipboard? "Six feet square!"
If you won't understand what six feet mean,
Compute and purchase stores accordingly—
And if in pique because he overhauls
Your Jerome, piano and bath, you come on board
Bare—why you cut a figure at the first
While sympathetic landsmen see you off;
Not afterwards, when, long ere half seas o'er,
You peep up from your utterly naked boards

BISHOP BLOUGRAM'S APOLOGY

Into some snug and well-appointed berth
Like mine, for instance (try the cooler jug—
Put back the other, but don't jog the ice)
And mortified you mutter "Well and good—
He sits enjoying his sea-furniture—
'Tis stout and proper, and there's store of it,
Though I've the better notion, all agree,
Of fitting rooms up! hang the carpenter,
Neat ship-shape fixings and contrivances—
I would have brought my Jerome, frame and all!"
And meantime you bring nothing: never mind—
You've proved your artist-nature: what you don't,
You might bring, so despise me, as I say.

Now come, let's backward to the starting place.
See my way: we're two college friends, suppose—
Prepare together for our voyage, then,
Each note and check the other in his work,—
Here's mine, a bishop's outfit; criticise!
What's wrong? why won't you be a bishop too?

Why, first, you don't believe, you don't and can't,
(Not statedly, that is, and fixedly
And absolutely and exclusively)
In any revelation called divine.
No dogmas nail your faith—and what remains
But say so, like the honest man you are?
First, therefore, overhaul theology!
Nay, I too, not a fool, you please to think,
Must find believing every whit as hard,
And if I do not frankly say as much,
The ugly consequence is clear enough.

Now, wait, my friend: well, I do not believe—
If you'll accept no faith that is not fixed,
Absolute and exclusive, as you say.
(You're wrong—I mean to prove it in due time)
Meanwhile, I know where difficulties lie

BISHOP BLOUGRAM'S APOLOGY

I could not, cannot solve, nor ever shall,
So give up hope accordingly to solve—
(To you, and over the wine).   Our dogmas then
With both of us, tho' in unlike degree,
Missing full credence—overboard with them!
I mean to meet you on your own premise—
Good, there go mine in company with yours!

    And now what are we? unbelievers both,
Calm and complete, determinately fixed
To-day, to-morrow, and for ever, pray?
You'll guarantee me that?   Not so, I think.
In no-wise! all we've gained is, that belief,
As unbelief before, shakes us by fits,
Confounds us like its predecessor.   Where's
The gain? how can we guard our unbelief,
Make it bear fruit to us?—the problem here.
Just when we are safest, there's a sunset-touch,
A fancy from a flower-bell, some one's death,
A chorus-ending from Euripides,—
And that's enough for fifty hopes and fears
As old and new at once as Nature's self,
To rap and knock and enter in our soul,
Take hands and dance there, a fantastic ring,
Round the ancient idol, on his base again,—
The grand Perhaps! we look on helplessly,—
There the old misgivings, crooked questions are—
This good God,—what he could do, if he would,
Would, if he could—then must have done long since:
If so, when, where, and how? some way must be,—
Once feel about, and soon or late you hit
Some sense, in which it might be, after all.
Why not, " The Way, the Truth, the Life? "

                                        —That way
Over the mountain, which who stands upon
Is apt to doubt if it's indeed a road ;

While if he views it from the waste itself,
Up goes the line there, plain from base to brow,
Not vague, mistakeable! what's a break or two
Seen from the unbroken desert either side?
And then (to bring in fresh philosophy)
What if the breaks themselves should prove at last
The most consummate of contrivances
To train a man's eye, teach him what is faith,—
And so we stumble at truth's very test?
What have we gained then by our unbelief
But a life of doubt diversified by faith,
For one of faith diversified by doubt.
We called the chess-board white,—we call it black.

"Well," you rejoin, "the end's no worse, at least,
We've reason for both colours on the board.
Why not confess, then, where I drop the faith
And you the doubt, that I'm as right as you?"

Because, friend, in the next place, this being so,
And both things even,—faith and unbelief
Left to a man's choice,—we'll proceed a step,
Returning to our image, which I like.

A man's choice, yes—but a cabin-passenger's—
The man made for the special life of the world—
Do you forget him? I remember though!
Consult our ship's conditions and you find
One and but one choice suitable to all,
The choice that you unluckily prefer
Turning things topsy-turvy—they or it
Going to the ground. Belief or unbelief
Bears upon life, determines its whole course,
Begins at its beginning. See the world
Such as it is,—you made it not, nor I;
I mean to take it as it is,—and you
Not so you'll take it,—though you get nought else.

BISHOP BLOUGRAM'S APOLOGY

I know the special kind of life I like,
What suits the most my idiosyncrasy,
Brings out the best of me and bears me fruit
In power, peace, pleasantness, and length of days.
I find that positive belief does this
For me, and unbelief, no whit of this.
—For you, it does, however—that we'll try!
'Tis clear, I cannot lead my life, at least
Induce the world to let me peaceably,
Without declaring at the outset, " Friends,
I absolutely and peremptorily
Believe!"—I say faith is my waking life.
One sleeps, indeed, and dreams at intervals,
We know, but waking 's the main point with us,
And my provision 's for life's waking part.
Accordingly, I use heart, head and hands
All day, I build, scheme, study and make friends;
And when night overtakes me, down I lie,
Sleep, dream a little, and get done with it,
The sooner the better, to begin afresh.
What 's midnight's doubt before the dayspring's faith?
You, the philosopher, that disbelieve,
That recognise the night, give dreams their weight—
To be consistent you should keep your bed,
Abstain from healthy acts that prove you a man,
For fear you drowse perhaps at unawares!
And certainly at night you'll sleep and dream,
Live through the day and bustle as you please.
And so you live to sleep as I to wake,
To unbelieve as I to still believe?
Well, and the common sense of the world calls you
Bed-ridden,—and its good things come to me.
Its estimation, which is half the fight,
That 's the first cabin-comfort I secure—
The next . . . but you perceive with half an eye!
Come, come, it 's best believing, if we can—
You can't but own that.

BISHOP BLOUGRAM'S APOLOGY

Next, concede again—
If once we choose belief, on all accounts
We can't be too decisive in our faith,
Conclusive and exclusive in its terms,
To suit the world which gives us the good things.
In every man's career are certain points
Whereon he dares not be indifferent;
The world detects him clearly, if he is,
As baffled at the game, and losing life.
He may care little or he may care much
For riches, honour, pleasure, work, repose,
Since various theories of life and life's
Success are extant which might easily
Comport with either estimate of these,
And whoso chooses wealth or poverty,
Labour or quiet, is not judged a fool
Because his fellows would choose otherwise.
We let him choose upon his own account
So long as he's consistent with his choice.
But certain points, left wholly to himself,
When once a man has arbitrated on,
We say he must succeed there or go hang.
Thus, he should wed the woman he loves most
Or needs most, whatsoe'er the love or need—
For he can't wed twice.   Then, he must avouch
Or follow, at the least, sufficiently,
The form of faith his conscience holds the best,
Whate'er the process of conviction was.
For nothing can compensate his mistake
On such a point, the man himself being judge—
He cannot wed twice, nor twice lose his soul.

Well now—there's one great form of Christian faith
I happened to be born in—which to teach
Was given me as I grew up, on all hands,
As best and readiest means of living by;
The same on examination being proved

BISHOP BLOUGRAM'S APOLOGY

The most pronounced moreover, fixed, precise
And absolute form of faith in the whole world—
Accordingly, most potent of all forms
For working on the world.   Observe, my friend,
Such as you know me, I am free to say,
In these hard latter days which hamper one,
Myself, by no immoderate exercise
Of intellect and learning, and the tact
To let external forces work for me,
Bid the street's stones be bread and they are bread,
Bid Peter's creed, or, rather, Hildebrand's,
Exalt me o'er my fellows in the world
And make my life an ease and joy and pride,
It does so,—which for me 's a great point gained,
Who have a soul and body that exact
A comfortable care in many ways.
There 's power in me and will to dominate
Which I must exercise, they hurt me else :
In many ways I need mankind's respect,
Obedience, and the love that 's born of fear :
While at the same time, there 's a taste I have,
A toy of soul, a titillating thing,
Refuses to digest these dainties crude.
The naked life is gross till clothed upon :
I must take what men offer, with a grace
As though I would not, could I help it, take !
A uniform to wear though over-rich—
Something imposed on me, no choice of mine ;
No fancy-dress worn for pure fashion's sake
And despicable therefore ! now men kneel
And kiss my hand—of course the Church's hand.
Thus I am made, thus life is best for me,
And thus that it should be I have procured ;
And thus it could not be another way,
I venture to imagine.

You 'll reply—

So far my choice, no doubt, is a success ;

But were I made of better elements,
With nobler instincts, purer tastes, like you,
I hardly would account the thing success
Though it do all for me I say. ✗

But, friend,
We speak of what is—not of what might be,
And how 'twere better if 'twere otherwise.
I am the man you see here plain enough—
Grant I'm a beast, why beasts must lead beasts' lives!
Suppose I own at once to tail and claws—
The tailless man exceeds me; but being tailed
I'll lash out lion-fashion, and leave apes
To dock their stump and dress their haunches up.
My business is not to remake myself,
But make the absolute best of what God made.
Or—our first simile—though you proved me doomed
To a viler berth still, to the steerage-hole,
The sheep-pen or the pig-stye, I should strive
To make what use of each were possible;
And as this cabin gets upholstery,
That hutch should rustle with sufficient straw.

But, friend, I don't acknowledge quite so fast
I fail of all your manhood's lofty tastes
Enumerated so complacently,
On the mere ground that you forsooth can find
In this particular life I choose to lead
No fit provision for them.   Can you not?
Say you, my fault is I address myself
To grosser estimators than I need,
And that's no way of holding up the soul—
Which, nobler, needs men's praise perhaps, yet knows
One wise man's verdict outweighs all the fools',—
Would like the two, but, forced to choose, takes that?
I pine among my million imbeciles
(You think) aware some dozen men of sense

BISHOP BLOUGRAM'S APOLOGY

Eye me and know me, whether I believe
In the last winking Virgin, as I vow,
And am a fool, or disbelieve in her
And am a knave,—approve in neither case,
Withhold their voices though I look their way:
Like Verdi when, at his worst opera's end
(The thing they gave at Florence,—what's its name?)
While the mad houseful's plaudits near out-bang
His orchestra of salt-box, tongs and bones,
He looks through all the roaring and the wreaths
Where sits Rossini patient in his stall.

    Nay, friend, I meet you with an answer here—
For even your prime men who appraise their kind
Are men still, catch a thing within a thing,
See more in a truth than the truth's simple self,
Confuse themselves. You see lads walk the streets
Sixty the minute; what's to note in that?
You see one lad o'erstride a chimney-stack;
Him you must watch—he's sure to fall, yet stands!
Our interest's on the dangerous edge of things.
The honest thief, the tender murderer,
The superstitious atheist, demireps
That love and save their souls in new French books—
We watch while these in equilibrium keep
The giddy line midway: one step aside,
They're classed and done with. I, then, keep the line
Before your sages,—just the men to shrink
From the gross weights, coarse scales, and labels broad
You offer their refinement. Fool or knave?
Why needs a bishop be a fool or knave
When there's a thousand diamond weights between?
So I enlist them. Your picked Twelve, you'll find,
Profess themselves indignant, scandalised
At thus being held unable to explain
How a superior man who disbelieves
May not believe as well: that's Schelling's way!

BISHOP BLOUGRAM'S APOLOGY

It's through my coming in the tail of time,
Nicking the minute with a happy tact.
Had I been born three hundred years ago   [believes "
They'd say, "What's strange?   Blougram of course
And, seventy years since, " disbelieves of course."
But now, " He may believe; and yet, and yet
How can he? "—All eyes turn with interest.
Whereas, step off the line on either side—
You, for example, clever to a fault,
The rough and ready man that write apace,
Read somewhat seldomer, think perhaps even less—
You disbelieve!   Who wonders and who cares?
Lord So-and-So—his coat bedropt with wax,
All Peter's chains about his waist, his back
Brave with the needlework of Noodledom,
Believes!   Again, who wonders and who cares?
But I, the man of sense and learning too,
The able to think yet act, the this, the that,
I, to believe at this late time of day!
Enough; you see, I need not fear contempt.

   —Except it's yours! admire me as these may,
You don't.   But what at least do you admire?
Present your own perfections, your ideal,
Your pattern man for a minute—oh, make haste!
Is it Napoleon you would have us grow?
Concede the means; allow his head and hand,
(A large concession, clever as you are)
Good!—In our common primal element
Of unbelief (we can't believe, you know—
We're still at that admission, recollect)
Where do you find—apart from, towering-o'er
The secondary temporary aims
Which satisfy the gross tastes you despise—
Where do you find his star?—his crazy trust
God knows through what or in what? it's alive
And shines and leads him and that's all we want

BISHOP BLOUGRAM'S APOLOGY

Have we aught in our sober night shall point
Such ends as his were, and direct the means
Of working out our purpose straight as his
Nor bring a moment's trouble on success
With after-care to justify the same?
—Be a Napoleon and yet disbelieve!
Why, the man's mad, friend, take his light away.
What's the vague good of the world for which you'd
    dare
With comfort to yourself blow millions up?
We neither of us see it! we do see
The blown-up millions—spatter of their brains
And writhing of their bowels and so forth,
In that bewildering entanglement
Of horrible eventualities
Past calculation to the end of time!
Can I mistake for some clear word of God
(Which were my ample warrant for it all)
His puff of hazy instincts, idle talk,
"The state, that's I," quack-nonsense about kings,
And (when one beats the man to his last hold)
The vague idea of setting things to rights,
Policing people efficaciously,
More to their profit, most of all to his own ;
The whole to end that dismallest of ends
By an Austrian marriage, cant to us the church,
And resurrection of the old *régime*.
Would I, who hope to live a dozen years,
Fight Austerlitz for reasons such and such?
No : for, concede me but the merest chance
Doubt may be wrong—there's judgment, life to come!
With just that chance, I dare not. Doubt proves
    right?
This present life is all? you offer me
Its dozen noisy years with not a chance
That wedding an Arch-Duchess, wearing lace,
And getting called by divers new-coined names,

BISHOP BLOUGRAM'S APOLOGY

Will drive off ugly thoughts and let me dine,
Sleep, read and chat in quiet as I like!
Therefore, I will not.

               Take another case;
Fit up the cabin yet another way.
What say you to the poet's? shall we write
Hamlets, Othellos—make the world our own,
Without a risk to run of either sort?
I can't!—to put the strongest reason first.
"But try," you urge, "the trying shall suffice:
The aim, if reached or not, makes great the life.
Try to be Shakespeare, leave the rest to fate!"
Spare my self-knowledge—there's no fooling me!
If I prefer remaining my poor self,
I say so not in self-dispraise but praise.
If I'm a Shakespeare, let the well alone—
Why should I try to be what now I am?
If I'm no Shakespeare, as too probable,—
His power and consciousness and self-delight
And all we want in common, shall I find—
Trying for ever? while on points of taste
Wherewith, to speak it humbly, he and I
Are dowered alike—I'll ask you, I or he,
Which in our two lives realises most?
Much, he imagined—somewhat, I possess.
He had the imagination; stick to that!
Let him say "In the face of my soul's works
Your world is worthless and I touch it not
Lest I should wrong them"—I withdraw my plea.
But does he say so? look upon his life!
Himself, who only can, gives judgment there.
He leaves his towers and gorgeous palaces
To build the trimmest house in Stratford town;
Saves money, spends it, owns the worth of things,
Giulio Romano's pictures, Dowland's lute;
Enjoys a show, respects the puppets, too,

BISHOP BLOUGRAM'S APOLOGY

And none more, had he seen its entry once,
Than "Pandulph, of fair Milan cardinal."
Why then should I who play that personage,
The very Pandulph Shakespeare's fancy made,
Be told that had the poet chanced to start
From where I stand now (some degree like mine
Being just the goal he ran his race to reach)
He would have run the whole race back, forsooth,
And left being Pandulph, to begin write plays?
Ah, the earth's best can be but the earth's best!
Did Shakespeare live, he could but sit at home
And get himself in dreams the Vatican,
Greek busts, Venetian paintings, Roman walls,
And English books, none equal to his own,
Which I read, bound in gold, (he never did).
—Terni and Naples' bay and Gothard's top—
Eh, friend? I could not fancy one of these—
But, as I pour this claret, there they are—
I've gained them—crossed St. Gothard last July
With ten mules to the carriage and a bed
Slung inside; is my hap the worse for that?
We want the same things, Shakespeare and myself,
And what I want, I have: he, gifted more,
Could fancy he too had it when he liked,
But not so thoroughly that if fate allowed
He would not have it also in my sense.
We play one game. I send the ball aloft
No less adroitly that of fifty strokes
Scarce five go o'er the wall so wide and high
Which sends them back to me: I wish and get.
He struck balls higher and with better skill,
But at a poor fence level with his head,
And hit—his Stratford house, a coat of arms,
Successful dealings in his grain and wool,—
While I receive heaven's incense in my nose
And style myself the cousin of Queen Bess.
Ask him, if this life's all, who wins the game?

BISHOP BLOUGRAM'S APOLOGY

Believe—and our whole argument breaks up.
Enthusiasm's the best thing, I repeat;
Only, we can't command it; fire and life
Are all, dead matter's nothing, we agree:
And be it a mad dream or God's very breath,
The fact's the same,—belief's fire once in us,
Makes of all else mere stuff to show itself.
We penetrate our life with such a glow
As fire lends wood and iron—this turns steel,
That burns to ash—all's one, fire proves its power
For good or ill, since men call flare success.
But paint a fire, it will not therefore burn.
Light one in me, I'll find it food enough!
Why, to be Luther—that's a life to lead,
Incomparably better than my own.
He comes, reclaims God's earth for God, he says,
Sets up God's rule again by simple means,
Re-opens a shut book, and all is done.
He flared out in the flaring of mankind;
Such Luther's luck was—how shall such be mine?
If he succeeded, nothing's left to do:
And if he did not altogether—well,
Strauss is the next advance. All Strauss should be
I might be also. But to what result?
He looks upon no future: Luther did.
What can I gain on the denying side?
Ice makes no conflagration. State the facts,
Read the text right, emancipate the world—
The emancipated world enjoys itself
With scarce a thank-you—Blougram told it first
It could not owe a farthing,—not to him
More than St. Paul! 'twould press its pay, you think?
Then add there's still that plaguey hundredth chance
Strauss may be wrong. And so a risk is run—
For what gain? not for Luther's, who secured
A real heaven in his heart throughout his life,
Supposing death a little altered things!

BISHOP BLOUGRAM'S APOLOGY

"Ay, but since really I lack faith," you cry,
"I run the same risk really on all sides,
In cool indifference as bold unbelief.
As well be Strauss as swing 'twixt Paul and him.
It's not worth having, such imperfect faith,
Nor more available to do faith's work
Than unbelief like yours.   Whole faith, or none!"

Softly, my friend! I must dispute that point.
Once own the use of faith, I'll find you faith.
We're back on Christian ground.   You call for faith:
I show you doubt, to prove that faith exists.
The more of doubt, the stronger faith, I say,
If faith o'ercomes doubt.   How I know it does?
By life and man's free will, God gave for that!
To mould life as we choose it, shows our choice:
That's our one act, the previous work's His own.
You criticise the soil? it reared this tree—
This broad life and whatever fruit it bears!
What matter though I doubt at every pore,
Head-doubts, heart-doubts, doubts at my fingers' ends,
Doubts in the trivial work of every day,
Doubts at the very bases of my soul
In the grand moments when she probes herself—
If finally I have a life to show,
The thing I did, brought out in evidence
Against the thing done to me underground
By Hell and all its brood, for aught I know?
I say, whence sprang this? shows it faith or doubt?
All's doubt in me; where's break of faith in this?
It is the idea, the feeling and the love
God means mankind should strive for and show forth,
Whatever be the process to that end,—
And not historic knowledge, logic sound,
And metaphysical acumen, sure!
"What think ye of Christ," friend? when all's done and
        said,

BISHOP BLOUGRAM'S APOLOGY

You like this Christianity or not?
It may be false, but will you wish it true?
Has it your vote to be so if it can?
Trust you an instinct silenced long ago
That will break silence and enjoin you love
What mortified philosophy is hoarse,
And all in vain, with bidding you despise?
If you desire faith—then you've faith enough.
What else seeks God—nay, what else seek ourselves?
You form a notion of me, we'll suppose,
On hearsay; it's a favourable one:
"But still," (you add) "there was no such good man,
Because of contradictions in the facts.
One proves, for instance, he was born in Rome,
This Blougram—yet throughout the tales of him
I see he figures as an Englishman."
Well, the two things are reconcileable.
But would I rather you discovered that,
Subjoining—"Still, what matter though they be?
Blougram concerns me nought, born here or there."

Pure faith indeed—you know not what you ask!
Naked belief in God the Omnipotent,
Omniscient, Omnipresent, sears too much
The sense of conscious creatures to be borne.
It were the seeing him, no flesh shall dare.
Some think, Creation's meant to show him forth:
I say, it's meant to hide him all it can,
And that's what all the blessed Evil's for.
Its use in time is to environ us,
Our breath, our drop of dew, with shield enough
Against that sight till we can bear its stress.
Under a vertical sun, the exposed brain
And lidless eye and disemprisoned heart
Less certainly would wither up at once
Than mind, confronted with the truth of Him.
But time and earth case-harden us to live;

BISHOP BLOUGRAM'S APOLOGY

The feeblest sense is trusted most ; the child
Feels God a moment, ichors o'er the place,
Plays on and grows to be a man like us.
With me, faith means perpetual unbelief
Kept quiet like the snake 'neath Michael's foot
Who stands calm just because he feels it writhe.
Or, if that's too ambitious,—here's my box—
I need the excitation of a pinch
Threatening the torpor of the inside-nose
Nigh on the imminent sneeze that never comes.
"Leave it in peace" advise the simple folk—
Make it aware of peace by itching fits,
Say I—let doubt occasion still more faith !

You'll say, once all believed, man, woman, child,
In that dear middle-age these noodles praise.
How you'd exult if I could put you back
Six hundred years, blot out cosmogony,
Geology, ethnology, what not,
(Greek endings with the little passing-bell
That signifies some faith's about to die)
And set you square with Genesis again,—
When such a traveller told you his last news,
He saw the ark a-top of Ararat
But did not climb there since 'twas getting dusk
And robber-bands infest the mountain's foot !
How should you feel, I ask, in such an age,
How act ?   As other people felt and did ;
With soul more blank than this decanter's knob,
Believe—and yet lie, kill, rob, fornicate
Full in belief's face, like the beast you'd be !

No, when the fight begins within himself,
A man's worth something.   God stoops o'er his head,
Satan looks up between his feet—both tug—
He's left, himself, in the middle : the soul wakes
And grows.   Prolong that battle through his life !

BISHOP BLOUGRAM'S APOLOGY

Never leave growing till the life to come!
Here, we've got callous to the Virgin's winks
That used to puzzle people wholesomely—
Men have outgrown the shame of being fools.
What are the laws of Nature, not to bend
If the Church bid them, brother Newman asks.
Up with the Immaculate Conception, then—
On to the rack with faith—is my advice!
Will not that hurry us upon our knees
Knocking our breasts, "It can't be—yet it shall!
Who am I, the worm, to argue with my Pope?
Low things confound the high things!" and so forth.
That's better than acquitting God with grace
As some folks do.   He's tried—no case is proved,
Philosophy is lenient—He may go!

You'll say—the old system's not so obsolete
But men believe still: ay, but who and where?
King Bomba's lazzaroni foster yet
The sacred flame, so Antonelli writes;
But even of these, what ragamuffin-saint
Believes God watches him continually,
As he believes in fire that it will burn,
Or rain that it will drench him?   Break fire's law,
Sin against rain, although the penalty
Be just a singe or soaking?   No, he smiles;
Those laws are laws that can enforce themselves.

The sum of all is—yes, my doubt is great,
My faith's the greater—then my faith's enough.
I have read much, thought much, experienced much,
Yet would die rather than avow my fear
The Naples' liquefaction may be false,
When set to happen by the palace-clock
According to the clouds or dinner-time.
I hear you recommend, I might at least
Eliminate, decrassify my faith

BISHOP BLOUGRAM'S APOLOGY

Since I adopt it; keeping what I must
And leaving what I can—such points as this i
I won't—that is, I can't throw one away.
Supposing there's no truth in what I said
About the need of trials to man's faith,
Still, when you bid me purify the same,
To such a process I discern no end,
Clearing off one excrescence to see two;
There's ever a next in size, now grown as big,
That meets the knife—I cut and cut again!
First cut the Liquefaction, what comes last
But Fichte's clever cut at God himself?
Experimentalize on sacred things?
I trust nor hand nor eye nor heart nor brain
To stop betimes: they all get drunk alike.
The first step, I am master not to take.

You'd find the cutting-process to your taste
As much as leaving growths of lies unpruned,
Nor see more danger in it, you retort.
Your taste's worth mine; but my taste proves more wise
When we consider that the steadfast hold
On the extreme end of the chain of faith
Gives all the advantage, makes the difference,
With the rough purblind mass we seek to rule.
We are their lords, or they are free of us
Just as we tighten or relax that hold.
So, other matters equal, we'll revert
To the first problem—which if solved my way
And thrown into the balance turns the scale—
How we may lead a comfortable life,
How suit our luggage to the cabin's size.

Of course you are remarking all this time
How narrowly and grossly I view life,
Respect the creature-comforts, care to rule
The masses, and regard complacently

BISHOP BLOUGRAM'S APOLOGY

"The cabin," in our old phrase! Well, I do.
I act for, talk for, live for this world now,
As this world calls for action, life and talk—
No prejudice to what next world may prove,
Whose new laws and requirements my best pledge
To observe then, is that I observe these now,
Doing hereafter what I do meanwhile.
Let us concede (gratuitously though)
Next life relieves the soul of body, yields
Pure spiritual enjoyments : well, my friend,
Why lose this life in the meantime, since its use
May be to make the next life more intense?

Do you know, I have often had a dream
(Work it up in your next month's article)
Of man's poor spirit in its progress still
Losing true life for ever and a day
Through ever trying to be and ever being
In the evolution of successive spheres,
Before its actual sphere and place of life,
Half way into the next, which having reached,
It shoots with corresponding foolery
Half way into the next still, on and off!
As when a traveller, bound from north to south,
Scouts fur in Russia—what's its use in France?
In France spurns flannel—where's its need in Spain?
In Spain drops cloth—too cumbrous for Algiers!
Linen goes next, and last the skin itself,
A superfluity at Timbuctoo.
When, through his journey, was the fool at ease?
I'm at ease now, friend—worldly in this world
I take and like its way of life; I think
My brothers who administer the means
Live better for my comfort—that's good too;
And God, if he pronounce upon it all,
Approves my service, which is better still.
If He keep silence,—why for you or me

BISHOP BLOUGRAM'S APOLOGY

Or that brute-beast pulled-up in to-day's "Times,"
What odds is 't, save to ourselves, what life we lead?

   You meet me at this issue—you declare,
All special-pleading done with, truth is truth,
And justifies itself by undreamed ways.
You don't fear but it's better, if we doubt,
To say so, acting up to our truth perceived
However feebly.   Do then,—act away!
'Tis there I'm on the watch for you!   How one acts
Is, both of us agree, our chief concern:
And how you'll act is what I fain would see
If, like the candid person you appear,
You dare to make the most of your life's scheme
As I of mine, live up to its full law
Since there's no higher law that counterchecks.
Put natural religion to the test
You've just demolished the revealed with—quick,
Down to the root of all that checks your will,
All prohibition to lie, kill, and thieve
Or even to be an atheistic priest!
Suppose a pricking to incontinence—
Philosophers deduce you chastity
Or shame, from just the fact that at the first
Whoso embraced a woman in the plain,
Threw club down, and forewent his brains beside,
So stood a ready victim in the reach
Of any brother-savage club in hand—
Hence saw the use of going out of sight
In wood or cave to prosecute his loves—
I read this in a French book t' other day.
Does law so analyzed coerce you much?
Oh, men spin clouds of fuzz where matters end,
But you who reach where the first thread begins,
You'll soon cut that!—which means you can, but won't
Through certain instincts, blind, unreasoned-out,
You dare not set aside, you can't tell why,

BISHOP BLOUGRAM'S APOLOGY

But there they are, and so you let them rule.
Then, friend, you seem as much a slave as I,
A liar, conscious coward and hypocrite,
Without the good the slave expects to get,
Suppose he has a master after all!
You own your instincts—why what else do I,
Who want, am made for, and must have a God
Ere I can be aught, do aught?—no mere name
Want, but the true thing with what proves its truth,
To wit, a relation from that thing to me,
Touching from head to foot—which touch I feel,
And with it take the rest, this life of ours!
I live my life here; yours you dare not live.

Not as I state it, who (you please subjoin)
Disfigure such a life and call it names,
While, in your mind, remains another way
For simple men: knowledge and power have rights,
But ignorance and weakness have rights too.
There needs no crucial effort to find truth
If here or there or anywhere about—
We ought to turn each side, try hard and see,
And if we can't, be glad we've earned at least
The right, by one laborious proof the more,
To graze in peace earth's pleasant pasturage.
Men are not gods, but, properly, are brutes.
Something we may see, all we cannot see—
What need of lying? I say, I see all,
And swear to each detail the most minute
In what I think a man's face—you, mere cloud:
I swear I hear him speak and see him wink,
For fear, if once I drop the emphasis,
Mankind may doubt if there's a cloud at all.
You take the simpler life—ready to see,
Willing to see—for no cloud's worth a face—
And leaving quiet what no strength can move,
And which, who bids you move? who has the right?

284

BISHOP BLOUGRAM'S APOLOGY

I bid you; but you are God's sheep, not mine—
"*Pastor est tui Dominus.*"   You find
In these the pleasant pastures of this life
Much you may eat without the least offence,
Much you don't eat because your maw objects,
Much you would eat but that your fellow-flock
Open great eyes at you and even butt,
And thereupon you like your friends so much
You cannot please yourself, offending them—
Though when they seem exorbitantly sheep,
You weigh your pleasure with their butts and kicks
And strike the balance.   Sometimes certain fears
Restrain you—real checks since you find them so—
Sometimes you please yourself and nothing checks;
And thus you graze through life with not one lie,
And like it best.

              But do you, in truth's name?
If so, you beat—which means—you are not I—
Who needs must make earth mine and feed my fill
Not simply unbutted at, unbickered with,
But motioned to the velvet of the sward
By those obsequious wethers' very selves.
Look at me, sir; my age is double yours.
At yours, I knew beforehand, so enjoyed,
What now I should be—as, permit the word,
I pretty well imagine your whole range
And stretch of tether twenty years to come.
We both have minds and bodies much alike.
In truth's name, don't you want my bishopric,
My daily bread, my influence and my state?
You're young, I'm old, you must be old one day;
Will you find then, as I do hour by hour,
Women their lovers kneel to, that cut curls
From your fat lap-dog's ears to grace a brooch—
Dukes, that petition just to kiss your ring—
With much beside you know or may conceive?

BISHOP BLOUGRAM'S APOLOGY

Suppose we die to-night : well, here am I,
Such were my gains, life bore this fruit to me,
While writing all the same my articles
On music, poetry, the fictile vase
Found at Albano, or Anacreon's Greek.
But you—the highest honour in your life,
The thing you 'll crown yourself with, all your days,
Is—dining here and drinking this last glass
I pour you out in sign of amity,
Before we part for ever.   Of your power
And social influence, worldly worth in short,
Judge what 's my estimation by the fact—
I do not condescend to enjoin, beseech,
Hint secrecy on one of all these words!
You 're shrewd and know that should you publish it
The world would brand the lie—my enemies first,
" Who 'd sneer—the bishop 's an arch-hypocrite,
And knave perhaps, but not so frank a fool."
Whereas I should not dare fcr both my ears
Breathe one such syllable, smile one such smile,
Before my chaplain who reflects myself—
My shade 's so much more potent than your flesh.
What 's your reward, self-abnegating friend ?
Stood you confessed of those exceptional
And privileged great natures that dwarf mine—
A zealot with a mad ideal in reach,
A poet just about to print his ode,
A statesman with a scheme to stop this war,
An artist whose religion is his art,
I should have nothing to object ! such men
Carry the fire, all things grow warm to them,
Their drugget 's worth my purple, they beat me.
But you,—you 're just as little those as I—
You, Gigadibs, who, thirty years of age,
Write stately for Blackwood's Magazine,
Believe you see two points in Hamlet's soul
Unseized by the Germans yet—which view you 'll print—

BISHOP BLOUGRAM'S APOLOGY

Meantime the best you have to show being still
That lively lightsome article we took
Almost for the true Dickens,—what's the name?
"The Slum and Cellar—or Whitechapel life
Limned after dark!" it made me laugh, I know,
And pleased a month and brought you in ten pounds.
—Success I recognise and compliment,
And therefore give you, if you please, three words
(The card and pencil-scratch is quite enough)
Which whether here, in Dublin, or New York,
Will get you, prompt as at my eyebrow's wink,
Such terms as never you aspired to get
In all our own reviews and some not ours.
Go write your lively sketches—be the first
"Blougram, or The Eccentric Confidence"—
Or better simply say, "The Outward-bound."
Why, men as soon would throw it in my teeth
As copy and quote the infamy chalked broad
About me on the church-door opposite.
You will not wait for that experience though,
I fancy, howsoever you decide,
To discontinue—not detesting, not
Defaming, but at least—despising me!

———————

Over his wine so smiled and talked his hour
Sylvester Blougram, styled *in partibus*
Episcopus, nec non—(the deuce knows what
It's changed to by our novel hierarchy)
With Gigadibs the literary man,
Who played with spoons, explored his plate's design,
And ranged the olive stones about its edge,
While the great bishop rolled him out his mind.

For Blougram, he believed, say, half he spoke.
The other portion, as he shaped it thus

BISHOP BLOUGRAM'S APOLOGY

For argumentatory purposes,
He felt his foe was foolish to dispute.
Some arbitrary accidental thoughts
That crossed his mind, amusing because new,
He chose to represent as fixtures there,
Invariable convictions (such they seemed
Beside his interlocutor's loose cards
Flung daily down, and not the same way twice)
While certain hell-deep instincts, man's weak tongue
Is never bold to utter in their truth
Because styled hell-deep ('tis an old mistake
To place hell at the bottom of the earth)
He ignored these,—not having in readiness
Their nomenclature and philosophy:
He said true things, but called them by wrong names.
"On the whole," he thought, "I justify myself
On every point where cavillers like this
Oppugn my life: he tries one kind of fence—
I close—he's worsted, that's enough for him;
He's on the ground! if the ground should break away
I take my stand on, there's a firmer yet
Beneath it, both of us may sink and reach.
His ground was over mine and broke the first.
So let him sit with me this many a year!"

   He did not sit five minutes.   Just a week
Sufficed his sudden healthy vehemence.
(Something had struck him in the "Outward-bound"
Another way than Blougram's purpose was)
And having bought, not cabin-furniture
But settler's-implements (enough for three)
And started for Australia—there, I hope,
By this time he has tested his first plough,
And studied his last chapter of St. John.

MEMORABILIA

I

AH, did you once see Shelley plain,
  And did he stop and speak to you?
And did you speak to him again?
  How strange it seems, and new!

II

But you were living before that,
  And you are living after,
And the memory I started at—
  My starting moves your laughter!

III

I crossed a moor with a name of its own
  And a use in the world no doubt,
Yet a hand's-breadth of it shines alone
  'Mid the blank miles round about—

IV

For there I picked up on the heather
  And there I put inside my breast
A moulted feather, an eagle-feather—
  Well, I forget the rest.

ANDREA DEL SARTO

ANDREA DEL SARTO

(CALLED "THE FAULTLESS PAINTER")

BUT do not let us quarrel any more,
No, my Lucrezia; bear with me for once:
Sit down and all shall happen as you wish.
You turn your face, but does it bring your heart?
I'll work then for your friend's friend, never fear,
Treat his own subject after his own way,
Fix his own time, accept too his own price,
And shut the money into this small hand
When next it takes mine. Will it? tenderly?
Oh, I'll content him,—but to-morrow, Love!
I often am much wearier than you think,
This evening more than usual, and it seems
As if—forgive now—should you let me sit
Here by the window with your hand in mine
And look a half hour forth on Fiesole,
Both of one mind, as married people use,
Quietly, quietly, the evening through,
I might get up to-morrow to my work
Cheerful and fresh as ever. Let us try.
To-morrow how you shall be glad for this!
Your soft hand is a woman of itself,
And mine the man's bared breast she curls inside.
Don't count the time lost, either; you must serve
For each of the five pictures we require—
It saves a model. So! keep looking so—
My serpentining beauty, rounds on rounds!
—How could you ever prick those perfect ears,
Even to put the pearl there! oh, so sweet—
My face, my moon, my everybody's moon,
Which everybody looks on and calls his,
And, I suppose, is looked on by in turn,
While she looks—no one's: very dear, no less!
You smile? why, there's my picture ready made.

290

ANDREA DEL SARTO

There's what we painters call our harmony !
A common greyness silvers everything,—
All in a twilight, you and I alike
—You, at the point of your first pride in me
(That's gone you know),—but I, at every point ,
My youth, my hope, my art, being all toned down
To yonder sober pleasant Fiesole.
There's the bell clinking from the chapel-top ;
That length of convent-wall across the way
Holds the trees safer, huddled more inside ;
The last monk leaves the garden ; days decrease
And autumn grows, autumn in everything.
Eh ? the whole seems to fall into a shape
As if I saw alike my work and self
And all that I was born to be and do,
A twilight-piece. Love, we are in God's hand.
How strange now, looks the life he makes us lead !
So free we seem, so fettered fast we are :
I feel he laid the fetter : let it lie !
This chamber for example—turn your head—
All that's behind us ! you don't understand
Nor care to understand about my art,
But you can hear at least when people speak ;
And that cartoon, the second from the door
—It is the thing, Love ! so such things should be—
Behold Madonna, I am bold to say.
I can do with my pencil what I know,
What I see, what at bottom of my heart
I wish for, if I ever wish so deep—
Do easily, too—when I say perfectly
I do not boast, perhaps : yourself are judge
Who listened to the Legate's talk last week,
And just as much they used to say in France.
At any rate 'tis easy, all of it,
No sketches first, no studies, that's long past—
I do what many dream of all their lives
—Dream ? strive to do, and agonise to do,

ANDREA DEL SARTO

And fail in doing. I could count twenty such
On twice your fingers, and not leave this town,
Who strive—you don't know how the others strive
To paint a little thing like that you smeared
Carelessly passing with your robes afloat,
Yet do much less, so much less, some one says,
(I know his name, no matter) so much less!
Well, less is more, Lucrezia! I am judged.
There burns a truer light of God in them,
In their vexed, beating, stuffed and stopped-up brain,
Heart, or whate'er else, than goes on to prompt
This low-pulsed forthright craftsman's hand of mine.
Their works drop groundward, but themselves, I know,
Reach many a time a heaven that's shut to me,
Enter and take their place there sure enough,
Though they come back and cannot tell the world.
My works are nearer heaven, but I sit here.
The sudden blood of these men! at a word—
Praise them, it boils, or blame them, it boils too.
I, painting from myself and to myself,
Know what I do, am unmoved by men's blame
Or their praise either. Somebody remarks
Morello's outline there is wrongly traced,
His hue mistaken—what of that? or else,
Rightly traced and well ordered—what of that?
Ah, but a man's reach should exceed his grasp,
Or what's a Heaven for? all is silver-grey
Placid and perfect with my art—the worse!
I know both what I want and what might gain—
And yet how profitless to know, to sigh
" Had I been two, another and myself,
Our head would have o'erlooked the world!" No
        doubt.
Yonder's a work, now, of that famous youth
The Urbinate who died five years ago.
('Tis copied, George Vasari sent it me.)
Well, I can fancy how he did it all,

ANDREA DEL SARTO

Pouring his soul, with kings and popes to see,
Reaching, that Heaven might so replenish him,
Above and through his art—for it gives way;
That arm is wrongly put—and there again—
A fault to pardon in the drawing's lines,
Its body, so to speak! its soul is right,
He means right—that, a child may understand.
Still, what an arm! and I could alter it.
But all the play, the insight and the stretch—
Out of me! out of me!   And wherefore out?
Had you enjoined them on me, given me soul,
We might have risen to Rafael, I and you.
Nay, Love, you did give all I asked, I think—
More than I merit, yes, by many times.
But had you—oh, with the same perfect brow,
And perfect eyes, and more than perfect mouth,
And the low voice my soul hears, as a bird
The fowler's pipe, and follows to the snare—
Had you, with these the same, but brought a mind!
Some women do so.   Had the mouth there urged
"God and the glory! never care for gain.
The present by the future, what is that?
Live for fame, side by side with Angelo—
Rafael is waiting.   Up to God all three!"
I might have done it for you.   So it seems—
Perhaps not.   All is as God over-rules.
Besides, incentives come from the soul's self;
The rest avail not.   Why do I need you?
What wife had Rafael, or has Angelo?
In this world, who can do a thing, will not—
And who would do it, cannot, I perceive:
Yet the will's somewhat—somewhat, too, the power—
And thus we half-men struggle.   At the end,
God, I conclude, compensates, punishes.
'Tis safer for me, if the award be strict,
That I am something underrated here,
Poor this long while, despised, to speak the truth.

ANDREA DEL SARTO

I dared not, do you know, leave home all day,
For fear of chancing on the Paris lords.
The best is when they pass and look aside;
But they speak sometimes; I must bear it all.
Well may they speak! That Francis, that first time,
And that long festal year at Fontainebleau!
I surely then could sometimes leave the ground,
Put on the glory, Rafael's daily wear,
In that humane great monarch's golden look,—
One finger in his beard or twisted curl
Over his mouth's good mark that made the smile,
One arm about my shoulder, round my neck,
The jingle of his gold chain in my ear,
You painting proudly with his breath on me,
All his court round him, seeing with his eyes,
Such frank French eyes, and such a fire of souls
Profuse, my hand kept plying by those hearts,—
And, best of all, this, this, this face beyond,
This in the back-ground, waiting on my work,
To crown the issue with a last reward!
A good time, was it not, my kingly days?
And had you not grown restless—but I know—
'Tis done and past; 'twas right, my instinct said;
Too live the life grew, golden and not grey—
And I'm the weak-eyed bat no sun should tempt
Out of the grange whose four walls make his world.
How could it end in any other way?
You called me, and I came home to your heart.
The triumph was to have ended there—then if
I reached it ere the triumph, what is lost?
Let my hands frame your face in your hair's gold,
You beautiful Lucrezia that are mine!
"Rafael did this, Andrea painted that—
The Roman's is the better when you pray,
But still the other's Virgin was his wife—"
Men will excuse me. I am glad to judge
Both pictures in your presence; clearer grows

ANDREA DEL SARTO

My better fortune, I resolve to think.
For, do you know, Lucrezia, as God lives,
Said one day Angelo, his very self,
To Rafael . . . I have known it all these years . . .
(When the young man was flaming out his thoughts
Upon a palace-wall for Rome to see,
Too lifted up in heart because of it)
" Friend, there's a certain sorry little scrub
Goes up and down our Florence, none cares how,
Who, were he set to plan and execute
As you are pricked on by your popes and kings,
Would bring the sweat into that brow of yours!"
To Rafael's!—And indeed the arm is wrong.
I hardly dare—yet, only you to see,
Give the chalk here—quick, thus the line should go!
Ay, but the soul! he's Rafael! rub it out!
Still, all I care for, if he spoke the truth,
(What he? why, who but Michael Angelo?
Do you forget already words like those?)
If really there was such a chance, so lost,
Is, whether you 're—not grateful—but more pleased.
Well, let me think so. And you smile indeed!
This hour has been an hour! Another smile?
If you would sit thus by me every night
I should work better, do you comprehend?
I mean that I should earn more, give you more.
See, it is settled dusk now; there's a star;
Morello's gone, the watch-lights shew the wall,
The cue-owls speak the name we call them by.
Come from the window, Love,—come in, at last,
Inside the melancholy little house
We built to be so gay with. God is just.
King Francis may forgive me. Oft at nights
When I look up from painting, eyes tired out,
The walls become illumined, brick from brick
Distinct, instead of mortar fierce bright gold,
That gold of his I did cement them with!

297

ANDREA DEL SARTO

Let us but love each other. Must you go?
That Cousin here again? he waits outside?
Must see you—you, and not with me? Those loans!
More gaming debts to pay? you smiled for that?
Well, let smiles buy me! have you more to spend?
While hand and eye and something of a heart
Are left me, work's my ware, and what's it worth?
I'll pay my fancy. Only let me sit
The grey remainder of the evening out,
Idle, you call it, and muse perfectly
How I could paint were I but back in France,
One picture, just one more—the Virgin's face,
Not yours this time! I want you at my side
To hear them—that is, Michael Angelo—
Judge all I do and tell you of its worth.
Will you? To-morrow, satisfy your friend.
I take the subjects for his corridor,
Finish the portrait out of hand—there, there,
And throw him in another thing or two
If he demurs; the whole should prove enough
To pay for this same Cousin's freak. Beside,
What's better and what's all I care about,
Get you the thirteen scudi for the ruff.
Love, does that please you? Ah, but what does he,
The Cousin! what does he to please you more?

I am grown peaceful as old age to-night.
I regret little, I would change still less.
Since there my past life lies, why alter it?
The very wrong to Francis! it is true
I took his coin, was tempted and complied,
And built this house and sinned, and all is said.
My father and my mother died of want.
Well, had I riches of my own? you see
How one gets rich! Let each one bear his lot.
They were born poor, lived poor, and poor they died:
And I have laboured somewhat in my time

ANDREA DEL SARTO

And not been paid profusely.   Some good son
Paint my two hundred pictures—let him try!
No doubt, there's something strikes a balance.   Yes,
You loved me quite enough, it seems to-night.
This must suffice me here.   What would one have?
In heaven, perhaps, new chances, one more chance—
Four great walls in the New Jerusalem
Meted on each side by the angel's reed,
For Leonard, Rafael, Angelo and me
To cover—the three first without a wife,
While I have mine!   So—still they overcome
Because there's still Lucrezia,—as I choose.

Again the Cousin's whistle! Go, my Love.

BEFORE

BEFORE

I

LET them fight it out, friend! things have gone too far.
God must judge the couple! leave them as they are
—Whichever one's the guiltless, to his glory,
And whichever one the guilt's with, to my story.

II

Why, you would not bid men, sunk in such a slough,
Strike no arm out further, stick and stink as now,
Leaving right and wrong to settle the embroilment,
Heaven with snaky Hell, in torture and entoilment?

III

Which of them's the culprit, how must he conceive
God's the queen he caps to, laughing in his sleeve!
'Tis but decent to profess oneself beneath her.
Still, one must not be too much in earnest either.

IV

Better sin the whole sin, sure that God observes,
Then go live his life out! life will try his nerves,
When the sky which noticed all, makes no disclosure,
And the earth keeps up her terrible composure.

V

Let him pace at pleasure, past the walls of rose,
Pluck their fruits when grape-trees graze him as he goes.
For he 'gins to guess the purpose of the garden,
With the sly mute thing beside there for a warden.

VI

What's the leopard-dog-thing, constant to his side,
A leer and lie in every eye on its obsequious hide?
When will come an end of all the mock obeisance,
And the price appear that pays for the misfeasance?

300

AFTER

VII

So much for the culprit.   Who's the martyred man?
Let him bear one stroke more, for be sure he can.
He that strove thus evil's lump with good to leaven,
Let him give his blood at last and get his heaven.

VIII

All or nothing, stake it! trusts he God or no?
Thus far and no farther? farther? be it so.
Now, enough of your chicane of prudent pauses,
Sage provisos, sub-intents, and saving-clauses.

IX

Ah, "forgive" you bid him?   While God's champion
   lives,
Wrong shall be resisted : dead, why he forgives.
But you must not end my friend ere you begin him ;
Evil stands not crowned on earth, while breath is in him.

X

Once more—Will the wronger, at this last of all,
Dare to say "I did wrong," rising in his fall?
No?—Let go, then—both the fighters to their places—
While I count three, step you back as many paces.

AFTER

TAKE the cloak from his face, and at first
   Let the corpse do its worst.

How he lies in his rights of a man !
   Death has done all death can.
And absorbed in the new life he leads,
   He recks not, he heeds
Nor his wrong nor my vengeance—both strike
   On his senses alike,

301

AFTER

And are lost in the solemn and strange
 Surprise of the change.
Ha, what avails death to erase
 His offence, my disgrace?
I would we were boys as of old
 In the field, by the fold—
His outrage, God's patience, man's scorn
 Were so easily borne.

I stand here now, he lies in his place—
 Cover the face.

IN THREE DAYS

I

So, I shall see her in three days
And just one night, but nights are short,
Then two long hours, and that is morn.
See how I come, unchanged, unworn—
Feel, where my life broke off from thine,
How fresh the splinters keep and fine,—
Only a touch and we combine!

II

Too long, this time of year, the days!
But nights—at least the nights are short.
As night shows where her one moon is,
A hand's-breadth of pure light and bliss,
So, life's night gives my lady birth
And my eyes hold her! what is worth
The rest of heaven, the rest of earth?

302

IN THREE DAYS

III

O loaded curls, release your store
Of warmth and scent as once before
The tingling hair did, lights and darks
Out-breaking into fairy sparks
When under curl and curl I pried
After the warmth and scent inside
Thro' lights and darks how manifold—
The dark inspired, the light controlled!
As early Art embrowned the gold

IV

What great fear—should one say, " Three days
That change the world, might change as well
Your fortune; and if joy delays,
Be happy that no worse befell."
What small fear—if another says,
" Three days and one short night beside
May throw no shadow on your ways;
But years must teem with change untried,
With chance not easily defied,
With an end somewhere undescried."
No fear!—or if a fear be born
This minute it dies out in scorn.
Fear? I shall see her in three days
And one night, now the nights are short
Then just two hours, and that is morn.

IN A YEAR

IN A YEAR

I

NEVER any more
  While I live,
Need I hope to see his face
  As before.
Once his love grown chill,
  Mine may strive—
Bitterly we re-embrace,
  Single still.

II

Was it something said,
  Something done,
Vexed him? was it touch of hand,
  Turn of head?
Strange! that very way
  Love begun.
I as little understand
  Love's decay.

III

When I sewed or drew,
  I recall
How he looked as if I sang,
  —Sweetly too.
If I spoke a word,
  First of all
Up his cheek the colour sprang,
  Then he heard.

IV

Sitting by my side,
  At my feet,
So he breathed the air I breathed,
  Satisfied!

IN A YEAR,

IN A YEAR

I, too, at love's brim
  Touched the sweet :
I would die if death bequeathed
  Sweet to him.

V

"Speak, I love thee best !"
  He exclaimed.
"Let thy love my own foretell,—"
  I confessed :
"Clasp my heart on thine
  Now unblamed,
Since upon thy soul as well
  Hangeth mine !"

VI

Was it wrong to own,
  Being truth ?
Why should all the giving prove
  His alone ?
I had wealth and ease,
  Beauty, youth—
Since my lover gave me love,
  I gave these.

VII

That was all I meant,
  —To be just,
And the passion I had raised
  To content.
Since he chose to change
  Gold for dust,
If I gave him what he praised
  Was it strange ?

IN A YEAR

Would he loved me yet,
  On and on,
While I found some way undreamed
  —Paid my debt!
Gave more life and more
  Till, all gone,
He should smile "She never seemed
  Mine before.

IX

"What—she felt the while,
  Must I think?
Love's so different with us men,"
  He should smile.
"Dying for my sake—
  White and pink!
Can't we touch these bubbles then
  But they break?"

Dear, the pang is brief,
  Do thy part,
Have thy pleasure.   How perplext
  Grows belief!
Well, this cold clay clod
  Was man's heart.
Crumble it—and what comes next?
  Is it God?

OLD PICTURES IN FLORENCE

I

THE morn when first it thunders in March,
  The eel in the pond gives a leap, they say.
As I leaned and looked over the aloed arch
  Of the villa-gate, this warm March day,
No flash snapt, no dumb thunder rolled
  In the valley beneath, where, white and wide,
Washed by the morning's water-gold,
  Florence lay out on the mountain-side.

II

River and bridge and street and square
  Lay mine, as much at my beck and call,
Through the live translucent bath of air,
  As the sights in a magic crystal ball.
And of all I saw and of all I praised,
  The most to praise and the best to see,
Was the startling bell-tower Giotto raised:
  But why did it more than startle me?

III

Giotto, how, with that soul of yours,
  Could you play me false who loved you so?
Some slights if a certain heart endures
  It feels, I would have your fellows know!
'Faith—I perceive not why I should care
  To break a silence that suits them best,
But the thing grows somewhat hard to bear
  When I find a Giotto join the rest.

IV

On the arch where olives overhead
  Print the blue sky with twig and leaf,
(That sharp-curled leaf they never shed)
  'Twixt the aloes I used to lean in chief,

OLD PICTURES IN FLORENCE

And mark through the winter afternoons,
  By a gift God grants me now and then,
In the mild decline of those suns like moons,
  Who walked in Florence, besides her men.

V

They might chirp and chaffer, come and go
  For pleasure or profit, her men alive—
My business was hardly with them, I trow,
  But with empty cells of the human hive ;
—With the chapter-room, the cloister-porch,
  The church's apsis, aisle or nave,
Its crypt, one fingers along with a torch—
  Its face, set full for the sun to shave.

VI

Wherever a fresco peels and drops,
  Wherever an outline weakens and wanes
Till the latest life in the painting stops,
  Stands One whom each fainter pulse-tick pains !
One, wishful each scrap should clutch its brick,
  Each tinge not wholly escape the plaster,
—A lion who dies of an ass's kick,
  The wronged great soul of an ancient Master.

VII

For oh, this world and the wrong it does !
  They are safe in heaven with their backs to it,
The Michaels and Rafaels, you hum and buzz
  Round the works of, you of the little wit !
Do their eyes contract to the earth's old scope,
  Now that they see God face to face,
And have all attained to be poets, I hope ?
  'Tis their holiday now, in any case.

OLD PICTURES IN FLORENCE

VIII

Much they reck of your praise and you!
  But the wronged great souls—can they be quit
Of a world where all their work is to do,
  Where you style them, you of the little wit,
Old Master this and Early the other,
  Not dreaming that Old and New are fellows,
That a younger succeeds to an elder brother,
  Da Vincis derive in good time from Dellos.

IX

And here where your praise would yield returns
  And a handsome word or two give help,
Here, after your kind, the mastiff girns
  And the puppy pack of poodles yelp.
What, not a word for Stefano there
  —Of brow once prominent and starry,
Called Nature's ape and the world's despair
  For his peerless painting (see Vasari)?

X

There he stands now. Study, my friends,
  What a man's work comes to! so he plans it,
Performs it, perfects it, makes amends
  For the toiling and moiling, and there 's its transit!
Happier the thrifty blind-folk labour,
  With upturned eye while the hand is busy,
Not sidling a glance at the coin of their neighbour!
  'Tis looking downward makes one dizzy.

XI

If you knew their work you would deal your dole.
  May I take upon me to instruct you?
When Greek Art ran and reached the goal,
  Thus much had the world to boast *in fructu—*

OLD PICTURES IN FLORENCE

The truth of Man, as by God first spoken,
   Which the actual generations garble,
Was re-uttered,—and Soul (which Limbs betoken)
   And Limbs (Soul informs) were made new in marble.

XII

So you saw yourself as you wished you were,
   As you might have been, as you cannot be ;
And bringing your own shortcomings there,
   You grew content in your poor degree
With your little power, by those statues' godhead,
   And your little scope, by their eyes' full sway,
And your little grace, by their grace embodied,
   And your little date, by their forms that stay.

XIII

You would fain be kinglier, say than I am?
   Even so, you will not sit like Theseus.
You 'd fain be a model? The Son of Priam
   Has yet the advantage in arms' and knees' use.
You 're wroth—can you slay your snake like Apollo?
   You 're grieved—still Niobe 's the grander !
You live—there 's the Racers' frieze to follow—
   You die—there 's the dying Alexander.

XIV

So, testing your weakness by their strength,
   Your meagre charms by their rounded beauty,
Measured by Art in your breadth and length,
   You learn—to submit is the worsted's duty.
—When I say "you" 'tis the common soul,
   The collective, I mean—the race of Man
That receives life in parts to live in a whole,
   And grow here according to God's own plan.

OLD PICTURES IN FLORENCE

XV

Growth came when, looking your last on them all,
  You turned your eyes inwardly one fine day
And cried with a start—What if we so small
  Are greater, ay, greater the while than they !
Are they perfect of lineament, perfect of stature ?
  In both, of such lower types are we
Precisely because of our wider nature ;
  For time, theirs—ours, for eternity.

XVI

To-day's brief passion limits their range,
  It seethes with the morrow for us and more.
They are perfect—how else ? they shall never change :
  We are faulty—why not ? we have time in store.
The Artificer's hand is not arrested
  With us—we are rough-hewn, no-wise polished :
They stand for our copy, and, once invested
  With all they can teach, we shall see them abolished.

XVII

'Tis a life-long toil till our lump be leaven—
  The better ! what's come to perfection perishes.
Things learned on earth, we shall practise in heaven.
  Works done least rapidly, Art most cherishes.
Thyself shall afford the example, Giotto !
  Thy one work, not to decrease or diminish,
Done at a stroke, was just (was it not ?) "O !"
  Thy great Campanile is still to finish.

XVIII

Is it true, we are now, and shall be hereafter,
  And what—is depending on life's one minute ?
Hails heavenly cheer or infernal laughter
  Our first step out of the gulf or in it ?

313

OLD PICTURES IN FLORENCE

And Man, this step within his endeavour,
  His face, have no more play and action
Than joy which is crystallized for ever,
  Or grief, an eternal petrifaction!

XIX

On which I conclude, that the early painters,
  To cries of "Greek Art and what more wish you?"—
Replied, " Become now self-acquainters,
  And paint man, man,—whatever the issue!
Make the hopes shine through the flesh they fray,
  New fears aggrandise the rags and tatters.
So bring the invisible full into play,
  Let the visible go to the dogs—what matters?"

XX

Give these, I say, full honour and glory
  For daring so much, before they well did it.
The first of the new, in our race's story,
  Beats the last of the old, 'tis no idle quiddit.
The worthies began a revolution
  Which if on the earth we intend to acknowledge
Honour them now—(ends my allocution)
  Nor confer our degree when the folks leave college.

XXI

There's a fancy some lean to and others hate—
  That, when this life is ended, begins
New work for the soul in another state,
  Where it strives and gets weary, loses and wins—
Where the strong and the weak, this world's
      congeries,
  Repeat in large what they practised in small,
Through life after life in unlimited series;
  Only the scale's to be changed, that's all.

314

OLD PICTURES IN FLORENCE

XXII

Yet I hardly know. When a soul has seen
  By the means of Evil that Good is best,
And through earth and its noise, what is heaven's
    serene,—
  When its faith in the same has stood the test—
Why, the child grown man, you burn the rod,
  The uses of labour are surely done.
There remaineth a rest for the people of God,
  And I have had troubles enough for one.

XXIII

But at any rate I have loved the season
  Of Art's spring-birth so dim and dewy,
My sculptor is Nicolo the Pisan ;
  My painter—who but Cimabue?
Nor ever was man of them all indeed,
  From these to Ghiberti and Ghirlandajo,
Could say that he missed my critic-meed.
  So now to my special grievance—heigh ho!

XXIV

Their ghosts now stand, as I said before,
  Watching each fresco flaked and rasped,
Blocked up, knocked out, or whitewashed o'er
  —No getting again what the church has grasped!
The works on the wall must take their chance,
  "Works never conceded to England's thick clime!"
(I hope they prefer their inheritance
  Of a bucketful of Italian quick-lime.)

XXV

When they go at length, with such a shaking
  Of heads o'er the old delusions, sadly
Each master his way through the black streets taking,
  Where many a lost work breathes though badly—

315

OLD PICTURES IN FLORENCE

Why don't they bethink them of who has merited?
  Why not reveal, while their pictures dree
Such doom, that a captive's to be out-ferreted?
  Why do they never remember me?

XXVI

Not that I expect the great Bigordi
  Nor Sandro to hear me, chivalric, bellicose;
Nor wronged Lippino—and not a word I
  Say of a scrap of Fra Angelico's.
But are you too fine, Taddeo Gaddi,
  To grant you a taste of your intonaco—
Some Jerome that seeks the heaven with a sad eye?
  No churlish saint, Lorenzo Monaco?

XXVII

Could not the ghost with the close red cap,
  My Pollajolo, the twice a craftsman,
Save me a sample, give me the hap
  Of a muscular Christ that shows the draughtsman?
No Virgin by him, the somewhat petty,
  Of finical touch and tempera crumbly—
Could not Alesso Baldovinetti
  Contribute so much, I ask him humbly?

XXVIII

Margheritone of Arezzo,
  With the grave-clothes garb and swaddling barret,
(Why purse up mouth and beak in a pet so.
  You bald, saturnine, poll-clawed parrot?)
No poor glimmering Crucifixion,
  Where in the foreground kneels the donor?
If such remain, as is my conviction,
  The hoarding does you but little honour.

OLD PICTURES IN FLORENCE

XXIX

They pass: for them the panels may thrill,
  The tempera grow alive and tinglish—
Rot or are left to the mercies still
  Of dealers and stealers, Jews and the English!
Seeing mere money's worth in their prize,
  Who sell it to some one calm as Zeno
At naked Art, and in ecstacies
  Before some clay-cold, vile Carlino!

XXX

No matter for these! But Giotto, you,
  Have you allowed, as the town-tongues babble it,
Never! it shall not be counted true—
  That a certain precious little tablet
Which Buonarroti eyed like a lover,—
  Buried so long in oblivion's womb,
Was left for another than I to discover,—
  Turns up at last, and to whom?—to whom?

XXXI

I, that have haunted the dim San Spirito,
  (Or was it rather the Ognissanti?)
Stood on the altar-steps, patient and weary too!
  Nay, I shall have it yet, *detur amanti!*
My Koh-i-noor—or (if that's a platitude)
  Jewel of Giamschid, the Persian Sofi's eye!
So, in anticipative gratitude,
  What if I take up my hope and prophesy?

XXXII

When the hour is ripe, and a certain dotard
  Pitched, no parcel that needs invoicing,
To the worst side of the Mont St. Gothard,
  Have, to begin by way of rejoicing,

317

OLD PICTURES IN FLORENCE

None of that shooting the sky (blank cartridge),
   No civic guards, all plumes and lacquer,
Hunting Radetzky's soul like a partridge
   Over Morello with squib and cracker.

XXXIII

We'll shoot this time better game and bag 'em hot—
   No display at the stone of Dante,
But a kind of Witan-agemot
   ("Casa Guidi," quod videas ante)
To ponder Freedom restored to Florence,
   How Art may return that departed with her.
Go, hated house, go each trace of the Loraine's!
   And bring us the days of Orgagna hither.

XXXIV

How we shall prologize, how we shall perorate,
   Say fit things upon art and history—
Set truth at blood-heat and the false at a zero rate,
   Make of the want of the age no mystery!
Contrast the fructuous and sterile eras,
   Show, monarchy its uncouth cub licks
Out of the bear's shape to the chimæra's—
   Pure Art's birth being still the republic's!

XXXV

Then one shall propose (in a speech, curt Tuscan,
   Sober, expurgate, spare of an *"issimo,"*)
Ending our half-told tale of Cambuscan,
   Turning the Bell-tower's altaltissimo.
And fine as the beak of a young beccaccia
   The Campanile, the Duomo's fit ally,
Soars up in gold its full fifty braccia,
   Completing Florence, as Florence, Italy.

SAUL

XXXVI

Shall I be alive that morning the scaffold
  Is broken away, and the long-pent fire
Like the golden hope of the world unbaffled
  Springs from its sleep, and up goes the spire—
As, "God and the People" plain for its motto,
  Thence the new tricolor flaps at the sky?
Foreseeing the day that vindicates Giotto
  And Florence together, the first am I!

SAUL

I

SAID Abner, "At last thou art come! Ere I tell, ere
        thou speak,
Kiss my cheek, wish me well!" Then I wished it, and did
        kiss his cheek.
And he, "Since the King, O my friend, for thy countenance
        sent,
Neither drunken nor eaten have we; nor until from his
        tent
Thou return with the joyful assurance the King liveth yet,
Shall our lip with the honey be bright, with the water
        be wet.
For out of the black mid-tent's silence, a space of three
        days,
Not a sound hath escaped to thy servants, of prayer or
        of praise,
To betoken that Saul and the Spirit have ended their
        strife,
And that, faint in his triumph, the monarch sinks back
        upon life.

SAUL

II

Yet now my heart leaps, O beloved ! God's child, with
his dew
On thy gracious gold hair, and those lilies still living and
blue
Just broken to twine round thy harp-strings, as if no wild
heat
Were now raging to torture the desert ! "

III

Then I, as was meet,
Knelt down to the God of my fathers, and rose on my
feet,
And ran o'er the sand burnt to powder. The tent was
unlooped ;
I pulled up the spear that obstructed, and under I
stooped ;
Hands and knees on the slippery grass-patch, all withered
and gone,
That extends to the second enclosure, I groped my way
on
Till I felt where the foldskirts fly open. Then once more
I prayed,
And opened the foldskirts and entered, and was not afraid,
But spoke, " Here is David, thy servant ! " And no voice
replied.
At the first I saw nought but the blackness ; but soon I
descried
A something more black than the blackness—the vast the
upright
Main prop which sustains the pavilion : and slow into
sight
Grew a figure against it, gigantic and blackest of all ;—
Then a sunbeam, that burst thro' the tent-roof,—showed
Saul.

SAUL.

SAUL

IV

He stood as erect as that tent-prop ; both arms stretched
out wide
On the great cross-support in the centre, that goes to
each side :
He relaxed not a muscle, but hung there,—as, caught in
his pangs
And waiting his change the king-serpent all heavily hangs,
Far away from his kind, in the pine, till deliverance come
With the spring-time,—so agonized Saul,—drear and stark,
blind and dumb.

V

Then I tuned my harp,—took off the lilies we twine round
its chords
Lest they snap 'neath the stress of the noontide—those
sunbeams like swords !
And I first played the tune all our sheep know, as, one
after one,
So docile they come to the pen-door, till folding be done.
They are white and untorn by the bushes, for lo, they have
fed
Where the long grasses stifle the water within the stream's
bed ;
And now one after one seeks its lodging, as star follows
star
Into eve and the blue far above us,—so blue and so far !

VI

—Then the tune, for which quails on the cornland will
each leave his mate
To fly after the player ; then what makes the crickets
elate,
Till for boldness they fight one another : and then, what
has weight

SAUL

To set the quick jerboa a-musing outside his sand
house—
There are none such as he for a wonder, half bird and
half mouse!—
God made all the creatures and gave them our love and
our fear,
To give sign, we and they are his children, one family
here.

VII

Then I played the help-tune of our reapers, their wine-
song, when hand
Grasps at hand, eye lights eye in good friendship, and
great hearts expand
And grow one in the sense of this world's life.—And then,
the last song
When the dead man is praised on his journey—" Bear,
bear him along
With his few faults shut up like dead flowerets! are balm-
seeds not here
To console us? The land has none left, such as he on
the bier.
Oh, would we might keep thee, my brother!"—And then,
the glad chaunt
Of the marriage,—first go the young maidens, next, she
whom we vaunt
As the beauty, the pride of our dwelling.—And then, the
great march
Wherein man runs to man to assist him and buttress an
arch
Nought can break; who shall harm them, our friends?
—Then, the chorus intoned
As the Levites go up to the altar in glory enthroned . . .
But I stopped here — for here in the darkness, Saul
groaned.

SAUL

And I paused, held my breath in such silence, and listened
    apart ;
And the tent shook, for mighty Saul shuddered,—and
    sparkles 'gan dart
From the jewels that woke in his turban at once with a
    start—
All its lordly male-sapphires, and rubies courageous at
    heart.
So the head—but the body still moved not, still hung there
    erect.
And I bent once again to my playing, pursued it
    unchecked,
As I sang,—

IX

    "Oh, our manhood's prime vigour! no
    spirit feels waste,
Not a muscle is stopped in its playing, nor sinew unbraced.
Oh the wild joys of living! the leaping from rock up to
    rock—
The strong rending of boughs from the fir-tree,—the cool
    silver shock
Of the plunge in a pool's living water,—the hunt of the
    bear,
And the sultriness showing the lion is couched in his lair.
And the meal—the rich dates—yellowed over with gold
    dust divine,
And the locust's-flesh steeped in the pitcher; the full
    draught of wine,
And the sleep in the dried river-channel where bull-rushes
    tell
That the water was wont to go warbling so softly and
    well.
How good is man's life, the mere living! how fit to
    employ
All the heart and the soul and the senses, for ever in joy!

SAUL

Hast thou loved the white locks of thy father, whose
                sword thou didst guard
When he trusted thee forth with the armies, for glorious
                reward ?
Didst thou see the thin hands of thy mother, held up as
                men sung
The low song of the nearly-departed, and heard her faint
                tongue
Joining in while it could to the witness, 'Let one more
                attest,
I have lived, seen God's hand thro' a lifetime, and all was
                for best . . .'
Then they sung thro' their tears in strong triumph, not
                much,—but the rest.
And thy brothers, the help and the contest, the working
                whence grew
Such result as from seething grape-bundles, the spirit
                strained true !
And the friends of thy boyhood—that boyhood of wonder
                and hope,
Present promise, and wealth of the future beyond the eye's
                scope,—
Till lo, thou art grown to a monarch ; a people is thine ;
And all gifts which the world offers singly, on one head
                combine !
On one head, all the beauty and strength, love and rage,
                like the throe
That, a-work in the rock, helps its labour, and lets the gold
                go :
High ambition and deeds which surpass it, fame crowning
                it,—all
Brought to blaze on the head of one creature—King Saul ! "

X

And lo, with that leap of my spirit, heart, hand, harp and
                voice,
Each lifting Saul's name out of sorrow, each bidding rejoice

SAUL

Saul's fame in the light it was made for—as when, dare I
say,
The Lord's army in rapture of service, strains through its
array,
And upsoareth the cherubim-chariot—" Saul!" cried I, and
stopped,
And waited the thing that should follow.   Then Saul, who
hung propt
By the tent's cross-support in the centre, was struck by his
name.
Have ye seen when Spring's arrowy summons goes right
to the aim,
And some mountain, the last to withstand her, that held,
(he alone,
While the vale laughed in freedom and flowers) on a broad
bust of stone
A year's snow bound about for a breastplate,—leaves grasp
of the sheet ?
Fold on fold all at once it crowds thunderously down to
his feet,
And there fronts you, stark, black but alive yet, your
mountain of old,
With his rents, the successive bequeathings of ages
untold—
Yea, each harm got in fighting your battles, each furrow
and scar
Of his head thrust 'twixt you and the tempest—all hail,
there they are !
Now again to be softened with verdure, again hold the
nest
Of the dove, tempt the goat and its young to the green on
its crest
For their food in the ardours of summer !   One long
shudder thrilled
All the tent till the very air tingled, then sank and was
stilled,

SAUL

At the King's self left standing before me, released and
  aware.
What was gone, what remained? all to traverse 'twixt
  hope and despair—
Death was past, life not come—so he waited. Awhile his
  right hand
Held the brow, helped the eyes left too vacant forthwith to
  remand
To their place what new objects should enter: 'twas Saul
  as before.
I looked up and dared gaze at those eyes, nor was hurt any
  more
Than by slow pallid sunsets in autumn, ye watch from the
  shore
At their sad level gaze o'er the ocean—a sun's slow decline
Over hills which, resolved in stern silence, o'erlap and
  entwine
Base with base to knit strength more intense: so, arm
  folded in arm
O'er the chest whose slow heavings subsided.

XI
                    What spell or what charm,
(For, awhile there was trouble within me) what next
  should I urge
To sustain him where song had restored him?—Song filled
  to the verge
His cup with the wine of this life, pressing all that it yields
Of mere fruitage, the strength and the beauty! Beyond,
  on what fields,
Glean a vintage more potent and perfect to brighten the
  eye
And bring blood to the lip, and commend them the cup
  they put by?
He saith, "It is good"; still he drinks not—he lets me
  praise life,
Gives assent, yet would die for his own part.

328

SAUL

XII

Then fancies grew rife
Which had come long ago on the pastures, when round me
the sheep
Fed in silence—above, the one eagle wheeled slow as in
sleep,
And I lay in my hollow, and mused on the world that
might lie
'Neath his ken, though I saw but the strip 'twixt the hill
and the sky:
And I laughed—" Since my days are ordained to be passed
with my flocks,
Let me people at least with my fancies, the plains and the
rocks,
Dream the life I am never to mix with, and image the show
Of mankind as they live in those fashions I hardly shall
know!
Schemes of life, its best rules and right uses, the courage
that gains,
And the prudence that keeps what men strive for."
And now these old trains
Of vague thought came again; I grew surer; so once
more the string
Of my harp made response to my spirit, as thus—

XIII

" Yea, my king,"
I began—" thou dost well in rejecting mere comforts that
spring
From the mere mortal life held in common by man and
by brute:
In our flesh grows the branch of this life, in our soul it
bears fruit.
Thou hast marked the slow rise of the tree,—how its stem
trembled first
Till it passed the kid's lip, the stag's antler; then safely
outburst

329

SAUL

The fan-branches all round ; and thou mindedst when
these too, in turn
Broke a-bloom and the palm-tree seemed perfect ; yet
more was to learn,
Ev'n the good that comes in with the palm-fruit. Our
dates shall we slight,
When their juice brings a cure for all sorrow ? or care for
the plight
Of the palm's self whose slow growth produced them ?
Not so ! stem and branch
Shall decay, nor be known in their place, while the palm-
wine shall staunch
Every wound of man's spirit in winter. I pour thee such
wine.
Leave the flesh to the fate it was fit for ! the spirit be
thine !
By the spirit, when age shall o'ercome thee, thou still shalt
enjoy
More indeed, than at first when inconscious, the life of
a boy.
Crush that life, and behold its wine running ! each deed
thou hast done
Dies, revives, goes to work in the world ; until e'en as the
sun
Looking down on the earth, though clouds spoil him,
though tempests efface,
Can find nothing his own deed produced not, must everywhere trace
The results of his past summer-prime,—so, each ray of
thy will,
Every flash of thy passion and prowess, long over, shall
thrill
Thy whole people the countless, with ardour, till they too
give forth
A like cheer to their sons, who in turn, fill the south and
the north

SAUL

With the radiance thy deed was the germ of. Carouse
in the past.
But the license of age has its limit; thou diest at last.
As the lion when age dims his eye-ball, the rose at her
height,
So with man—so his power and his beauty for ever take
flight.
No! again a long draught of my soul-wine! look forth o'er
the years—
Thou hast done now with eyes for the actual; begin with
the seer's!
Is Saul dead? in the depth of the vale make his tomb—
bid arise
A grey mountain of marble heaped four-square, till built to
the skies.
Let it mark where the great First King slumbers—whose
fame would ye know?
Up above see the rock's naked face, where the record shall go
In great characters cut by the scribe,—Such was Saul, so
he did;
With the sages directing the work, by the populace chid,—
For not half, they'll affirm, is comprised there! Which fault
to amend,
In the grove with his kind grows the cedar, whereon they
shall spend
(See, in tablets 'tis level before them) their praise, and
record
With the gold of the graver, Saul's story,—the statesman's
great word
Side by side with the poet's sweet comment. The river's
a-wave
With smooth paper-reeds grazing each other when prophet
winds rave:
So the pen gives unborn generations their due and their
part
In thy being! Then, first of the mighty, thank God that
thou art."

331

SAUL

And behold while I sang . . But O Thou who didst grant
me that day,
And before it not seldom hast granted, thy help to essay
Carry on and complete an adventure,—my Shield and my
Sword
In that act where my soul was thy servant, thy word was
my word,—
Still be with me, who then at the summit of human
endeavour
And scaling the highest man's thought could, gazed
hopeless as ever
On the new stretch of Heaven above me—till, Mighty to
save,
Just one lift of thy hand cleared that distance—God's
throne from man's grave!
Let me tell out my tale to its ending—my voice to my
heart,
Which can scarce dare believe in what marvels that night
I took part,
As this morning I gather the fragments, alone with my
sheep,
And still fear lest the terrible glory evanish like sleep!
For I wake in the grey dewy covert, while Hebron
upheaves
The dawn struggling with night on his shoulder, and
Kidron retrieves
Slow the damage of yesterday's sunshine.

XV

I say then,—my song
While I sang thus, assuring the monarch, and ever more
strong
Made a proffer of good to console him—he slowly resumed
His old motions and habitudes kingly. The right hand
replumed

SAUL

His black locks to their wonted composure adjusted the
        swathes
Of his turban, and see—the huge sweat that his counten-
        ance bathes,
He wipes off with the robe ; and he girds now his loins as
        of yore,
And feels slow for the armlets of price, with the clasp set
        before,
He is Saul, ye remember in glory,—ere error had bent
The broad brow from the daily communion ; and still,
        though much spent
Be the life and the bearing that front you, the same, God
        did choose,
To receive what a man may waste, desecrate, never quite
        lose.
So sank he along by the tent-prop, till, stayed by the pile
Of his armour and war-cloak and garments, he leaned
        there awhile,
And so sat out my singing,—one arm round the tent-prop,
        to raise
His bent head, and the other hung slack—till I touched on
        the praise
I foresaw from all men in all times, to the man patient
        there,
And thus ended, the harp falling forward. Then first I
        was 'ware
That he sat, as I say, with my head just above his vast
        knees
Which were thrust out on each side around me, like oak-
        roots which please
To encircle a lamb when it slumbers. I looked up to
        know
If the best I could do had brought solace : he spoke not,
        but slow
Lifted up the hand slack at his side, till he laid it with care
Soft and grave, but in mild settled will, on my brow : thro'
        my hair

SAUL

The large fingers were pushed, and he bent back my head,
      with kind power—
All my face back, intent to peruse it, as men do a flower.
Thus held he me there with his great eyes that scrutinised
      mine—
And oh, all my heart how it loved him! but where was the
      sign?
I yearned—"Could I help thee, my father, inventing a
      bliss,
I would add to that life of the past, both the future and
      this.
I would give thee new life altogether, as good, ages hence,
As this moment,—had love but the warrant, love's heart to
      dispense!"

XVI

Then the truth came upon me. No harp more—no song
      more! out-broke—

XVII

"I have gone the whole round of Creation: I saw and I
      spoke!
I, a work of God's hand for that purpose, received in my
      brain
And pronounced on the rest of his handwork—returned
      him again
His creation's approval or censure: I spoke as I saw.
I report, as a man may of God's work—all's love, yet all's
      law!
Now I lay down the judgeship he lent me. Each faculty
      tasked
To perceive him, has gained an abyss, where a dew-drop
      was asked.
Have I knowledge? confounded it shrivels at wisdom laid
      bare.
Have I forethought? how purblind, how blank, to the
      Infinite care!

SAUL

Do I task any faculty highest, to image success?
I but open my eyes,—and perfection, no more and no less,
In the kind I imagined, full-fronts me, and God is seen
                        God
In the star, in the stone, in the flesh, in the soul and the
                        clod.
And thus looking within and around me, I ever renew
(With that stoop of the soul which in bending upraises
                        it too)
The submission of Man's nothing-perfect to God's All-
                        Complete,
As by each new obeisance in spirit, I climb to his feet!
Yet with all this abounding experience, this Deity known,
I shall dare to discover some province, some gift of my
                        own.
There's one faculty pleasant to exercise, hard to hoodwink
I am fain to keep still in abeyance, (I laugh as I think)
Lest, insisting to claim and parade in it, wot ye, I worst
E'en the Giver in one gift.—Behold! I could love if I
                        durst!
But I sink the pretension as fearing a man may o'ertake
God's own speed in the one way of love: I abstain, for
                        love's sake!
—What, my soul? see thus far and no farther? when
                        doors great and small,
Nine-and-ninety flew ope at our touch, should the
                        hundredth appal?
In the least things, have faith, yet distrust in the greatest
                        of all?
Do I find love so full in my nature, God's ultimate gift,
That I doubt his own love can compete with it? here, the
                        parts shift?
Here, the creatures surpass the Creator, the end, what
                        Began?—
Would I fain in my impotent yearning do all this for man,
And dare doubt He alone shall not help him, who yet
                        alone can?

SAUL

Would it ever have entered my mind, the bare will, much
less power,
To bestow on this Saul what I sang of, the marvellous
dower
Of the life he was gifted and filled with? to make such a
soul,
Such a body, and then such an earth for insphering the
whole?
And doth it not enter my mind (as my warm tears attest)
These good things being given, to go on, and give one
more, the best?
Ay, to save and redeem and restore him, maintain at the
height
This perfection, — succeed with life's dayspring, death's
minute of night?
Interpose at the difficult minute, snatch Saul, the mistake,
Saul, the failure, the ruin he seems now,—and bid him
awake,
From the dream, the probation, the prelude, to find himself
set
Clear and safe in new light and new life,—a new harmony
yet
To be run, and continued, and ended—who knows?—or
endure!
The man taught enough by life's dream, of the rest to
make sure.
By the pain - throb, triumphantly winning intensified
bliss,
And the next world's reward and repose, by the struggle
in this.

XVIII

"I believe it! 'tis Thou, God, that givest, 'tis I who
receive:
In the first is the last, in thy will is my power to believe.

SAUL

All's one gift: thou canst grant it moreover, as prompt to
my prayer
As I breathe out this breath, as I open these arms to the
air.
From thy will, stream the worlds, life and nature, thy
dread Sabaoth:
I will?—the mere atoms despise me! and why am I loth
To look that, even that in the face too? why is it I dare
Think but lightly of such impuissance? what stops my
despair?
This;—'tis not what man Does which exalts him, but what
man Would do!
See the king—I would help him but cannot, the wishes
fall through.
Could I wrestle to raise him from sorrow, grow poor to
enrich,
To fill up his life, starve my own out, I would—knowing
which,
I know that my service is perfect.—Oh speak through me
now!
Would I suffer for him that I love? So wilt Thou—so
wilt Thou!
So shall crown thee the topmost, ineffablest, uttermost
Crown—
And thy love fill infinitude wholly, nor leave up nor down
One spot for the creature to stand in! It is by no breath,
Turn of eye, wave of hand, that Salvation joins issue with
death!
As thy Love is discovered almighty, almighty be proved
Thy power, that exists with and for it, of Being beloved!
He who did most, shall bear most; the strongest shall
stand the most weak.
'Tis the weakness in strength that I cry for! my flesh, that
I seek
In the Godhead! I seek and I find it. O Saul, it shall be
A Face like my face that receives thee: a Man like to
me,

SAUL

Thou shalt love and be loved by, for ever! a Hand like
this hand
Shall throw open the gates of new life to thee! See the
Christ stand!"

XIX

I know not too well how I found my way home in the
night.
There were witnesses, cohorts about me, to left and to
right,
Angels, powers, the unuttered, unseen, the alive—the
aware—
I repressed, I got through them as hardly, as strugglingly
there,
As a runner beset by the populace famished for news—
Life or death. The whole earth was awakened, hell loosed
with her crews;
And the stars of night beat with emotion, and tingled and
shot
Out in fire the strong pain of pent knowledge: but I
fainted not.
For the Hand still impelled me at once and supported—
suppressed
All the tumult, and quenched it with quiet, and holy
behest,
Till the rapture was shut in itself, and the earth sank to rest.
Anon at the dawn, all that trouble had withered from
earth—
Not so much, but I saw it die out in the day's tender
birth;
In the gathered intensity brought to the grey of the hills;
In the shuddering forests' new awe; in the sudden wind-
thrills;
In the startled wild beasts that bore off, each with eye
sidling still
Tho' averted, in wonder and dread; and the birds stiff and
chill

"DE GUSTIBUS"

That rose heavily, as I approached them, made stupid
with awe!
E'en the serpent that slid away silent,—he felt the new
Law.
The same stared in the white humid faces upturned by
the flowers ;
The same worked in the heart of the cedar, and moved
the vine-bowers.
And the little brooks witnessing murmured, persistent and
low,
With their obstinate, all but hushed voices—E'en so! it
is so.

"DE GUSTIBUS"

I

YOUR ghost will walk, you lover of trees,
    (If loves remain)
    In an English lane,
By a cornfield-side a-flutter with poppies.
Hark, those two in the hazel coppice—
A boy and a girl, if the good fates please,
    Making love, say,—
    The happier they!
Draw yourself up from the light of the moon,
And let them pass, as they will too soon,
    With the beanflowers' boon,
    And the blackbird's tune,
    And May, and June!

II

What I love best in all the world,
Is, a castle, precipice-encurled,
In a gash of the wind-grieved Apennine.
Or look for me, old fellow of mine,

339

"DE GUSTIBUS"

(If I get my head from out the mouth
O' the grave, and loose my spirit's bands,
And come again to the land of lands)—
In a sea-side house to the farther south,
Where the baked cicalas die of drouth,
And one sharp tree ('tis a cypress) stands,
By the many hundred years red-rusted,
Rough iron-spiked, ripe fruit-o'ercrusted,
My sentinel to guard the sands
To the water's edge.   For, what expands
Without the house, but the great opaque
Blue breadth of sea, and not a break?
While, in the house, for ever crumbles
Some fragment of the frescoed walls,
From blisters where a scorpion sprawls.
A girl bare-footed brings and tumbles
Down on the pavement, green-flesh melons,
And says there's news to-day—the king
Was shot at, touched in the liver-wing,
Goes with his Bourbon arm in a sling.
—She hopes they have not caught the felons.
     Italy, my Italy!
Queen Mary's saying serves for me—
     (When fortune's malice
     Lost her, Calais.)
Open my heart and you will see
Graved inside of it, "Italy."
Such lovers old are I and she;
So it always was, so it still shall be!

PROTVS

BYAM SHAW

AMONG these latter busts we count by scores,
Half-emperors and quarter-emperors,
Each with his bay-leaf fillet, loose-thonged vest,
Loric and low-browed Gorgon on the breast
One loves a baby face, with violets there,
Violets instead of laurel in the hair,
As those were all the little locks could bear.

Now read here. " Protus ends a period
Of empery beginning with a god :
Born in the porphyry chamber at Byzant ;
Queens by his cradle, proud and ministrant.
And if he quickened breath there, 'twould like
    fire
Pantingly through the dim vast realm transpire.
A fame that he was missing, spread afar—
The world, from its four corners, rose in war,
Till he was borne out on a balcony
To pacify the world when it should see.
The captains ranged before him, one, his hand
Made baby points at, gained the chief command.
And day by day more beautiful he grew
In shape, all said, in feature and in hue,
While young Greek sculptors gazing on the child
Were, so, with old Greek sculpture, reconciled.
Already sages laboured to condense
In easy tomes a life's experience :
And artists took grave counsel to impart
In one breath and one hand-sweep, all their art—
To make his graces prompt as blossoming
Of plentifully-watered palms in spring :
Since well beseems it, whoso mounts the throne,

PROTUS

For beauty, knowledge, strength, should stand alone,
And mortals love the letters of his name."

—Stop! Have you turned two pages? Still the same.
New reign, same date. The scribe goes on to say
How that same year, on such a month and day,
"John the Pannonian, groundedly believed
A blacksmith's bastard, whose hard hand reprieved
The Empire from its fate the year before,—
Came, had a mind to take the crown, and wore
The same for six years, (during which the Huns
Kept off their fingers from us) till his sons
Put something in his liquor"—and so forth.
Then a new reign. Stay—"Take at its just worth"
(Subjoins an annotator) "what I give
As hearsay. Some think John let Protus live
And slip away. 'Tis said he reached man's age
At some blind northern court ; made first a page,
Then, tutor to the children—last, of use
About the hunting-stables. I deduce.
He wrote the little tract 'On worming dogs,'
Whereof the name in sundry catalogues
Is extant yet. A Protus of the Race
Is rumoured to have died a monk in Thrace,—
And if the same, he reached senility."

Here's John the Smith's rough-hammered head. Great eye,
Gross jaw and griped lips do what granite can
To give you the crown-grasper. What a man !

THE GUARDIAN-ANGEL

THE GUARDIAN-ANGEL

(A PICTURE AT FANO)

I

DEAR and great Angel, wouldst thou only leave
  That child, when thou hast done with him, for me!
Let me sit all the day here, that when eve
  Shall find performed thy special ministry
And time come for departure, thou, suspending
Thy flight, mayst see another child for tending,
  Another still, to quiet and retrieve.

II

Then I shall feel thee step one step, no more,
  From where thou standest now, to where I gaze,
And suddenly my head be covered o'er
  With those wings, white above the child who prays
Now on that tomb—and I shall feel thee guarding
Me, out of all the world; for me, discarding
  Yon heaven thy home, that waits and opes its door!

III

I would not look up thither past thy head
  Because the door opes, like that child, I know,
For I should have thy gracious face instead,
  Thou bird of God! And wilt thou bend me low
Like him, and lay, like his, my hands together,
And lift them up to pray, and gently tether
  Me, as thy lamb there, with thy garment's spread?

IV

If this was ever granted, I would rest
  My head beneath thine, while thy healing hands
Close-covered both my eyes beside thy breast,
  Pressing the brain, which too much thought expands,
Back to its proper size again, and smoothing
Distortion down till every nerve had soothing,
  And all lay quiet, happy and supprest.

343

THE GUARDIAN-ANGEL

V

How soon all worldly wrong would be repaired!
   I think how I should view the earth and skies
And sea, when once again my brow was bared
   After thy healing, with such different eyes.
O, world, as God has made it! all is beauty:
And knowing this, is love, and love is duty.
   What further may be sought for or declared?

VI

Guercino drew this angel I saw teach
   (Alfred, dear friend)—that little child to pray,
Holding the little hands up, each to each
   Pressed gently,—with his own head turned away
Over the earth where so much lay before him
Of work to do, though heaven was opening o'er him,
   And he was left at Fano by the beach.

VII

We were at Fano, and three times we went
   To sit and see him in his chapel there,
And drink his beauty to our soul's content
   —My angel with me too: and since I care
For dear Guercino's fame, (to which in power
And glory comes this picture for a dower,
   Fraught with a pathos so magnificent)

VIII

And since he did not work so earnestly
   At all times, and has else endured some wrong,—
I took one thought his picture struck from me,
   And spread it out, translating it to song.
My Love is here. Where are you, dear old friend?
How rolls the Wairoa at your world's far end?
   This is Ancona, yonder is the sea.

344

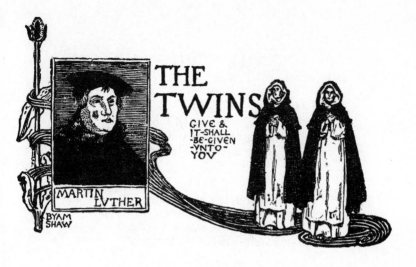

THE TWINS

GIVE &
IT·SHALL
·BE·GIVEN
·VNTO·
YOV

MARTIN
LVTHER

BYAM
SHAW

I

GRAND rough old Martin Luther
    Bloomed fables—flowers on furze,
The better the uncouther:
    Do roses stick like burrs?

II

A beggar asked an alms
    One day at an abbey-door,
Said Luther; but, seized with qualms,
    The Abbot replied, "We're poor!"

III

"Poor, who had plenty once,
    "When gifts fell thick as rain:
"But they give us nought, for the nonce,
    "And how should we give again?"

IV

Then the beggar, "See your sins!
    "Of old, unless I err,
"Ye had brothers for inmates, twins,
    "Date and Dabitur."

345

THE TWINS

V

" While Date was in good case
  " Dabitur flourished too :
" For Dabitur's lenten face,.
  " No wonder if Date rue."

VI

" Would ye retrieve the one ?
  " Try and make plump the other !
" When Date's penance is done,
  " Dabitur helps his brother."

VII

" Only, beware relapse ! "
  The Abbot hung his head.
This beggar might be, perhaps,
  An angel, Luther said.

CLEON

" As certain also of your own poets have said "—

CLEON the poet, (from the sprinkled isles,
Lily on lily, that o'erlace the sea,
And laugh their pride when the light wave lisps
  " Greece ")—
To Protos in his Tyranny : much health !

They give thy letter to me, even now :
I read and seem as if I heard thee speak.
The master of thy galley still unlades
Gift after gift ; they block my court at last
And pile themselves along its portico
Royal with sunset, like a thought of thee :
And one white she-slave from the group dispersed
Of black and white slaves, (like the chequer-work

CLEON

Pavement, at once my nation's work and gift,
Now covered with this settle-down of doves)
One lyric woman, in her crocus vest
Woven of sea-wools, with her two white hands
Commends to me the strainer and the cup
Thy lip hath bettered ere it blesses mine.

Well-counselled, king, in thy munificence!
For so shall men remark, in such an act
Of love for him whose song gives life its joy,
Thy recognition of the use of life;
Nor call thy spirit barely adequate
To help on life in straight ways, broad enough
For vulgar souls, by ruling and the rest.
Thou, in the daily building of thy tower,
Whether in fierce and sudden spasms of toil,
Or through dim lulls of unapparent growth,
Or when the general work 'mid good acclaim
Climbed with the eye to cheer the architect,
Didst ne'er engage in work for mere work's sake—
Hadst ever in thy heart the luring hope
Of some eventful rest a-top of it,
Whence, all the tumult of the building hushed,
Thou first of men mightst look out to the east.
The vulgar saw thy tower; thou sawest the sun. *THE GRAMMARIAN?*
For this, I promise on thy festival
To pour libation, looking o'er the sea,
Making this slave narrate thy fortunes, speak
Thy great words, and describe thy royal face—
Wishing thee wholly where Zeus lives the most
Within the eventual element of calm.

Thy letter's first requirement meets me here.
It is as thou hast heard: in one short life
I, Cleon, have effected all those things
Thou wonderingly dost enumerate.
That epos on thy hundred plates of gold
Is mine,—and also mine the little chaunt,

CLEON

So sure to rise from every fishing-bark
When, lights at prow, the seamen haul their nets.
The image of the sun-god on the phare
Men turn from the sun's self to see, is mine;
The Pœcile, o'er-storied its whole length,
As thou didst hear, with painting, is mine too
I know the true proportions of a man
And woman also, not observed before;
And I have written three books on the soul,
Proving absurd all written hitherto,
And putting us to ignorance again.
For music,—why, I have combined the moods,
Inventing one. In brief, all arts are mine;
Thus much the people know and recognise,
Throughout our seventeen islands. Marvel not.
We of these latter days, with greater mind
Than our forerunners, since more composite,
Look not so great (beside their simple way)
To a judge who only sees one way at once,
One mind-point, and no other at a time,—
Compares the small part of a man of us
With some whole man of the heroic age,
Great in his way,—not ours, nor meant for ours,
And ours is greater, had we skill to know.
Yet, what we call this life of men on earth,
This sequence of the soul's achievements here,
Being, as I find much reason to conceive,
Intended to be viewed eventually
As a great whole, not analysed to parts,
But each part having reference to all,—
How shall a certain part, pronounced complete,
Endure effacement by another part?
Was the thing done?—Then what's to do again?
See, in the chequered pavement opposite,
Suppose the artist made a perfect rhomb,
And next a lozenge, then a trapezoid—
He did not overlay them, superimpose
The new upon the old and blot it out,

CLEON

But laid them on a level in his work,
Making at last a picture; there it lies.
So, first the perfect separate forms were made,
The portions of mankind—and after, so,
Occurred the combination of the same.
Or where had been a progress, otherwise? ←
Mankind, made up of all the single men,—
In such a synthesis the labour ends.
Now, mark me—those divine men of old time
Have reached, thou sayest well, each at one point
The outside verge that rounds our faculty;
And where they reached, who can do more than reach?
It takes but little water just to touch
At some one point the inside of a sphere,
And, as we turn the sphere, touch all the rest
In due succession: but the finer air
Which not so palpably nor obviously,
Though no less universally, can touch
The whole circumference of that emptied sphere,
Fills it more fully than the water did;
Holds thrice the weight of water in itself
Resolved into a subtler element.
And yet the vulgar call the sphere first full
Up to the visible height—and after, void;
Not knowing air's more hidden properties.
And thus our soul, misknown, cries out to Zeus
To vindicate his purpose in its life—
Why stay we on the earth unless to grow?
Long since, I imaged, wrote the fiction out,
That he or other God, descended here
And, once for all, showed simultaneously
What, in its nature, never can be shown
Piecemeal or in succession;—showed, I say,
The worth both absolute and relative
Of all His children from the birth of time,
His instruments for all appointed work.
I now go on to image,—might we hear
The judgment which should give the due to each,

CLEON

Shew where the labour lay and where the ease,
And prove Zeus' self, the latent, everywhere!
This is a dream. But no dream, let us hope,
That years and days, the summers and the springs
Follow each other with unwaning powers—
The grapes which dye thy wine, are richer far
Through culture, than the wild wealth of the rock;
The suave plum than the savage-tasted drupe;
The pastured honey-bee drops choicer sweet;
The flowers turn double, and the leaves turn flowers;
That young and tender crescent-moon, thy slave,
Sleeping upon her robe as if on clouds,
Refines upon the women of my youth.
What, and the soul alone deteriorates?
I have not chanted verse like Homer's, no—
Nor swept string like Terpander, no—nor carved
And painted men like Phidias and his friend:
I am not great as they are, point by point:
But I have entered into sympathy
With these four, running these into one soul,
Who, separate, ignored each others' arts.
Say, is it nothing that I know them all?
The wild flower was the larger—I have dashed
Rose-blood upon its petals, pricked its cup's
Honey with wine, and driven its seed to fruit,
And show a better flower if not so large.
I stand, myself. Refer this to the gods
Whose gift alone it is! which, shall I dare
(All pride apart) upon the absurd pretext
That such a gift by chance lay in my hand,
Discourse of lightly or depreciate?
It might have fallen to another's hand—what then?
I pass too surely—let at least truth stay!

And next, of what thou followest on to ask.
This being with me as I declare, O king,
My works, in all these varicoloured kinds,
So done by me, accepted so by men—

CLEON

Thou askest if (my soul thus in men's hearts)
I must not be accounted to attain
The very crown and proper end of life.
Inquiring thence how, now life closeth up,
I face death with success in my right hand :
Whether I fear death less than dost thyself
The fortunate of men.   "For" (writest thou)
"Thou leavest much behind, while I leave nought :
Thy life stays in the poems men shall sing,
The pictures men shall study ; while my life,
Complete and whole now in its power and joy,
Dies altogether with my brain and arm,
Is lost indeed ; since,—what survives myself?
The brazen statue that o'erlooks my grave,
Set on the promontory which I named.
And that—some supple courtier of my heir
Shall use its robed and sceptred arm, perhaps,
To fix the rope to, which best drags it down.
I go, then : triumph thou, who dost not go!"

Nay, thou art worthy of hearing my whole mind.
Is this apparent, when thou turn'st to muse
Upon the scheme of earth and man in chief,
That admiration grows as knowledge grows?
That imperfection means perfection hid,
Reserved in part, to grace the after-time?
If, in the morning of philosophy,
Ere aught had been recorded, aught perceived,
Thou, with the light now in thee, couldst have looked
On all earth's tenantry, from worm to bird,
Ere man had yet appeared upon the stage—
Thou wouldst have seen them perfect, and deduced
The perfectness of others yet unseen.
Conceding which,—had Zeus then questioned thee
"Wilt thou go on a step, improve on this,
Do more for visible creatures than is done?"
Thou wouldst have answered, "Ay, by making each
Grow conscious in himself—by that alone.

CLEON

All's perfect else : the shell sucks fast the rock,
The fish strikes through the sea, the snake both swims
And slides ; the birds take flight, forth range the beasts,
Till life's mechanics can no further go—
And all this joy in natural life, is put,
Like fire from off Thy finger into each,
So exquisitely perfect is the same.
But 'tis pure fire—and they mere matter are ;
It has them, not they it : and so I choose,
For man, Thy last premeditated work
(If I might add a glory to this scheme)
That a third thing should stand apart from both,
A quality arise within the soul,
Which, intro-active, made to supervise
And feel the force it has, may view itself,
And so be happy." Man might live at first
The animal life : but is there nothing more ?
In due time, let him critically learn
How he lives ; and, the more he gets to know
Of his own life's adaptabilities,
The more joy-giving will his life become.
The man who hath this quality, is best

But thou, king, hadst more reasonably said :
" Let progress end at once,—man make no step
Beyond the natural man, the better beast,
Using his senses, not the sense of sense."
In man there 's failure, only since he left
The lower and inconscious forms of life.
We called it an advance, the rendering plain
A spirit might grow conscious of that life,
And, by new lore so added to the old,
Take each step higher over the brute's head.
This grew the only life, the pleasure-house,
Watch-tower and treasure-fortress of the soul
Which whole surrounding flats of natural life
Seemed only fit to yield subsistence to ;
A tower that crowns a country. But alas !

CLEON

The soul now climbs it just to perish there,
For thence we have discovered ('tis no dream—
We know this, which we had not else perceived)
That there's a world of capability
For joy, spread round about us, meant for us,
Inviting us; and still the soul craves all,
And still the flesh replies, "Take no jot more
Than ere you climbed the tower to look abroad!
Nay, so much less, as that fatigue has brought
Deduction to it." We struggle—fain to enlarge
Our bounded physical recipiency,
Increase our power, supply fresh oil to life,
Repair the waste of age and sickness. No,
It skills not: life's inadequate to joy,
As the soul sees joy, tempting life to take.
They praise a fountain in my garden here
Wherein a Naiad sends the water-spurt
Thin from her tube; she smiles to see it rise.
What if I told her, it is just a thread
From that great river which the hills shut up,
And mock her with my leave to take the same?
The artificer has given her one small tube
Past power to widen or exchange—what boots
To know she might spout oceans if she could?
She cannot lift beyond her first straight thread.
And so a man can use but a man's joy
While he sees God's. Is it for Zeus to boast
"See, man, how happy I live, and despair—
That I may be still happier—for thy use!"
If this were so, we could not thank our Lord,
As hearts beat on to doing: 'tis not so—
Malice it is not. Is it carelessness?
Still, no. If care—where is the sign, I ask—
And get no answer: and agree in sum,
O king, with thy profound discouragement,
Who seest the wider but to sigh the more.
Most progress is most failure! thou sayest well.

CLEON

The last point now :—thou dost except a case—
Holding joy not impossible to one
With artist-gifts—to such a man as I—
Who leave behind me living works indeed ;
For, such a poem, such a painting lives.
What ? dost thou verily trip upon a word,
Confound the accurate view of what joy is
(Caught somewhat clearer by my eyes than thine)
With feeling joy ? confound the knowing how
And showing how to live (my faculty)
With actually living ?—Otherwise
Where is the artist's vantage o'er the king ?
Because in my great epos I display
How divers men young, strong, fair, wise, can act—
Is this as though I acted ? if I paint,
Carve the young Phœbus, am I therefore young ?
Methinks I'm older that I bowed myself
The many years of pain that taught me art !
Indeed, to know is something, and to prove
How all this beauty might be enjoyed, is more :
But, knowing nought, to enjoy is something too.
Yon rower with the moulded muscles there
Lowering the sail, is nearer it than I.
I can write love-odes—thy fair slave's an ode.
I get to sing of love, when grown too grey
For being beloved : she turns to that young man
The muscles all a-ripple on his back.
I know the joy of kingship : well—thou art king !

  " But," sayest thou—(and I marvel, I repeat,
To find thee tripping on a mere word) " what
Thou writest, paintest, stays : that does not die :
Sappho survives, because we sing her songs,
And Æschylus, because we read his plays ! "
Why, if they live still, let them come and take
Thy slave in my despite—drink from thy cup—
Speak in my place. Thou diest while I survive ?

CLEON

Say rather that my fate is deadlier still,—
In this, that every day my sense of joy
Grows more acute, my soul (intensified
In power and insight) more enlarged, more keen ;
While every day my hairs fall more and more,
My hand shakes, and the heavy years increase—
The horror quickening still from year to year,
The consummation coming past escape
When I shall know most, and yet least enjoy—
When all my works wherein I prove my worth,
Being present still to mock me in men's mouths,
Alive still, in the phrase of such as thou,
I, I, the feeling, thinking, acting man,
The man who loved his life so over much,
Shall sleep in my urn.   It is so horrible,
I dare at times imagine to my need
Some future state revealed to us by Zeus,
Unlimited in capability
For joy, as this is in desire for joy,
To seek which, the joy-hunger forces us.
That, stung by straitness of our life, made strait
On purpose to make sweet the life at large—
Freed by the throbbing impulse we call death
We burst there as the worm into the fly,
Who, while a worm still, wants his wings.   But, no !
Zeus has not yet revealed it ; and, alas !
He must have done so—were it possible !

    Live long and happy, and in that thought die,
Glad for what was.   Farewell.   And for the rest,
I cannot tell thy messenger aright
Where to deliver what he bears of thine
To one called Paulus—we have heard his fame
Indeed, if Christus be not one with him—
I know not, nor am troubled much to know.
Thou canst not think a mere barbarian Jew,
As Paulus proves to be, one circumcised,

CLEON

Hath access to a secret shut from us?
Thou wrongest our philosophy, O king,
In stooping to inquire of such an one,
As if his answer could impose at all.
He writeth, doth he? well, and he may write.
Oh, the Jew findeth scholars! certain slaves
Who touched on this same isle, preached him and Christ;
And (as I gathered from a bystander)
Their doctrines could be held by no sane man.

POPULARITY

POPULARITY

I

STAND still, true poet that you are,
  I know you; let me try and draw you.
Some night you'll fail us.   When afar
  You rise, remember one man saw you,
Knew you, and named a star.

II

My star, God's glow-worm! Why extend
  That loving hand of His which leads you,
Yet locks you safe from end to end
  Of this dark world, unless He needs you—
Just saves your light to spend?

III

His clenched Hand shall unclose at last
  I know, and let out all the beauty.
My poet holds the future fast,
  Accepts the coming ages' duty,
Their present for this past.

IV

That day, the earth's feast-master's brow
  Shall clear, to God the chalice raising;
"Others give best at first, but Thou
  For ever set'st our table praising,—
Keep'st the good wine till now."

V

Meantime, I'll draw you as you stand,
  With few or none to watch and wonder.
I'll say—a fisher (on the sand
  By Tyre the Old) his ocean-plunder,
A netful, brought to land.

POPULARITY

VI

Who has not heard how Tyrian shells
  Enclosed the blue, that dye of dyes
Whereof one drop worked miracles,
  And coloured like Astarte's eyes
Raw silk the merchant sells?

VII

And each bystander of them all
  Could criticise, and quote tradition
How depths of blue sublimed some pall,
  To get which, pricked a king's ambition;
Worth sceptre, crown and ball.

VIII

Yet there's the dye,—in that rough mesh,
  The sea has only just o'er-whispered!
Live whelks, the lip's-beard dripping fresh,
  As if they still the water's lisp heard
Through foam the rock-weeds thresh.

IX

Enough to furnish Solomon
  Such hangings for his cedar-house,
That when gold-robed he took the throne
  In that abyss of blue, the Spouse
Might swear his presence shone

X

Most like the centre-spike of gold
  Which burns deep in the blue-bell's womb,
What time, with ardours manifold,
  The bee goes singing to her groom,
Drunken and overbold.

TWO IN THE CAMPAGNA

XI

Mere conchs! not fit for warp or woof!
  Till art comes,—comes to pound and squeeze
And clarify,—refines to proof
  The liquor filtered by degrees,
While the world stands aloof.

XII

And there's the extract, flasked and fine,
  And priced, and saleable at last!
And Hobbs, Nobbs, Stokes and Nokes combine
  To paint the future from the past,
Put blue into their line.

XIII

Hobbs hints blue,—straight he turtle eats.
  Nobbs prints blue,—claret crowns his cup.
Nokes outdares Stokes in azure feats,—
  Both gorge. Who fished the murex up?
What porridge had John Keats?

TWO IN THE CAMPAGNA

I

I WONDER do you feel to-day
  As I have felt, since, hand in hand,
We sat down on the grass, to stray
  In spirit better through the land,
This morn of Rome and May?

II

For me, I touched a thought, I know,
  Has tantalised me many times,
(Like turns of thread the spiders throw
  Mocking across our path) for rhymes
To catch at and let go.

TWO IN THE CAMPAGNA

III

Help me to hold it : first it left
    The yellowing fennel, run to seed
There, branching from the brickwork's cleft,
    Some old tomb's ruin : yonder weed
Took up the floating weft,

IV

Where one small orange cup amassed
    Five beetles,—blind and green they grope
Among the honey-meal,—and last
    Everywhere on the grassy slope
I traced it.   Hold it fast !

V

The champaign with its endless fleece
    Of feathery grasses everywhere !
Silence and passion, joy and peace,
    An everlasting wash of air—
Rome's ghost since her decease.

VI

Such life there, through such lengths of hours,
    Such miracles performed in play,
Such primal naked forms of flowers,
    Such letting Nature have her way
While Heaven looks from its towers.

VII

How say you ?   Let us, O my dove,
    Let us be unashamed of soul,
As earth lies bare to heaven above.
    How is it under our control
To love or not to love ?

TWO IN THE CAMPAGNA

VIII

I would that you were all to me,
   You that are just so much, no more—
Nor yours, nor mine,—nor slave nor free!
   Where does the fault lie? what the core
Of the wound, since wound must be?

IX

I would I could adopt your will,
   See with your eyes, and set my heart
Beating by yours, and drink my fill
   At your soul's springs,—your part, my part
In life, for good and ill.

X

No.   I yearn upward—touch you close,
   Then stand away.   I kiss your cheek,
Catch your soul's warmth,—I pluck the rose
   And love it more than tongue can speak—
Then the good minute goes.

XI

Already how am I so far
   Out of that minute?   Must I go
Still like the thistle-ball, no bar,
   Onward, whenever light winds blow,
Fixed by no friendly star?

XII

Just when I seemed about to learn!
   Where is the thread now?   Off again!
The old trick!   Only I discern—
   Infinite passion and the pain
Of finite hearts that yearn.

361

A GRAMMARIAN'S FUNERAL

A GRAMMARIAN'S FUNERAL

[*Time*—Shortly after the revival of learning in Europe]

LET us begin and carry up this corpse,
 Singing together.
Leave we the common crofts, the vulgar thorpes,
 Each in its tether
Sleeping safe on the bosom of the plain,
 Cared-for till cock-crow.
Look out if yonder's not the day again
 Rimming the rock-row!
That's the appropriate country—there, man's thought,
 Rarer, intenser,
Self-gathered for an outbreak, as it ought,
 Chafes in the censer!
Leave we the unlettered plain its herd and crop;
 Seek we sepulture
On a tall mountain, citied to the top,
 Crowded with culture!
All the peaks soar, but one the rest excels;
 Clouds overcome it;
No, yonder sparkle is the citadel's
 Circling its summit!
Thither our path lies—wind we up the heights—
 Wait ye the warning?
Our low life was the level's and the night's;
 He's for the morning!
Step to a tune, square chests, erect the head,
 'Ware the beholders!
This is our master, famous, calm, and dead,
 Borne on our shoulders.

Sleep, crop and herd! sleep, darkling thorpe and croft,
 Safe from the weather!
He, whom we convoy to his grave aloft,
 Singing together,

A GRAMMARIAN'S FUNERAL

He was a man born with thy face and throat,
    Lyric Apollo!
Long he lived nameless: how should spring take note
    Winter would follow?
Till lo, the little touch, and youth was gone!
    Cramped and diminished,
Moaned he, " New measures, other feet anon!
    My dance is finished?"
No, that 's the world's way! (keep the mountain-side,
    Make for the city.)
He knew the signal, and stepped on with pride
    Over men's pity;
Left play for work, and grappled with the world
    Bent on escaping:
" What 's in the scroll," quoth he, " thou keepest furled?
    Shew me their shaping,
Theirs, who most studied man, the bard and sage,—
    Give!"—So he gowned him,
Straight got by heart that book to its last page:
    Learned, we found him!
Yea, but we found him bald too—eyes like lead,
    Accents uncertain:
" Time to taste life," another would have said,
    " Up with the curtain!"
This man said rather, " Actual life comes next?
    Patience a moment!
Grant I have mastered learning's crabbed text
    Still, there 's the comment.
Let me know all. Prate not of most or least,
    Painful or easy:
Even to the crumbs I'd fain eat up the feast,
    Ay, nor feel queasy!"
Oh, such a life as he resolved to live,
    When he had learned it,
When he had gathered all books had to give
    Sooner, he spurned it!

A GRAMMARIAN'S FUNERAL

Image the whole, then execute the parts—
    Fancy the fabric
Quite, ere you build, ere steel strike fire from quartz,
    Ere mortar dab brick!

(Here's the town-gate reached : there's the market-place
    Gaping before us.)
Yea, this in him was the peculiar grace
    (Hearten our chorus)
Still before living he'd learn how to live—
    No end to learning.
Earn the means first—God surely will contrive
    Use for our earning.
Others mistrust and say—"But time escapes,—
    "Live now or never!"
He said, "What's Time? leave Now for dogs and apes ı
    Man has For ever."
Back to his book then : deeper drooped his head ;
    Calculus racked him :
Leaden before, his eyes grew dross of lead ;
    Tussis attacked him.
"Now, Master, take a little rest!"—not he!
    (Caution redoubled!
Step two a-breast, the way winds narrowly.)
    Not a whit troubled,
Back to his studies, fresher than at first,
    Fierce as a dragon
He, (soul-hydroptic with a sacred thirst)
    Sucked at the flagon.
Oh, if we draw a circle premature,
    Heedless of far gain,
Greedy for quick returns of profit, sure,
    Bad is our bargain!
Was it not great? did not he throw on God,
    (He loves the burthen)—
God's task to make the heavenly period
    Perfect the earthen?

THE TREE OF KNOWLEDGE

A GRAMMARIAN'S FUNERAL

BYAM·SHAW·

A GRAMMARIAN'S FUNERAL

Did not he magnify the mind, shew clear
    Just what it all meant?
He would not discount life, as fools do here,
    Paid by instalment!
He ventured neck or nothing—heaven's success
    Found, or earth's failure:
" Wilt thou trust death or not ? " he answered " Yes.
    " Hence with life's pale lure!"
That low man seeks a little thing to do,
    Sees it and does it:
This high man, with a great thing to pursue,
    Dies ere he knows it.
That low man goes on adding one to one,
    His hundred's soon hit:
This high man, aiming at a million,
    Misses an unit.
That, has the world here—should he need the next,
    Let the world mind him!
This, throws himself on God, and unperplext
    Seeking shall find Him.
So, with the throttling hands of Death at strife,
    Ground he at grammar;
Still, thro' the rattle, parts of speech were rife.
    While he could stammer
He settled *Hoti's* business—let it be!—
    Properly based *Oun*—
Gave us the doctrine of the enclitic *De*,
    Dead from the waist down.
Well, here's the platform, here's the proper place.
    Hail to your purlieus
All ye highfliers of the feathered race,
    Swallows and curlews!
Here's the top-peak! the multitude below
    Live, for they can there.
This man decided not to Live but Know—
    Bury this man there ?

A GRAMMARIAN'S FUNERAL

Here—here's his place, where meteors shoot, clouds form,
    Lightnings are loosened,
Stars come and go! let joy break with the storm—
    Peace let the dew send!
Lofty designs must close in like effects:
    Loftily lying,
Leave him—still loftier than the world suspects,
    Living and dying.

ONE WAY OF LOVE

I

ALL June I bound the rose in sheaves.
Now, rose by rose, I strip the leaves,
And strew them where Pauline may pass
She will not turn aside?   Alas!
Let them lie.   Suppose they die?
The chance was they might take her eye.

II

How many a month I strove to suit
These stubborn fingers to the lute!
To-day I venture all I know.
She will not hear my music?   So!
Break the string—fold music's wing.
Suppose Pauline had bade me sing!

III

My whole life long I learned to love.
This hour my utmost art I prove
And speak my passion.—Heaven or hell?
She will not give me heaven?   'Tis well!
Lose who may—I still can say,
Those who win heaven, blest are they.

ANOTHER WAY OF LOVE

ANOTHER WAY OF LOVE

I

JUNE was not over,
        Though past the full,
And the best of her roses
        Had yet to blow,
        When a man I know
(But shall not discover,
        Since ears are dull,
        And time discloses)
Turned him and said with a man's true air,
Half sighing a smile in a yawn, as 'twere,
" If I tire of your June, will she greatly care?"

II

Well, Dear, in-doors with you!
        True, serene deadness
Tries a man's temper.
        What's in the blossom
        June wears on her bosom?
Can it clear scores with you?
        Sweetness and redness,
        Eadem semper!
Go, let me care for it greatly or slightly!
If June mends her bowers now, your hand left unsightly
By plucking their roses,—my June will do rightly.

III

And after, for pastime,
        If June be refulgent
With flowers in completeness,
        All petals, no prickles,
        Delicious as trickles
Of wine poured at mass-time,—
        And choose One indulgent
        To redness and sweetness:
Or if, with experience of man and of spider,
She use my June-lightning, the strong insect-ridder,
To stop the fresh spinning,—why, June will consider.

369

MISCONCEPTIONS

I

THIS is a spray the Bird clung to,
    Making it blossom with pleasure,
Ere the high tree-top she sprung to,
    Fit for her nest and her treasure.
    Oh, what a hope beyond measure
Was the poor spray's, which the flying feet hung to,—
So to be singled out, built in, and sung to!

II

This is a heart the Queen leant on,
    Thrilled in a minute erratic,
Ere the true bosom she bent on,
    Meet for love's regal dalmatic.
    Oh, what a fancy ecstatic
Was the poor heart's, ere the wanderer went on—
Loved to be saved for it, proffered to, spent on!

370

ONE WORD MORE

ONE WORD MORE

TO E. B. B.

I

THERE they are, my fifty men and women
Naming me the fifty poems finished!
Take them, Love, the book and me together.
Where the heart lies, let the brain lie also.

II

Rafael made a century of sonnets,
Made and wrote them in a certain **volume**
Dinted with the silver-pointed pencil
Else he only used to draw Madonnas:
These, the world might view—but One, the volume.
Who that one, you ask? Your heart instructs you.
Did she live and love it all her life-time?
Did she drop, his lady of the sonnets,
Die, and let it drop beside her pillow
Where it lay in place of Rafael's glory,
Rafael's cheek so duteous and so loving—
Cheek, the world was wont to hail a painter's,
Rafael's cheek, her love had turned a poet's?

III

You and I would rather read that volume,
(Taken to his beating bosom by it)
Lean and list the bosom-beats of Rafael,
Would we not? than wonder at Madonnas—
Her, San Sisto names, and Her, Foligno,
Her, that visits Florence in a vision,
Her, that's left with lilies in the Louvre—
Seen by us and all the world in circle.

371

ONE WORD MORE

IV

You and I will never read that volume.
Guido Reni, like his own eye's apple
Guarded long the treasure-book and loved it.
Guido Reni dying, all Bologna
Cried, and the world with it, " Ours—the treasure !"
Suddenly, as rare things will, it vanished.

V

Dante once prepared to paint an angel:
Whom to please?   You whisper " Beatrice."
While he mused and traced it and retraced it,
(Peradventure with a pen corroded
Still by drops of that hot ink he dipped for,
When, his left-hand i' the hair o' the wicked,
Back he held the brow and pricked its stigma,
Bit into the live man's flesh for parchment,
Loosed him, laughed to see the writing rankle,
Let the wretch go festering thro' Florence)—
Dante, who loved well because he hated,
Hated wickedness that hinders loving,
Dante standing, studying his angel,—
In there broke the folk of his Inferno.
Says he—" Certain people of importance "
(Such he gave his daily, dreadful line to)
Entered and would seize, forsooth, the poet.
Says the poet—" Then I stopped my painting."

VI

You and I would rather see that angel,
Painted by the tenderness of Dante,
Would we not?—than read a fresh Inferno.

VII

You and I will never see that picture.
While he mused on love and Beatrice,

ONE WORD MORE

While he softened o'er his outlined angel,
In they broke, those "people of importance":
We and Bice bear the loss forever.

VIII

What of Rafael's sonnets, Dante's picture?

IX

This: no artist lives and loves that longs not
Once, and only once, and for One only,
(Ah, the prize!) to find his love a language
Fit and fair and simple and sufficient—
Using nature that's an art to others,
Not, this one time, art that's turned his nature.
Ay, of all the artists living, loving,
None but would forego his proper dowry,—
Does he paint? he fain would write a poem,—
Does he write? he fain would paint a picture,
Put to proof art alien to the artist's,
Once, and only once, and for One only,
So to be the man and leave the artist,
Save the man's joy, miss the artist's sorrow.

X

Wherefore? Heaven's gift takes earth's abatement!
He who smites the rock and spreads the water,
Bidding drink and live a crowd beneath him,
Even he, the minute makes immortal,
Proves, perchance, his mortal in the minute,
Desecrates, belike, the deed in doing.
While he smites, how can he but remember,
So he smote before, in such a peril,
When they stood and mocked—"Shall smiting help us?"
When they drank and sneered—"A stroke is easy!"
When they wiped their mouths and went their journey,
Throwing him for thanks—"But drought was pleasant."

ONE WORD MORE

Thus old memories mar the actual triumph;
Thus the doing savours of disrelish;
Thus achievement lacks a gracious somewhat;
O'er-importuned brows becloud the mandate,
Carelessness or consciousness, the gesture.
For he bears an ancient wrong about him,
Sees and knows again those phalanxed faces,
Hears, yet one time more, the 'customed prelude—
" How should'st thou, of all men, smite, and save us? "
Guesses what is like to prove the sequel—
" Egypt's flesh-pots—nay, the drought was better."

XI

Oh, the crowd must have emphatic warrant!
Theirs, the Sinai-forehead's cloven brilliance,
Right-arm's rod-sweep, tongue's imperial fiat.
Never dares the man put off the prophet.

XII

Did he love one face from out the thousands,
(Were she Jethro's daughter, white and wifely,
Were she but the Æthiopian bondslave,)
He would envy yon dumb patient camel,
Keeping a reserve of scanty water
Meant to save his own life in the desert;
Ready in the desert to deliver
(Kneeling down to let his breast be opened)
Hoard and life together for his mistress.

XIII

I shall never, in the years remaining,
Paint you pictures, no, nor carve you statues,
Make you music that should all-express me;
So it seems: I stand on my attainment.

374

ONE WORD MORE

This of verse alone, one life allows me;
Verse and nothing else have I to give you.
Other heights in other lives, God willing—
All the gifts from all the heights, your own, Love!

XIV

Yet a semblance of resource avails us—
Shade so finely touched, love's sense must seize it.
Take these lines, look lovingly and nearly,
Lines I write the first time and the last time.
He who works in fresco, steals a hair-brush,
Curbs the liberal hand, subservient proudly,
Cramps his spirit, crowds its all in little,
Makes a strange art of an art familiar,
Fills his lady's missal-marge with flowerets.
He who blows thro' bronze, may breathe thro' silver,
Fitly serenade a slumbrous princess.
He who writes, may write for once, as I do.

XV

Love, you saw me gather men and women,
Live or dead or fashioned by my fancy,
Enter each and all, and use their service,
Speak from every mouth,—the speech, a poem.
Hardly shall I tell my joys and sorrows,
Hopes and fears, belief and disbelieving:
I am mine and yours—the rest be all men's.
Karshook, Cleon, Norbert and the fifty.
Let me speak this once in my true person,
Not as Lippo, Roland or Andrea,
Though the fruit of speech be just this sentence—
Pray you, look on these my men and women,
Take and keep my fifty poems finished;
Where my heart lies, let my brain lie also!
Poor the speech; be how I speak, for all things

ONE WORD MORE

XVI

Not but that you know me!   Lo, the moon's self!
Here in London, yonder late in Florence,
Still we find her face, the thrice-transfigured.
Curving on a sky imbrued with colour,
Drifted over Fiesole by twilight,
Came she, our new crescent of a hair's-breadth.
Full she flared it, lamping Samminiato,
Rounder 'twixt the cypresses and rounder,
Perfect till the nightingales applauded.
Now, a piece of her old self, impoverished,
Hard to greet, she traverses the houseroofs,
Hurries with unhandsome thrift of silver,
Goes dispiritedly,—glad to finish.

XVII

What, there's nothing in the moon note-worthy?
Nay—for if that moon could love a mortal,
Use, to charm him (so to fit a fancy)
All her magic ('tis the old sweet mythos)
She would turn a new side to her mortal,
Side unseen of herdsman, huntsman, steersman—
Blank to Zoroaster on his terrace,
Blind to Galileo on his turret,
Dumb to Homer, dumb to Keats—him, even!
Think, the wonder of the moonstruck mortal—
When she turns round, comes again in heaven,
Opens out anew for worse or better?
Proves she like some portent of an ice-berg
Swimming full upon the ship it founders,
Hungry with huge teeth of splintered chrystals?
Proves she as the paved-work of a sapphire
Seen by Moses when he climbed the mountain?
Moses, Aaron, Nadab and Abihu
Climbed and saw the very God, the Highest,
Stand upon the paved-work of a sapphire.

ONE WORD MORE

Like the bodied heaven in his clearness
Shone the stone, the sapphire of that paved-work,
When they ate and drank and saw God also!

XVIII

What were seen? None knows, none ever shall know.
Only this is sure—the sight were other,
Not the moon's same side, born late in Florence,
Dying now impoverished here in London.
God be thanked, the meanest of his creatures
Boasts two soul-sides, one to face the world with,
One to show a woman when he loves her.

XIX

This I say of me, but think of you, Love!
This to you—yourself my moon of poets!
Ah, but that's the world's side—there's the wonder
Thus they see you, praise you, think they know you.
There, in turn I stand with them and praise you.
Out of my own self, I dare to phrase it.
But the best is when I glide from out them
Cross a step or two of dubious twilight,
Come out on the other side, the novel
Silent silver lights and darks undreamed of,
Where I hush and bless myself with silence.

XX

Oh, their Rafael of the dear Madonnas,
Oh, their Dante of the dread Inferno,
Wrote one song—and in my brain I sing it,
Drew one angel—borne, see, on my bosom!

THE END